A Gentleman of Considerable Talent

Caitlin Press Inc.
3375 Ponderosa Way
Qualicum Beach, BC V9K 2J8
www.caitlinpress.com

Text and cover design by Vici Johnstone
Maps by Morgan Hite, Hesperus Arts, Victoria, BC
Cover image: *Winter Couriers of the North-West Fur Company*, 1877. Public domain via Wikimedia Commons.
Edited by Catherine Edwards
Printed in Canada

Caitlin Press Inc. acknowledges financial support from the Government of Canada and the Canada Council for the Arts, and the Province of British Columbia through the British Columbia Arts Council and the Book Publisher's Tax Credit.

A gentleman of considerable talent : William Brown and the fur trade, 1811-1827 / Geoff Mynett.
William Brown and the fur trade, 1811-1827
Mynett, Geoff, 1946- author.
Includes bibliographical references and index.
Canadiana 2024035267X | ISBN 9781773861524 (softcover)
LCSH: Brown, William, 1790-1827. | LCSH: Hudson's Bay Company. | LCSH: Fur traders—Canada—Biography. | LCSH: Fur trade—Canada—History—19th century. | LCGFT: Biographies.
LCC FC3212.1.B76 M96 2024 | DDC 971.2/01092—dc23

A Gentleman of Considerable Talent

WILLIAM BROWN AND THE FUR TRADE, 1811–1827

Geoff Mynett

Caitlin Press 2024

To the memory of my parents

"Mr. Brown, a Gentleman of Considerable Talent, is appointed
to the charge of the District."

—Governor George Simpson

"It is but justice to say that Mr. Brown's steady, careful and judicious
management, together with his firmness and activity under all
our difficulties merits my warmest acknowledgments, and
I do not know that the Honbl. Coy. has a more faithful
servant in their employ."

—Governor George Simpson

Contents

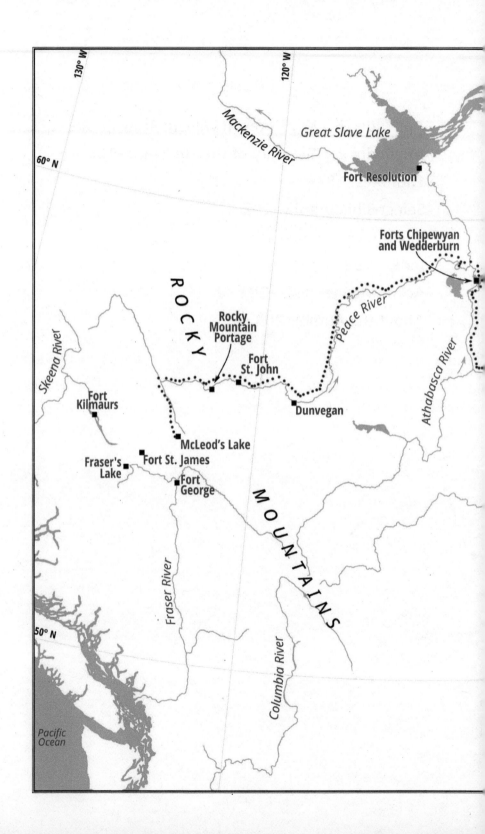

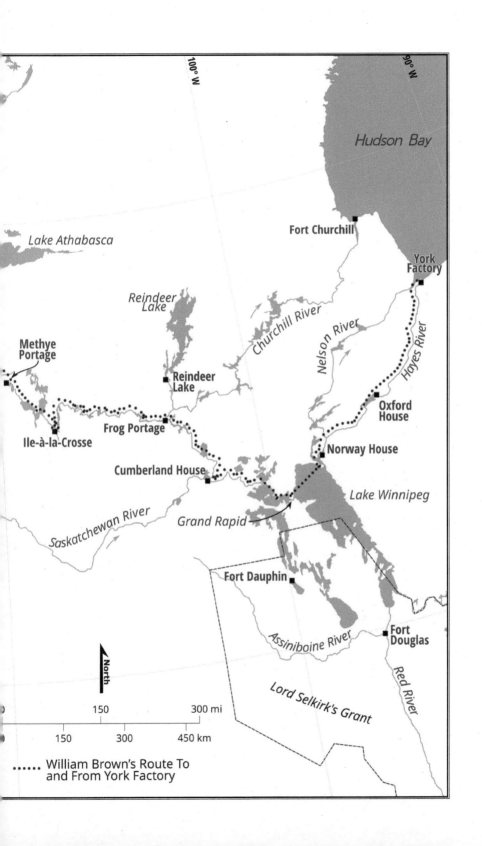

William Brown's Route To and From York Factory

Preface

The historian Stephen Bown has written that "The ghosts of Canada Past are all around us.... It is my job as a popular historian to bring these ghosts back to life."[1] The ghosts of the past, be they mighty or ordinary, have stories to tell us and information about their lives and times to share with us. Above all, they warn us to hold facts in reverence, for we ignore facts at our peril. They provide a lifeline to guide us from the past to our own times and help us understand the present.

The unimportant people often have stories as revealing as those of the mighty, but they are often harder to find. They remind us that in reality no one is ordinary. Here then is the ghost of William Brown, a Hudson's Bay Company (HBC) fur trader between 1811 and 1827. He steps out to us through the obscuring fogs of the past and tells his story. He was not a grand merchant from Montreal nor a hard-eyed capitalist from the boardrooms of London. He was a Scot from the village of Kilmaurs, nineteen miles southwest of Glasgow. He joined the Hudson's Bay Company (HBC) in 1811 and, aside from a few years back in Scotland, spent approximately a dozen years in its service. These years were among the most tumultuous in the history of the HBC and arguably of Canada. Returning to Scotland in the autumn of 1826, Brown died in Edinburgh early in 1827.

Brown's service with the HBC was one of survival during long, hard winters and short summers. He traded the goods of the Industrial Revolution for the furs so much sought after in Europe. Winters were ferocious. Men at the company's trading posts were frequently intensely cold. Mere survival was a challenge. Like so many others, Brown was often living on the edge of starvation.

In 1670, King Charles II of England had granted a charter to the HBC that gave it a monopoly of trade over all the land whose rivers drained into Hudson Bay. This land—named Rupert's Land in the company charter—was geographically and politically separate from both Upper and Lower Canada. The fur-trading posts in Rupert's Land were called factories because they were superintended by a factor. They were also called forts because protection was considered necessary. Many of them were set within stockades, with bastions at the corners and a supply of loaded muskets close by.

The years that Brown spent in Rupert's Land, Athabasca (the land west of Rupert's Land) and New Caledonia (the land west of the Rocky Mountains) were important ones in Canada's history. In these years, the disparate parts within the HBC's monopoly, including Rupert's Land,

Athabasca and New Caledonia, came together into one company under the governorship of George Simpson. Taking over after the merger, he held effective control of the company until his death in 1860. When Brown stepped ashore at York Factory in 1811, the future of these parts was uncertain; when he left in 1826, they were, for better or for worse, united under Simpson's de facto governance.

I have a strong prejudice against acronyms. Nevertheless, in the interests of efficiency, I refer to the Hudson's Bay Company as the HBC. Conveniently, I can use this both as a noun and as an adjective. The term HBC has been assigned many other meanings, the most famous of which is Here Before Christ. Another more prosaic but more accurate version is Here Before Canada. Except in quotations, I use the name Hudson Bay—without the apostrophe—to refer to the bay itself.

Men from the North West Company are often referred to as Nor'Westers, and I abide by that convention. Again, I use the term both as a noun and as an adjective. When an HBC trader referred to somebody as a Frenchman or a Canadian, he was talking of someone engaged by the North West Company in Lower Canada. After 1815, though, the HBC also recruited in Lower Canada. Many of its employees or servants, as they were called, spoke French as their first language.

In the period covered by this book, people often named a place where two rivers merged as the "forks." I use the term here to mean the forks at the confluence of the Skeena and the Bulkley Rivers. At the time, traders referred to the Bulkley River as Simpson's River and the Skeena River as the Babine River or, sometimes, McDougall's River. Gitanmaax, the central village of the Indigenous Gitxsan people, was located at these Forks. The Dakelh (Carrier) word for the Gitxsan people was Atnah, meaning outsiders or strangers. This is the term used in the HBC records at the time and therefore the one I use. The town of Hazelton, which is located at the Forks, was not established and named until 1871.

The North West Company fort of Stuart's Lake on the lake of the same name was renamed Fort St. James in 1822. William Brown established a fort on Babine Lake and named it Fort Kilmaurs. After his time there, it became known as Fort Babine, and later still, after a new post called Fort Babine was established farther north, as Old Fort. At the time the Wet'suwet'en (also spelled Wit'suwit'en) village of Witset was called Hotset and, much later, Moricetown. Although Stuart's Lake and McLeod's Lake are now spelled without the apostrophe, in the records of the time the apostrophe was used more often than not and I have used the old spelling.

This book is not about Indigenous people or specifically about the relations between them and the HBC. Nevertheless, they are an important part of Brown's story and he spent much of his time trading with them. I have attempted to include them in his story in as respectful a way as I can. The role of the HBC in the history of Canada has become controversial for many. It dislocated Indigenous societies and trading relations. It introduced firearms, liquor and new diseases, in too many cases with terrible consequences. Long after Brown's time, it led to the extension of Canadian law over Indigenous lands and peoples. To the extent that the HBC had a trading monopoly over one-twelfth of the land surface of the globe when absorbed into the Dominion of Canada in 1870, the HBC cannot escape part of any criticism directed at the Dominion.

The HBC journals and correspondence contain, alas, very little information about the social life of the men and women at the forts. The rule was strict and enforced. In a letter of December 9, 1823, John Stuart, at the HBC post at McLeod's Lake, wrote to the clerk in charge of Fort St. James, "I will beg leave to remind you that it was known to you to be very clear that nothing of a trifling nature should appear in the journal of any post unconnected with transactions of the place. A journal or diary is not a vehicle to convey either the libels or reveries of individuals and I now request that no letter (unless it be of importance) that is addressed you by any other than the chief factor in charge and then merely because they may be considered as instructions, with yours to him in answer, be inserted in the journal." No more than in the annual financial report of a company in modern times do we read about the women and children who participated in the social life of the organization. It is very tempting, but perhaps unwise, to jump to conclusions about what life was like at an HBC post in the early nineteenth century in the absence of persuasive evidence.

Indigenous people made many contributions to non-Indigenous culture and the English language. Among them are such words of Indigenous origin as canoe, muskeg, pemmican and toboggan as well as such place names as Athabasca (ayapaskah—place of rolling terrain), Chipewyan (ocliiweyen—painted skins) and Manitoba (manitou—the Creator.) These contributions include many plant-based medicines such as spruce juice, used to cure and prevent scurvy, and yarrow used to treat a wide variety of ailments.

In their journals and other writings, HBC traders and other contemporaries used language and names that, if used today, would cause offence and attract criticism. They were written at a time when differences between races, nationalities and classes were considered natural and unchallengeable. I have used their words only in quotations. They also used names that reflected their own cultures and history and not the names the Indigenous people themselves used or use. Thus the traders used the name

Carrier for the Dakelh. The Wet'suwet'en (Wit'suwit'en) people are a branch of the Dakelh. The Dene people consists of multiple nations—including the Chipewyan (Denesuline), Dogrib (Tlicho), the Yellowknife (T'atsaot'ine) and the Slavey (Dey cho.) For the quotations to refer to Indigenous people using one name and for me to refer to the same people by another name, though, would be confusing. To reduce possible confusion, I use the names the traders used. I do make an exception for the name Dakelh, using that name rather than Carrier. I have attempted to be guided by Gregory Young-ing's *Elements of Indigenous Style.*

I have relied on the abundance of contemporary records written by HBC employees—post journals, correspondence and financial accounts. We should keep in mind that all the records of the HBC, all the letters and diaries were written by non-Indigenous people. There is, consequently, a filter over everything we have received as facts. We seldom, if ever, hear the contemporary Indigenous voice. Moreover, the traders who wrote HBC journals and letters knew that what they wrote could be read by their superiors at York Factory and even in London, where these papers were sent. They would no doubt have been guarded in their criticisms of their seniors and careful to provide justification for their mistakes.

Among my challenges have been ones of transcription, selection and arrangement. Transcription presents its own problems. At a time when few could read or write, and accurate spelling, capitalization and punctuation were considered unimportant, the existing records varied considerably. I have made the spelling of names consistent and have inserted some punctuation to improve comprehension. Additionally, the men who wrote the journals were very casual about how they recorded the "Mcs and Macs" of Scottish names. Since a large number of the HBC were from Scotland, this makes the task of recording their names frustrating. I have tried to be consistent even when the original records were not. Lastly, I have maintained the imperial measurements used at the time because it would sound oddly out of place to state, for example, that a fur trader travelled ten kilometres.

William Brown was neither important nor powerful. As it turned out, his endeavours and his health eventually failed. He was intelligent, far-seeing and active, a man of brawn and a man of brain. His life gives us a rich picture of the Hudson's Bay Company at this important time in Canada's history.

Prologue

William Brown, standing on the deck of the Hudson's Bay Company's ship *Prince of Wales*, stared at the soft greens of the Hampshire coast as the ship passed along it and eased into the calmer waters of the Solent. As the ship approached Portsmouth Harbour, he pointed out to his four-year-old son, Daniel, the forest of masts and rigging of the ships crowding there. And there were the buildings and church spires of the town. Not old enough to comprehend what was he was looking at, Daniel peered out at the unfamiliar landscape. He knew only that they were going to a place called Scotland, to a home he had never known and to a family he had never met.

The pair had left York Factory on Hudson Bay on September 29, and after a long and at times tempestuous voyage, were now coming home. Rupert's Land, where Brown had worked for the Hudson's Bay Company for a dozen years, was very different from the verdant softness of England's south coast. It was a land of extremes. Of ice, and all too often, near-starvation. A land of rivers and lakes. A land of back-breaking portages between waterways. A land of startlingly different people. A land where danger was never far away. A land of loneliness. Brown thought back to the strife with the long-gone North West Company. The good times and bad times. And the people he had encountered who had changed his life: William Auld and Colin Robertson, both of whom had been so pivotal in his career; Simon McGillivray; and John Stuart, his old boss in New Caledonia, far away over the Rocky Mountains. And, of course, George Simpson, who was in charge of the whole company now and already changing it dramatically, making it even more bureaucratic, more focused on budgets and costs. Simpson was also becoming an autocrat.

And his time with the HBC? That was all over now. Had it all been worth it? Could he have done more? Was it his disagreements with Stuart and Connolly that had ended it for him? Or his ill health? He wasn't well, he knew that. Perhaps he could have risen higher in the company hierarchy. Once a rising man, he had stumbled. And that was that. Basically, he knew he was just an ordinary Scot, trying to do his best. But it hadn't been good enough.

He, Daniel and two other HBC factors were going ashore here in Portsmouth and then on to London by coach. From there it would be a long journey over bad roads in uncomfortable coaches to Brown's village of

Kilmaurs, near Glasgow, where he would meet his family after eight years. He recalled his last parting from his wife, Elizabeth.

As he watched the pilot boat that would take them ashore coming out to meet them from the harbour, Brown would have been wondering what he would find when he finally arrived back at Kilmaurs after so many years away.

1

A Second Chance at Reindeer Lake

1812

"A Mr. Brown who came out as a Writer, goes up with
the Boat for your House, and make no doubt, you will
find him a very agreeable messmate."

Thomas Topping, Chief Factor at Churchill Factory,
July 22, 1812

William Brown heard the pebbles grind as the canoe ran up onto the
shore at the Hudson's Bay Company's (HBC) post at Reindeer Lake.
As one of the canoe men jumped into the water to drag it up the bank,
he clambered out. His seven-week journey from York Factory, the HBC's
headquarters on Hudson Bay, was over. A slender, wiry man of five foot,
eight-and-a-half inches tall, Brown was intelligent, capable and curious.
Richard Sutherland, the chief there and his new boss, came down to welcome him. Knowing they would be working together for several years, the
two men would have greeted each other with eyes full of questions and
assessment. It was September 12, 1812.

Brown, a twenty-two-year-old clerk from Kilmaurs in Scotland, knew
he was lucky. When William Auld, the HBC superintendent at York Factory, decided not to send him back to Scotland for discipline and perhaps
trial, he knew that he had dodged severe discipline or worse, possibly even
conscription into the Royal Navy, engaged at that time in the grinding war
with Napoleonic France. Auld was allowing him to work out his contract
as the clerk for the HBC post at Reindeer Lake, sometimes also called Deer
Lake or, at this time, Clapham House.

Brown was well aware he had been given a second chance. Only luck
and the needs of the HBC had saved him. His experience on the Nelson
River that winter had been bad. He had come close to personal disaster.
But he had felt justified at the time. The conditions he and his comrades
had to live in there had been intolerable. When they had complained and
objected to orders, the HBC officers had called it an insurgency, a mutiny.
And Brown hated being bored; hanging around the encampment on the
Nelson River doing nothing much all day since the previous October had
been frustrating. If he did not make a success of this posting, though, his

life might still take a turn for the worse. Whether or not he made good was in his hands. Now it was up to him to prove himself.

Settling in at Reindeer Lake

After Auld had made his fateful decision, Brown had left York Factory and travelled up the coast to Fort Churchill, where, when he arrived on July 18, whaling was in full swing. He appears to have made himself popular because on July 22, in a routine business letter about furs, hatchet helves (handles) and the next boat to leave Churchill for Reindeer Lake, Thomas Topping, chief factor there, wrote to Sutherland. "A Mr. Brown who came out as a Writer," he said, "goes up with the Boat for your House, and make no doubt, you will find him a very agreeable messmate."[2] Leaving Churchill in a heavy fog on July 29 with thirteen men in two boats, Brown had taken almost seven weeks to get upriver. Sutherland wrote in the Reindeer Lake post journal on September 18: "This day our people arrived at this place from the Factory, viz, Mr. Brown accompanied by eight men for to Remain at the Deer's Lake."[3] These men included two of his fellow mutineers, William Anderson and Daniel Campbell, as well as William Loutit, now apparently recovered from the separate affray on New Year's Day.

A man from Barra in the Outer Hebrides, Sutherland was described in the HBC's books as a very reliable officer. In the strict hierarchy of HBC ranks, Brown, as a clerk, was below the chief factor but above the other employees. The HBC paid Sutherland £40 a year and Brown £30. At this time there were eleven HBC employees at the fort; only Sutherland and Brown were officers. Sutherland kept the post journal, which Brown maintained when Sutherland was away.

Brown would have looked around him eagerly. In area, Reindeer Lake is the twenty-fourth largest lake in the world and the ninth largest lake in what is now Canada. A great quiet lay over it, broken only by the slap of a fish jumping or the distant bark of a dog or call of a bird. Such few noises would have deepened the silence. At certain times of the year there was a background hum of insects. It is a flat landscape of water, with a shoreline deeply indented and with inlets beyond counting. Beyond the thin layer of trees and rocks lie low, smoke-blue hills and a vast sky. Between the countless islands can be seen stretches of water with more islands far away in the distance, shimmering in the light, tricking the imagination into disbelief. On the horizon, the water dissolves into the clouds. In one meteorite–struck place, now called Deep Bay, the lake is 720 feet deep. Indigenous legend has it that a mythical water monster lurks there, one that in prehistory had pulled a reindeer down through the ice into its depths.

Here at Reindeer Lake, Brown was out of the fractious cocoon of the

HBC on Hudson Bay. He had moved from the noise, bustle and politics of the forts there to the silence and endless vastness of the North. Was it forbidding or beckoning? He was now responsible for his own survival and would soon find himself tested. Would he too be sucked down like the reindeer into the darkness? His life would now have four objectives: first, to become acquainted with his new colleagues and district; second, to learn the business of fur-trading; third, to find provisions and help keep those at the fort alive—no small matter; and fourth, to compete in the fur trade with the rival North West Company. Trading in the store, keeping accounts, making nets and fishing would become the tenor of Brown's life.

Sutherland would have given him a tour of the post—their living quarters, the trading room, and the stores. He would no doubt have pointed out the Nor'Wester post not far away. This they called the French House and the men there Frenchmen. Brown would have started to learn about the different animals and their furs, the ins and outs of the trade, the difference between good furs and bad furs, and how to negotiate with the Indigenous hunters. Sutherland doubtless told the new arrivals that during the previous week they had caught only sixteen fish of all kinds at the fort. Their survival would, consequently, depend almost entirely on how good they were at making and repairing nets and using them to catch fish.[4] Sutherland gave everyone a few days to recover from their long journey. Then he set them all to work making more nets. Two days later they had finished two nets and put them into the water.

Sutherland thought they might have better luck at catching fish if they went farther up the lake, and so he sent several men there to set nets. Four men returned a few days later with 560 whitefish and trout, which was all they could catch. In early October, Sutherland sent Brown and five men with leather tents and six new nets up the lake to fish. Brown stayed there to fish, returning on October 19 with a good catch. By the end of October, they had put 1,600 fish into stock in their fish house.

By early November, winter was setting in and ice covered the lake as far as they could see. When the ice was thick enough, they set nets beneath it. One end of the net was fastened to the end of a long pole which passed by means of forked sticks through the hole and under the ice to another hole. There the other end of the net was secured.[5] Since these nets could be as long as 360 feet, the work of making the nets, setting them under the ice and picking the fish out of the nets was laborious and time-consuming. Fingers and hands froze in the icy water. At other times, Sutherland instructed the men to cut more firewood and search for wood to make snowshoes and sledges, or traineaux as they were called.

Brown set about learning about the fur trade: how to value, trade and pack the pelts brought into the fort. He would soon have to become expert in distinguishing good furs from bad and in identifying every defect he could use to reduce the price. When Indigenous people came to major HBC forts to trade, they often came in a brigade of canoes. They swept down a river to the fort with a flourish, following which the leader of the brigade and the chief factor for the HBC would give and receive gifts, share pipes, and engage in formal conversations and elaborate ceremonies. Not until these traditional greetings and rituals were over would trading begin. Most post journals make it clear, though, that trading was usually simpler and more informal.

Before shipment to York Factory and then on to Europe for processing and sale, the furs were pressed into a compact bale known as a pack or pièce. Each fort had one or more large fur presses to do this. Each pack weighed approximately ninety pounds and typically contained forty-five beaver pelts, twelve otter skins, five bear and six fisher skins. At York Factory, men would check them, dry them and repack them for shipment to London.

Brown now had to wear the HBC uniform—though perhaps at such an out-of-the-way place more in theory than in practice. John Tod, one of his shipmates on the voyage out, described the regulation dress of the HBC. According to Tod,

> light blue was the company's colour in attire, and I donned a coat of that colour, worn in this time of winter over a leather, flannel-lined doublet, worsted scarlet waist belt, smoked buckskin breeches, blue cloth leggings up to the knee, under which were three rolls of blanket socks, encased in moose moccasins. This soft and yielding, though tough footgear, by not impeding the circulation, lessened the risk of freezing which the use of hard leather boots would have caused.[6]

Because his life might depend on his ability to light a fire, each man also carried a fire-bag, with flint, steel and space for a pipe and tobacco. Like everyone else, Brown would have adjusted his clothing to the climate. Winters were so severe that he would have added layers of furs, mittens, socks and overshoes. Furs of every animal would have been typical of his winter clothing.

The Fur Trade

Brown would have been aware of the recent history of the HBC. He may not have known or cared that on May 2, 1670, King Charles II of England had granted a charter to a group of merchant adventurers led by his cousin Prince Rupert. This gave them the sole right to trade and commerce over all the lands whose rivers flowed into Hudson Bay—a land of one-and-a-half million square miles, a land named Rupert's Land. Brown would, though, undoubtedly have known that the rival North West Company, based in Montreal, was not only challenging the HBC in Rupert's Land but had a virtual monopoly on the land beyond: Athabasca, and also on the inland trade across the Rocky Mountains, in an area named New Caledonia. Both companies traded the industrial goods of Europe for the bounty of the rivers and forests brought to them by the Indigenous peoples. Inevitably, competition led to conflict, which in turn led to the violence that was already occurring sporadically.

Beavers bred more slowly than the number trapped and killed allowed for regeneration. The existential problem for the fur trade companies, therefore, was that over time hunting denuded an area of its beaver population. This pushed trappers to move ever outwards, lengthening the distances to be travelled. The El Dorado for the fur companies was Athabasca, with its abundance of beavers with thick fur and underhair. Geography gave the fur trade companies a gift. The drainage systems of Rupert's Land and beyond, by reason of their network of lakes and rivers with only short portages between them, enabled the fur traders to use them as highways for the carriage of goods. Both companies entered Lake Winnipeg, the HBC from the north and the North West Company from the southeast, and they shared the waterways going into Athabasca.

The North West Company had several important advantages over the HBC. In the first place, it had a deeper pool of men in Lower Canada to select employees from. In the second, it had a readily available source of food in pemmican. This was essential for the Nor'Westers in the late eighteenth century. It was made from buffalo (more accurately bison) meat, pulverized and mixed with melted tallow and Saskatoon berries. Nor'Westers ate it raw or coated with flour and fried. Generally, a man ate eight pounds of fish or fresh meat in a day. Pemmican provided the equivalent nourishment in one-and-a-half pounds. Conveniently packed into special bags thirty inches long and four inches wide, it could be stowed easily in canoes for long journeys. The Indigenous and Métis peoples hunted buffalo and made pemmican in the lands around the Assiniboine and Red Rivers. Any threat to the supply of pemmican threatened the existence of both the North West Company and the Métis. Furthermore, the North West Company had the more dynamic organization, being a partnership that, based in Montreal, could make decisions quickly. It was altogether more entrepreneurial than the HBC, which was bureaucratically micro-managed from the boardrooms on Fenchurch Street in London.

With these advantages and the closing of markets in Europe to the fur trade during the Napoleonic wars, the North West Company was increasingly seen to be the company most likely to survive. Many argued that the HBC had to change and become more assertive or it would cease to exist. Among these were William Auld and Colin Robertson, both of whom made pivotal decisions about Brown's future. The Shakespeare-loving Robertson had been a Nor'Wester. He brought its independent thinking and risk-taking mentality into the HBC and proposed more aggressive policies.

In 1811, Thomas Douglas, the 5th Earl of Selkirk, stepped into the story. With the wealth of a Scottish aristocrat and the benevolent rationalism of the Scottish enlightenment, he wanted to establish colonies in British North America where indigent Scots, ejected from their lands during the Highland clearances, could settle, farm and thrive. He asked the HBC to give him the right to establish a colony on the Red River, with a land area of 116,000 square miles. The shareholders of the HBC approved his application on May 30, 1811. By then, he had already been recruiting colonists in Scotland and Ireland. These he sent to Stornoway to wait for the ships that would take them to York Factory.

As naive as he was benevolent, Selkirk ignored the warnings that his new colony would inevitably lead to conflict. It would seriously disrupt the pemmican trade and arouse fierce opposition from the North West Company and the Métis, who also depended on the buffalo hunt. With better right than anyone, the Indigenous people of the region saw the land as theirs. They too would resist. In any event, they may have all thought, what chance would a few dozen crofters and clerks have of being able to establish farms on the Red River and survive the dry summers and savagely cold winters? Many in the HBC service, William Auld among them, with a firmer grasp of reality than Selkirk, believed that this venture, however well-intentioned, could not survive.

Indigenous People

A few days after Brown arrived at Reindeer Lake, two Indigenous men came to the fort and asked for ammunition and tobacco. Brown thus began his acquaintance with the local inhabitants, who were mostly Chipewyan people. The next day, four Indigenous families arrived at the fort and two others went to the nearby Nor'Wester post. Sutherland noted that they had no goods to trade but wanted credit.

The entry of the HBC into Rupert's Land, and later Athabasca and New Caledonia, profoundly changed Indigenous societies. The introduction of industrial goods, liquor, tobacco and guns dislocated age-old cultures. Over the previous one hundred and fifty years, though, the HBC had established and maintained a trading relationship with Indigenous people. With some exceptions, this was peaceful. Violence would not have helped either side in a trading relationship that benefitted both parties. Coexistence, not always comfortably, had been the norm for those one hundred and fifty years.

The Indigenous world beyond the immediate surroundings of the forts was, and is, complicated and sophisticated. The picture of an Indigenous man killing a beaver and merely bringing its pelt to the nearest fort is simplistic. A trapper would not necessarily bring the furs he had trapped to the fort himself but might pass them on in trade with other Indigenous people. A pelt might, therefore, have passed through an intricate trading system before it came through a fort's door. "The main reason the fur trade operated as smoothly as it did," Peter Newman, a historian of the HBC, wrote, "was that, without being aware of it, the HBC factors tapped into an existing Indian economic network dating back as much as five thousand years."[7]

The post journal faithfully recorded when Indigenous traders came to the post and what they brought. On July 5, 1813, for example, Brown wrote in the post's journal: "This day 5 Indian Men & a boy arrived at our house. They brought with them 2 Beaver Skins, 1 Otter, 4 lbs of Fat, 120 lbs of Green Meat, 225 lbs of Meat, dry and pounded. One Indian also went to the French House."[8] Among the items that Indigenous men brought to the fort were the delightfully named and undoubtedly useful shaganappies, which were raw-hide straps used to tie things together.

NORTH WEST COMPANY—THE FRENCH

Within sight of the HBC post on Reindeer Lake, the North West Company had a trading post manned by five men and a clerk. Relations between the two companies, which in places had already broken out into violence (and would grow worse), here at Reindeer Lake were relatively peaceful and civil. They were, nevertheless, competitors. They exchanged polite notes and conversed. But as all competitors do, however friendly, they watched each other closely and seized every opportunity to gain an advantage. Brown and Sutherland carefully noted which Indigenous hunters went to the Nor'Wester House and what they took with them. In turn, the Nor'Westers watched who came to the HBC. The Indigenous hunters and trappers were well able to play each company off against the other, and so they did.

Naturally, men of both companies tried to poach each other's Indigenous hunters and were insulted when the other poached theirs. Both companies believed they had claims to the exclusive loyalty of a specific group of Indigenous hunters. Both were offended when they noticed an Indigenous man whom they thought was committed to them going into the other's house. Both used tobacco and liquor as inducements and fists as weapons, though the Nor'Westers—at least by HBC accounts—seemed to be more violent. Brown recorded that Indigenous men came to him secretly and said they would only trade at night, somewhere secret, because they were afraid the Nor'Westers would severely beat them for disloyalty if they knew they were trading with the HBC. Sometimes Brown would go out to Indigenous villages and tents to forestall the Nor'Westers.

Neither company was above suborning each other's employees. Before changing sides, deserters, no doubt discreetly, would have made sure of their welcome. Sutherland recorded one incident that took place in early January 1813. He had just returned from a three-day trip up the lake to look for wood for snowshoes and sledges. On his return, he wrote that

> it is easier conceived than described how much I was surprised to hear that two of our Men, viz, Daniel Campbell & William Anderson had left the House on the Night between the 6th and 7th Inst. when every other person at the House was fast asleep. They did not leave a single article behind them excepting a Bible. In their hurry for getting over to the French House, as was supposed, they had carried every article belonging them without the door before they intended setting off for good & all. Consequently in their bustle & hurry they had left the door of the House open behind them, which gave free admittance to every one of the dogs & awakened some of the Men, but, they having no suspicion of any thing of the kind to have taken place, they got off unknown to every one until Morning.[9]

Next morning Sutherland sent a note to James Keith, the Nor'Wester chief, asking why he had received the men so clandestinely. Keith replied that both had wanted to serve with the North West Company and did not want to return to the HBC. Significantly, both Campbell and Anderson had been among the insurgents at the Nelson Encampment, having both signed an angry letter to William Auld that Brown had likely written. The dynamics of the relationship between Brown and the two men before their desertion might perhaps have been fraught.

Brown knew he would be spending the next three years here working out his contract. He now had to settle down to learn the trade and survive. Life at Reindeer Lake was quiet but hard. He and his colleagues would endure the winters as best they could and welcome spring when it arrived. Doubtless there were times when he would wonder what he had got himself into.

In his reflective moments, he may have thought back on how he had got there and how close his escape from being sent back to Scotland in disgrace had been. Memories of Stornoway harbour and the fractious winter on Nelson River would have still been fresh in his memory. So far, his time since leaving Glasgow had been full of strife, near-starvation and hardship. He would now be tested again. Would he swim, or would he, like the reindeer, sink down into the darkness?

2

Chaos in Stornoway Harbour

July 1811

"Damn my buttons. If you don't like the food, you may jump overboard."

John Davison, July 26, 1811

God knows, Brown had seen enough strife. His whole adventure in North America had started in Stornoway Harbour on the Isle of Lewis in the Outer Hebrides with one of the most chaotic scenes he had ever witnessed. He was in fact part of that chaos. The Glasgow clerks, among whom he was a notable member, were already being described as troublesome and dissipated. And his winter on the Nelson River had been a nightmare that had led him to a protest that the HBC had called an insurgency and treated as such.

Born in about 1790, Brown had grown up in Kilmaurs, a village about nineteen miles southwest of Glasgow. With a population of approximately 750, Kilmaurs had two principal industries: weaving and knife-making. Where Brown was going, he would need to be, as the popular saying had it, "as gleg as a Kilmaurs whittle." Gleg was an old Scottish term for sharp, clever or clear-sighted and a whittle was a knife. Here both his parents, Daniel and Elizabeth, had been born. We know little about young William's early life, but we do know that by 1811, he was literate and working as a clerk.

Always of an adventurous nature, Brown's explorations had led him to Elizabeth Armour. Their illegitimate daughter, also named Elizabeth, was born on November 12, 1810. The elders of the kirk were unhappy about this and took Elizabeth to task. On July 12, 1811, she admitted to them that she had dallied with William Brown and gave them his written acknowledgement of paternity. The elders disciplined her but may have allowed her to have her daughter christened two days later. By this time, though, Brown was far away. While Elizabeth was explaining her conduct to the elders, he was in Stornoway waiting for the HBC ships to arrive from Gravesend, the port downstream from London on the River Thames. Though we may speculate, we do not actually know why he decided to leave Scotland.

Kilmaurs in about 1900. This is the tollbooth of Kilmaurs, built about the time of Brown's birth. A tollbooth was the main municipal building in a Scottish town. Within it was the council chamber, the courthouse and the town gaol. Many of the buildings still exist.

Captain Roderick (probably Roderick MacDonald), a recruiting agent for the HBC since 1810, had been touring Scotland looking for likely young men to journey to Rupert's Land either to work for the HBC itself or to be among the first settlers of Lord Selkirk's colony on the Red River. In Glasgow he hired thirteen clerks, one of whom was Brown, together with thirty labourers. Whatever Brown's personal reasons, going to work for the HBC was a common way for many Scots to escape the restrictions and poverty of early nineteenth-century Scotland. Men enlisted on a three-year contract, intending to save their wages and then return to Scotland to build a better life for themselves.

Sometime in June, Brown, together with the other men from Glasgow, took passage to Stornoway. John Tod was one of the other Glasgow clerks. Chafing at parental restrictions, a boring job and armed with a copy of the Bible, a book of Robert Burns's verse, and William Buchan's *Domestic Medicine* given to him by his father, Tod had signed on with the HBC as an apprentice clerk. His wages would be £20 a year, with a raise of £5 every year of his contract. Tod admitted he did not really have much idea where he was going or what he would do when he got there. In Stornoway, the newly hired clerks waited for the settlers to assemble and, bored and with nothing to do, sought whatever dissipations Stornoway had to offer.

SELKIRK AND THE RED RIVER SETTLEMENT

What they were waiting for were the three HBC ships to arrive to take them to York Factory, the HBC's headquarters located on a low, swampy neck of land between the mouths of the Hayes and Nelson Rivers on Hudson Bay. The ships were coming from Gravesend, where the principals of the Selkirk colony were gathering. On June 15, 1811, the governor and officers of the HBC together with Selkirk's officers had bumped in chaises over the twenty-two miles from London to Gravesend. When they arrived, their ships, the *Edward and Ann*, the *Prince of Wales* and the *Eddystone,* each fired a seven-cannon salute to greet them. That evening, as was traditional, the governor held a dinner at the Falcon Inn for thirty-four of the HBC officers and gentlemen. After speeches, toasts and general bonhomie, Joseph Berens, the deputy governor of the HBC, formally announced the appointment of Captain Miles Macdonell to lead the expedition. He also named him the first governor of Assiniboine, the name of the proposed settlement on the Red River. He then announced that William Hillier would be second in command. However, there was a difference between them. Hillier was an HBC employee and would not be subject to Macdonell's orders on land. Rather, he had a separate HBC mission. Macdonell's orders were to sail to York Factory and take no fewer than thirty men upriver to establish the Red River Settlement before winter.

Bad weather delayed their departure. "The detention here is unfortunate," Macdonell wrote from Yarmouth on July 4, "& I fear will destroy our expectation of getting into the interior this winter. However, all that's possible shall be effected."[10] Any delay in reaching Stornoway meant the ships were likely to arrive at York Factory too late to establish the Red River Settlement before winter. If this were the case, the settlers would have to spend a long, cold winter on Hudson Bay. Lord Selkirk's venture was not off to a good start.

When the convoy eventually arrived at Stromness in the Orkney Isles, the *Prince of Wales* stayed to embark Orkney men, while the *Edward and Ann* and the *Eddystone,* with Macdonell aboard, carried on to Stornoway. Captain Thomas Gull brought the *Edward and Ann* into Stornoway Harbour and dropped anchor at noon on Tuesday, July 17. Macdonell then went ashore to find out how many settlers were waiting to embark. With the clerks and labourers from Glasgow were other Scots and Irishmen, all having their first experience of different cultures. Father Charles Bourke was an Irish Catholic priest. An enthusiastic settler, he told Macdonell he could recruit thousands more settlers where he came from. Nevertheless, instead of the seventy he had promised, he actually arrived in Stornoway with only fourteen, mainly recruited from his own parish of Killala. He

William Daniell, RA, *Stornoway on the Isle of Lewis*, 1819. Here the HBC ships collected the waiting settlers and new HBC recruits, including Brown, to take them to Hudson Bay.

enjoyed singing and relished convivial tippling. Macdonell, a little less politely, called him a tipsy priest.

STORNOWAY

Macdonell took stock of the men and their mood. His first problem was that Captain Roderick had promised higher wages to the Glasgow clerks and labourers than had been promised to the Irish. He proposed reducing the wages of the Glasgow men to be in line with those of the Irish. The Scots quickly made it abundantly clear that they would not under any circumstances agree to this. He wrote that the men, saying they would not have enlisted for any less, objected strongly to any reduction in their pay: "It was then necessary to address the whole body and assure them that no alteration would be made in their agreements. Others wanted an augmentation to their pay, saying that if I [Macdonell] had the power to reduce I could add."[11] Unable to reduce the wages and unwilling to raise them, Macdonell had to back down. With so few settlers, he felt he could not discharge any and send them home. This difference in wages for the labourers along national lines was bound to cause trouble, and indeed it did.

The Glasgow clerks (or writers as they were called), including Brown and Tod, were already proving troublesome. As clerks, they occupied a different position from the labourers, having been hired as the most junior officers in the HBC hierarchy. Macdonell noted they were already "dissatisfied from dissipation and idleness."[12] He had problems with them from the start. Macdonell did not quite know what to do with them because no one had told him whether or not they were going to go to York Factory and Churchill for the HBC or with him to the Red River. Referring to the Glasgow clerks, to whom he had paid a year's wages in advance, Macdonell wrote "they were, while on shore, with a few exceptions, as irregular in their conduct & troublesome as the common hired men."[13]

Since the HBC thought the Glasgow clerks were being paid too much, it now reneged on their contracts. Brown, one of these clerks, would probably have been out of a job. This could have left him stranded in the Outer Hebrides, after a month living in Stornoway with nothing to do and perhaps without much money left from his advance. Macdonell, though, obtained authority from Lord Selkirk to hire the clerks as settlers for the Red River Settlement. While in Stornoway, the clerks were, in effect, moved from the HBC service to Selkirk's. Their reactions to this were not recorded, but they were noted as being a grumpy lot and at times mutinous. At this point, Brown may have believed he was now going to the Red River. Or perhaps they didn't tell him anything.

Many in the HBC ships suspected—with good reason—that someone was trying to prevent the ships from sailing. And they knew who. Sir Alexander Mackenzie, the famous explorer, and Simon McGillivray, both senior partners in the North West Company, the HBC's powerful fur-trading rival in British North America, were both in England. Both believed Selkirk's settlement posed a significant threat to their company's existence, and both had publicly asserted they would do everything they could to wreck the settlement before it even started. Mackenzie had spent the first ten years of his life in Stornoway and had many relatives there willing to be aggressively helpful.

Their agents had been distributing copies of the *Inverness Journal* in the Hebrides. This contained an article written by McGillivray, under the nom de plume of the "Highlander." This disparaged Lord Selkirk's project and attempted to dissuade the emigrants from continuing. It was certainly effective in persuading many of the would-be settlers to slip away. Father Bourke and Macdonell saw the need to counter the article and both wrote spirited replies. While waiting in Stornoway, Father Bourke amused himself by writing songs and concerning himself with other forms of spirits. On July 13, he wrote: "I spent the evening with some friends. Seven bottles of wine, punch, accordingly were drank."[14] Father Bourke wrote one of the more lively accounts of the voyage and the events of the coming winter.

Macdonell invited local dignitaries to dinner on board the *Eddystone*. One of his guests was Mr. Reid, the collector of customs in Stornoway. Significantly, Reid was married to Sir Alexander Mackenzie's aunt. Macdonell later alleged that Captain John Mackenzie, who, a few days later, played a principal part in obstructing them, was Reid's son-in-law. He is a "mean fellow of the name McKenzie, called a Captain," Macdonell told Selkirk, leaving little doubt what he thought of this particular Mackenzie.[15]

EMBARKATION AND PREPARING TO SAIL

On Saturday, July 20, the *Prince of Wales* arrived in Stornoway Harbour with fifty-nine settlers from the Orkney Isles on board. Also on board was a woman disguised as a man, presumably stowing away to be with a paramour. Discovered, she was put ashore in Stornoway. The following day, the captains of the three ships gave orders to bring the provisions and stores on board. The ships were not yet quite ready to load the passengers, and so the men milled around Stornoway expectantly. But if any of them were looking for their last chance of more dissipation before boarding, the likelihood of their finding much in Stornoway on a Scottish Sunday would have been low.

Tuesday, July 23, was a day of confusion. In heavy rain, the captains commenced embarking the passengers. Some were drunk; some mutinous. A few of them had to be carried on board. Others absconded and hid. Since they had signed contracts—that is, were indentured—and had been given advances of as much as a year's wages, Macdonell thought they had no right to desert. They were, he maintained, under contract: therefore, they had to board. He called for support from the marines to enforce compliance. It was not only the labourers who deserted. One troublesome clerk, who went on shore "by stealth," did not return and sent for his belongings the next day. He later caused much trouble by publicly criticizing Selkirk's project in London.

By now it was clear that Reid, Mackenzie and others on shore were actively obstructing the ships' departure in any way they could. The authorities were enforcing the emigration rules strictly. Some have suggested they were doing so, not at the behest of the North West Company and the Mackenzies, but were merely performing their duties as officers of the law. Nevertheless, they enforced the rules with an energy and determination that suggests they had every intention of delaying the ships for as long as possible. One regulation, for example, was that each ship had to have a doctor on board. So the authorities on shore ordered the captains and doctors to come ashore so they could thoroughly check their papers with the most rigid scrutiny. Until the customs office issued a clearance, the ships could not leave. They also scrutinized the passenger lists in great detail.

The port authorities came to each ship for a muster which, perhaps surprisingly, went smoothly. The men by now, though, Macdonell said, were "very mutinous & turbulent."[16]

Eventually, all the passengers were on board. Macdonell wrote to Selkirk:

> All the men that we shall have are now embarked, but it has been a Herculean labour!... The Collector of this place, Mr. Reid, an old, weak & dissipated man (although I asked him to dinner & made him drunk) has thrown every impediment in our way, & has armed himself against us with all the formalities of the Customs to which he has exacted a rigid compliance from all the ships & to which we were fortunately able to conform.[17]

On July 25, 1811, it was raining, with squalls coming across the open harbour. Brown was one of the passengers on board the *Edward and Ann*. He may be forgiven if he had looked around him in dismay at the growing chaos. There were disputes about food. There were angry arguments about whether the clerks from Glasgow were to eat and sleep with common labourers or, as promised, in their own mess. They had to make do with a curtain.

The chaos continued through Thursday and into Friday, July 26. Captain Gull of the *Edward and Ann* went ashore to satisfy the Customs House on a minor regulation. Taking advantage of his absence, Captain Mackenzie came on board with a sergeant and a recruiting party to look for deserters from the army and also to try to persuade the passengers to enlist. Lord Wellington was winning battles against Napoleon's generals in Spain but needed more soldiers to finish the job. Mackenzie did recruit one man, Mathew Shiells, and gave him the King's shilling to seal the bargain. Macdonell, though, would not let Shiells leave the ship. The soldiers also tried to persuade men to abandon their plans of going to Rupert's Land.

Father Bourke wrote:

> One McKenzy commonly called Captain McKenzy came on board to spread sedition & mutiny among the Men, which in part he effected. He at first said he came to look for Diserters. He went into the forepart of the Ship, offering money to the Men to inlist them. An Irishman, Anthony Macdonell [no relation to Miles Macdonell], upon offering him a shilling told him *kur en da hone ee* [Gaelic], which is to say put it in your a—s. This happened a.m.

Capt. McDonell was not on board. Not succeeding in the forenoon, he resolved to try another attempt, in which he succeeded better, by corrupting some of the Men and having boats prepared for taking them ashore in the evening, and accordingly prevailed on ten of them, & would on a good many more, but for my prevalence with them. He & his accomplices insinuated that the Men would be starved on board, that their provisions would be curtailed when they put to sea. This language prevailed with ten of them &, as I have said, would with many more but for me. I reasoned with them & brought them over.[18]

Captain Mackenzie returned to the *Edward and Ann* for more obstruction in the afternoon. While Mr. McIver, the clerk in his party, was pleading for no violence, Mackenzie tried to climb up the side of the ship. Miles Macdonell, now back on board, was not prepared to allow him on deck because of his "ungentleman-like conduct" of that morning, and successfully prevented him. The two men shouted insults at each other. Macdonell wrote: "Some sharp words passed between us."[19] As indeed, they probably had. That evening, Macdonell went ashore to challenge Mackenzie to a duel but could not find him.

From one of the boats, McIver officiously read aloud the section of the Emigration Act to the effect that, despite their contracts, the passengers did not have to go if they did not want to. (Sir Alexander Mackenzie had married Isabella McIver and the family connection clearly helped.) On hearing this, some of those on board the *Edward and Ann* jumped down into Mackenzie's boat.

With Captain Gull feeling temporarily unwell, John Davison, the supercargo, was temporarily in charge. All he had given the passengers to eat so far was porridge. John Tod recounted that John Hamilton, one of the labourers, walked up to Davison and told him the passengers would not live any longer on porridge. "Damn my buttons," Tod quoted Davison as saying, "if you don't like the food, you may jump overboard."[20] Whereupon Hamilton threw off his bonnet, coat and boots, jumped into the sea—followed by five others—and started to swim to the shore one-and-a-half miles away.

Davison lowered boats to recapture the swimmers. Men on shore, seeing the commotion and afraid their friends had got among the Irish, also rowed to the scene. "The two flotillas reached the fugitives about the same time," Tod recalled, "and after a struggle in which, amusingly, the shoulders and feet of some of the swimmers were pulled in different directions by the contesting rescuers, the town party won and proceeded to the shore with their willing captives."[21] Macdonell wrote: "It was a complete scramble. Some going, others pulling them back & it being late in the evening, the Collector & Custom house officers got into their Boat & I thought I saw some of our runaway men brought to shore in it."[22]

Sailing

The next day, Friday, July 26, the wind was blowing from an inconvenient direction. Captain Gull, now feeling better, fearing more desertions and having a favourable breeze, put the *Edward and Ann* out to sea as soon as he could. His was no idle fear. As a result of the desertions, a quarter of those who had assembled in Stornoway for the voyage had already melted away. The three ships sailed with ninety labourers and fifteen clerks. From the first, the men from Glasgow were the most turbulent and the most dissatisfied. A small boat had managed to come out to them with confirmation of what they already suspected: there had indeed been a conspiracy in Stornoway to stop them. "I now learnt," Macdonell wrote, "that the business of yesterday was [a] pre-concerted matter between the Collector, Captain McKenzie & others."[23]

By the evening, they were off the Butt of Lewis and heading to Hudson Bay. They were sailing in a convoy with the other HBC ships and two others bound for Labrador, and for most of the voyage, the *Edward and Ann* kept within sight of the convoy. The passengers settled down to endure the journey as best they could and wondered about their futures.

Though the obstructions in Stornoway were now behind them, the perils of the voyage were ahead. Crossing the North Atlantic had its risks at any time of the year. With Great Britain still at war with Napoleonic France, there was a risk that they would be intercepted by a French warship and carried away to a French prison. More to the point, the *Edward and Ann* was scarcely sea-worthy. Captain Gull seemed incompetent, and the crew of sixteen, including the captain, mate and three small boys, was far too small to sail her. With rotting ropes and sails and far too small a crew for such an arduous voyage, it looked as though the ship could barely sail across Stornoway harbour, let alone the North Atlantic.

Selkirk and Macdonell were at least aware of the forces arrayed against them, even if they chose to ignore them. William Brown, setting out across the North Atlantic on the *Edward and Ann*, probably knew nothing whatsoever of such potential perils. He was perhaps merely hoping and praying to reach dry land safely. By now, Brown may have been wondering whether he had made the right decision. What misbegotten venture *had* he let himself in for? With heavy rain, a conspiracy of obstruction, mutinous passengers and an unseaworthy ship, his adventures in Rupert's Land had got off to a worrying start.

3

Survival, Scurvy and Strife
on the Nelson River

WINTER 1811

"A Clerk came to the factory with his toes, as I am told, frozen solid.... I hope they won't send any more of these soft-toed gentry here."

William Cook, December 23, 1811

The crossing had been long. But except for a storm or two, a huge comet that lit up the sky and became known as the Great Comet of 1811, a few strange sails on the horizon and the need for passengers to assist the crew, it had been uneventful. No French warship or privateer appeared out of nowhere to snap them up. At first, as might be expected, all the land-lubbers, including the doctor, were seasick. By August 5, though, most of them had found their sea legs. The fare, happily for them all, did get better. John Tod noted that the food "improved, and 'burgoo,' or oatmeal porridge without milk or any substitute was almost banished from the tables. I had no idea," he declared, "till I tried it, and saw the effect upon others, how distasteful oatmeal by itself soon becomes, excepting always cakes fried on the griddle."[24]

On September 3, the passengers saw shore birds and seaweed and understood they were approaching land. The commodore signalled to the other ships that he had seen ice, and the following day they had their first glimpse of North America. A week later, leaving the dangers of the North Atlantic behind them, they sailed into the Hudson Bay Straits. In these straits, which are five hundred miles long and forty to fifty miles wide, they had to be on the watch for icebergs with all their lurking dangers.

William Brown climbed carefully down the side of the ship. He found his footing in the small boat that was to take him across the icy waters of the Hudson Bay Straits to the *Eddystone*. Freezing spray blew over him across the unsheltered waters. There had been so much confusion in Stornoway that Macdonell found he had assigned men to the wrong ships. Since the *Eddystone* was going directly to Fort Churchill, he moved some of the passengers around. "Not conceiving it to be the intention of the Co.," he wrote to Selkirk on October 1, "that all the clerks or writers were for one part of

Robert Hood (1797-1821), *The Hudson's Bay Company Ships* Prince of Wales *and* Eddystone *Bartering with the Eskimos off the Upper Savage Islands, Hudson Strait, 1819.*

the Country, I permitted three to volunteer into the *Prince of Wales* for the service of the south[ern] Factories, and two others to go in the *Eddystone* to Churchill."[25] Brown was one of these two. This suggests that Brown may have chosen to stay with the HBC and go to Fort Churchill rather than risk of the rigours of the Red River.

Macdonell, mindful of Selkirk's belief that mixing the men from different nations would lead to greater harmony and understanding, complained that "none of the young men made any progress in learning the Gaelic or Irish languages on the voyage." He also tried arms drill with them but found that none of them knew much about guns. "There never was a more awkward squad," he grumbled. "Not a man or even officer of the party knew how to put a gun to his eye or had ever fired a shot."[26]

By now they would all have understood they would be arriving at York Factory too late in the season to journey south to the Red River and establish Selkirk's settlement. They would, consequently, have to remain somewhere on Hudson Bay doing not very much until spring. Their winter would be long and hard, and they were in no way prepared for it. Discontent, national animosities and fear of scurvy simmered in the community, and it led to violence and a mutiny in which Brown was deeply involved.

Arrival at York Factory

On September 24, after a voyage of sixty-one days, the convoy finally arrived at York Factory. "The longest ever known," Macdonell wrote to Selkirk about the voyage, "& the latest to H. Bay."[27] A little to Macdonell's surprise, the *Edward and Ann* had somehow managed to cross the Atlantic. But he was not at all satisfied with the ship's seaworthiness. "The passengers were of great assistance," he wrote. "Without them I do not know how she would have done. I am surprised the Co'y. would charter and send her off in that state."[28]

Because of the shallowness of the coastal waters, the closest to York

Factory the ships could anchor was Five Fathom Hole, approximately seven miles away. Sloops took the passengers and goods ashore the following day. The men of York Factory immediately started the work of unpacking, dividing and loading the goods for their inland destinations. Macdonell complained that all the stores for the Red River Settlement were hopelessly mixed with the HBC stores in the process of unloading. In the confusion, the grindstone he intended to take with him to the Red River was left on board. The *Eddystone,* with Brown on it, attempted to reach Fort Churchill. Stopped by ice, it had to turn back to York Factory. Brown now stepped foot on the land where he was to spend most of the next fifteen years.

York Factory was the headquarters of the HBC in Rupert's Land. The man in charge of the factory was William Cook. The person in charge of the HBC in Rupert's Land was also based there: this was the redoubtable William Auld.

John Tod described York Factory thus:

> York Factory, where we disembarked, was a large collection of buildings, some in disrepair owing to the swampiness of the locality, which indeed characterizes the whole coast. The factory was built partly on piles. It was within a large, oblong enclosure, walled by a timber stockade, with galleries to walk on, inside and out—a tower at each corner and a high "lookout" tower near the end of the main building. This latter was very large, containing a general room 300 feet long with the officers' and servants' rooms entered from it. Fur sheds, shipping warehouses, offices, stores, magazines, boat house and dwellings for the servants made thirty to forty buildings within the enclosure. There were cannons in the bastions, and facing the main entrance, chiefly now I was told, for defense against a possible raid by the rival Northwest Company.[29]

John McLeod was another of the clerks. He recalled that Cook and Auld were haughty. They sent the clerks, he wrote, to eat with the cooks in the kitchen rather than at the officers' table. This led to great discontent among the clerks, who felt that, as clerks they were gentlemen, albeit on the lowest rung of the HBC ladder. It was therefore their right to eat with the other officers, and they complained mightily about this mistreatment. Cook eventually permitted them to dine in a separate room in a small house. In an organization as formally bureaucratic as the HBC, where people ate and how they were treated was evidence of their status. The clerks, however lowly, could not accept the demotion of eating in the kitchen.

Peter Rindisbacher, *Departure of the Second Settler Transport from York Factory to Rockfort [Rock Fort]*, September 6, 1821.

Accompanying Brown on this venture in Rupert's Land were two other men from his own parish of Kilmaurs: Robert Montgomery and James Robertson. Although it is tempting to think they were friends, engaged in this great adventure together, there is in fact no evidence whatsoever to connect them other than the fact that they came from the same parish. The HBC now sent Brown's friend John Tod, whom it considered too young for the Red River, as apprentice clerk to its post at Severn Factory, eastwards along Hudson Bay. Perhaps they thought Tod was just the sort of impressionable—and therefore teachable—person they wanted.

Auld believed Selkirk's Red River Settlement was impractical, utopian and unlikely to succeed. He also thought it would actively impede the proper business of the HBC. At that time, there were only 320 HBC men in seventy-six posts in the whole of Rupert's Land. (The North West Company had twelve hundred.) Here now were a hundred more men to feed. He foresaw trouble, and he was right. Nevertheless, he was instructed to help them in any way he could and this, grumbling, and some say obstructing, he did.

Nelson Encampment

Auld seemed to have wanted the new arrivals away from York Factory as soon as he could arrange it. He decided they should spend the winter at a camp twenty-six miles away at a place near Seal Island on the Nelson River where there was already a rudimentary outpost. Macdonell wrote that the men were hurried off to Nelson River "promiscuously as they landed from the Ships."[30] At their new home for the winter, they would have to build houses for themselves and find their own food. Auld hoped they would be able to catch enough fish at Seal Island to sustain themselves.

Tod described the climate as being nine months of snow and ice and three months of bad weather. How would they survive the winter? *Would* they survive the winter? Few of them knew much about guns, and even fewer knew how to deal with the winter conditions they would be facing. Though they had been told the winters were no worse than Scotland's, they soon found out that they had been misled: it was considerably colder and far less hospitable.

On September 30, William Hillier took a party of men to Nelson River to start building houses. Macdonell went by boat around the point a few days later and had a hard time of it. On his first attempt, strong winds drove him back towards York Factory. "The water dashed into the Boat," he wrote, "which froze on the men's clothes like armour. Had to put back."[31] After several more attempts, he finally succeeded. But the men with him had to jump out of the boat in icy water up to their knees to pull the boat off shoals. The water was so slushy and full of ice that it had a clammy, tenacious quality. Father Bourke, going with them, likened the journey to rowing in thick mud. Macdonell wrote to Selkirk on October 7, 1811.

> Arrived in the evening at the place opposite the Seal Islands where Mr. Hillier & our people were encamped. The Men were quartered, some in Leather Tents & others in Tents formed of spruce branches. I had my Tent pitched & took Mr. Bourke with me into it. Found Mr. Hillier's house nearly built & the house intended for me & my officers, part of the wall raised. A narrow flat where the Houses are, behind which is a high bank to the North. Call the place Nelson Encampment.[32]

The first task was to finish building the houses to live in during the winter. Until the houses were completed, the men lived in tents. Father Bourke, who spent a few nights in Macdonell's tent, thought he would freeze to death. To his surprise, he was warm and snug under his blankets. He did note, though, that there was an inch of ice on the outside of his blanket every morning. Macdonell and his men continued to build the houses, and Bourke wrote "in little time had bulwarks to resist the intensest cold, & what was more surprising, he [Macdonell] lodged the Men before himself."[33]

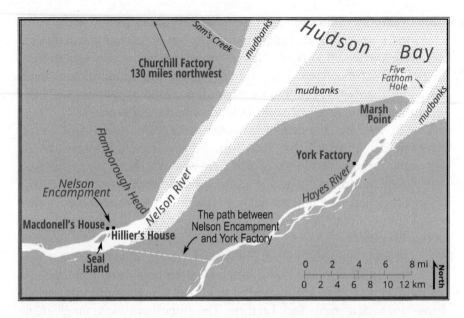

York Factory and Nelson Encampment. Brown spent the winter of 1811–1812 at Nelson Encampment and became a leader in an insurrection there.

RED RIVER SETTLERS AND HBC EMPLOYEES

For the rest of 1811, we hear nothing more of William Brown and the Glasgow clerks. We must assume they settled in to make the best of it, taking their part in necessary chores, learning what they could of the new country and, importantly, staying out of trouble. That would soon change.

The men assembled at Nelson Encampment for the winter were a diverse group of nationalities simmering with the prejudices of the time: Orkney men, Scots from the Highlands and Islands, fractious clerks and men from Glasgow, and Irishmen. The men were being paid different wages and this inevitably caused resentment. Why should a Scot, an Irishman would have thought, be paid more than he was for doing the same job?

Orkney men had been loyal, trusted, obedient servants of the HBC for over a century. For them it was a way of life to sign up for three years, serve their time, re-engage or not, and then return to the Orkney Isles. Of the 530 employees of the HBC in 1799, 416 were from Orkney. (At that time there were reportedly twice as many young women in Stromness as young men.[34]) The Irish were Catholics, with Father Bourke as their priest. Auld had prejudices—or premonitions—about these Irish. "The arrival of such Strangers as the Irish men is highly disgusting to every servant of the Company's, and I am much mistaken if we shall not find them more dangerous to us than our enemies.… [A] more fatal blow was never given nor ever will be again given to the H.B. Co'y. than employing Irishmen, the sweepings, I understand, of jails."[35] They all seemed to agree that the English were far too accustomed to the debaucheries and fleshpots of London to make good labourers. With a reputation for complaining, the English were often seen as troublemakers.

On the voyage out, Macdonell had been thinking about how to allocate the men between the Red River Settlement (his men) and the HBC (Hillier's men). Some of the men were going with Macdonell to the Red River Settlement. Others were staying with the HBC, many of whom would be going with Hillier to establish a new HBC post on the eastern side of Lake Winnipeg, north of the proposed settlement on the Red River. Hillier's men would be on contract there for three years before returning to Scotland.

But which of the men would go with Macdonell and which with Hillier? Almost as soon as they arrived at Nelson Encampment, Macdonell pounced. On October 10, he separated the men into two parties in the way he deemed appropriate: that is, he cherry-picked the best of them. He took thirty-eight men from the party to go with him to the Red River. Macdonell noted, almost with surprise, that Hillier was displeased at this. No wonder. Macdonell had chosen the most able men for the Red River, and assigned the old, the weak and the sick to Hillier. Auld wrote:

> C'n [Captain] Macdonell was a good many days after Mr. Hillier & the people at the factory when he arrived there at Seal Island. He immediately divided the Men in a most unequal & very improper manner without making the slightest notice of his design to Hillier who was confounded with the insult & then required arguments from me of a very peculiar nature to keep him yet from demanding satisfaction. [That is, a duel.] It was a most unwise & impolitic measure so unnecessarily to declare this superiority and alienate a person who is designed to be his chief support.[36]

Auld wrote again to William Cook, the chief factor at York Factory, on November 19.

> With regard to the affair of the division of the Men which Mr. Hillier first hinted at in a letter to you, I was not long there before I saw enough to dissipate anything like envy at their situation for, tho' so nearly connected as Capt. Macdonell & Mr. Hillier are, nothing but the

cold obligations of duty keep them from open war. ...It seems a day or two after C'n McD. got to the encampment where Mr. H. had been some time before a parcel of the rubbish consisting of Boys & useless old men came to Mr. Hillier's hut or tent and said they waited his pleasure. He at first did not understand them but they told him McD. had shared the people & his lot were standing before him. This Mr. H. says is a downright insult and a most public one. Talked of certain obligations & stuff I did not understand restraining him. He was in a stage of choaking suffocation for several days in swallowing the dose which continues to work upwards both loud & severely.[37]

Such a division of the workforce called for justification. When Auld asked, Macdonell replied: "The selection of Men for Red River Settlement was made in my mind on board of the Ships & once I learned the number to be given me for that service there could be no further delay."[38] Hillier did not forgive him.

Survival

Meanwhile, the men at Nelson Encampment settled down to learn how to survive the winter and, a task apparently just as hard, how to get along with each other. Macdonell wrote:

Tuesday, October 15

Cloudy weather & cold. Men employed at the buildings. Get up part of a chimney, which stood very firm with the frost, but when fire was made in it & that it began to thaw down it all tumbled. Get a Flagstaff of 33 feet long erected on the height behind the House. Hoisted the flag with 3 cheers. Gave a dram to the party who were at work on it.

October, Friday 18

Cloudy weather. Some snow fell. Mr. Bourke & Mr Edwards [Abel Edwards, the surgeon] ran for a Bet from the House uphill to the Flag Staff. Mr. B. won. Set up a Thermometer given me by Mr. Auld. It was 25 degrees below freezing Point at 10 at night. The river very full of ice.

Sunday, October 20

Our House being so forrard [I] do not insist on the
people working. Mr. Hillier obliges his party to work by
stripping the Tent from off their heads while they sat in
it. Thermometer at 8 o'clock morning 10 degrees below.
Mr. Bourke said Mass in the House & preached a few
words in Irish.[39]

By October 26, they had finished the buildings well enough for everyone to move in. Macdonell noted with evident satisfaction that he now
slept under a substantial roof. The houses, stretching in an irregular line
fronting the river, were made of round logs, the front high and sloping to
the rear, and were covered with moss and clay nearly a foot thick. The floors
were made of rough-cut boards, most of which had to be brought from
York Factory. Behind the houses rose a cliff 130 feet high. The land was
boggy and mossy. The few trees were spruce trees and mainly killed by fire.
Here they would spend the winter.

Auld recommended that Macdonell keep the men busy, or trouble
would result. This became increasingly difficult as winter wore on. At first,
they had been kept busy building houses. Then, amidst the snow, ice and intense cold, they were occupied in hunting for food or in making the twen-
ty-six-mile hike to and from York Factory for supplies. With nothing else
to do other than survive, they were basically waiting for the weather to
improve enough for them to travel to the Red River. This would likely be
possible by the end of the following June. They would have been bored, and
bored men can become surly and then mutinous. On October 16, Auld
wrote to Macdonell:

I strongly recommend you to keep your people employed. They ought to have tasks of fire wood to cut
down, no matter whether they require it for their own
use or not. Their poor country people may need it next
season. Running Races, games at foot ball or any thing
that your address can easily provide for their Employment. But recollect too that in that disease it is no slight
matter to provide for the employment of the mind as
well as the body for nothing is to be more guarded
against than that sullen & prostrate despondency which
unhappily accompanies the Scurvy.[40]

As winter set in, finding enough food to feed everyone became more of
a problem. Most of their provisions had to come from Auld's limited supplies

in York Factory. As soon as they arrived at Nelson River, Macdonell sent men there for food, which Auld supplied. Throughout the winter the York Factory post journal records the arrival of men from Macdonell requesting oatmeal and bacon. Auld's problem was that he had scarcely enough food to feed even his own men at York Factory. Since there was little fishing at York Factory at this time of the year, the men there had to live on what they could hunt or what the Indigenous people brought in.

Most of the new arrivals at Nelson Encampment were inexperienced and incapable of dealing with the rigours of a northern winter. Ice in the Nelson River precluded local fishing. None of the men knew how to hunt in these frozen wastes. True, they could ask Indigenous people living around the bay to help, which they did. But there were too few of them and the game was too scarce for them to be of great assistance. Furthermore, hunting for meat meant they had less time to hunt for pelts, thereby reducing the number of pelts that could be sent to London.

After his return, Macdonell settled into a much happier frame of mind and wrote that the chimney, which, after yet another attempt to build it, now worked and that his house was tolerably warm. A few days later, however, he was writing to Cook that at the end of the month their supplies would be exhausted, and their position would be most helpless: "With 12 officers and 58 men on the ground & by calculation only provisions in store for only one month & the supply from the resort of game quite uncertain, I felt apprehensive of a scarcity."[41] He believed the river would then be impossible to cross, and they would no longer be able to obtain supplies from either York Factory or Fort Churchill. He said they had tried to kill game but had only succeeded in killing three brace of wood partridges. He implied they were all going to starve.

Auld wasn't buying this. He spent much of his time travelling among the posts on Hudson Bay and thought he knew what was happening. He suspected that Macdonell was exaggerating the paucity of his food stocks in order to persuade him to send him more. Auld rather sourly compared their ample fare with his own at York Factory, where he had to subsist on the salt provisions that increased the risk of scurvy.

Relations between Auld and Macdonell deteriorated. They argued, for example, about whether or not the boats to be built to take Macdonell's men to the Red River should have keels. Macdonell was one of those people who always knows better than anyone else. He had a fixed opinion that the boat should not have a keel. The vastly more experienced Auld knew that a keel made portaging over land easier. William Cook was also exasperated by Macdonell's behaviour and complained "I am persecuted almost to distraction by Cap'n McD & his boats."[42] Auld replied consolingly a little later.

> First, regarding the Boats, be so good as to let C'n Mac-
> donell have his way entirely for if he has not, so ignorant
> is he of our characters that if we persist in thwart[ing]
> him, his failure (and I think with such men as he has
> must fail in any craft) will assuredly be placed to our
> account.... But never mind, let the boats be built as he
> wishes them. Only require, if you have not got it already,
> his request in writing.[43]

Since Macdonell had a direct relationship to Selkirk, one of the most powerful and active HBC heads at the time, Auld knew he had to tread lightly.

SCURVY

The threat of scurvy hung over them all. Scurvy resulted from insufficient vitamin C in the diet. It loosened men's teeth and, if not attended to, caused internal bleeding and death. Sufferers slowly lost the use of their limbs. Flesh turned black and blue. Although it is generally associated in the popular imagination with long voyages at sea, it was also common on land in Rupert's Land. In *Buchan's Domestic Medicine*, one of the three books John Tod had brought with him, Dr. Buchan had written, with questionable medical accuracy, that

> we know no method of curing this disease but by pur-
> suing a course directly opposite to that which brought
> it on. It proceeds from a vitiated state of the humours,
> occasioned by errors in diet, air or exercise.... Nothing
> has a greater tendency, either to prevent or remove this
> disease, than constant cheerfulness and good humour.
> But this alas! is seldom the lot of persons afflicted with
> the scurvy. They are generally surly, peevish, sour, mo-
> rose and dull.[44]

To his credit, Dr. Buchan did recommend fresh fruit and vegetables such as apples, oranges, lemons and tamarinds. But where were such fruits to be found on Hudson Bay? Auld, himself a doctor and wanting to help the men avoid the disease, sent lemon crystals to Nelson Encampment. Additionally, over the previous century men of the HBC had learned from Indigenous people that a liquid derived from the bark of the spruce tree was an effective remedy. It tasted foul but it worked.

One young man who had come ashore from the ship in a weak, debilitated state after the voyage from Scotland died of scurvy at York Factory on October 25. The men there suffered grievously from scurvy that winter, which was turning out to be one of the coldest anyone could recall. "Hunting has failed entirely & we have only got 50 lbs of fish last week," Cook told Auld. "Nothing but scarcity prevails. As for Partridges & Rabbits, the ground is in the most literal sense clear of them. Our firewood-hunters succeed better. Thank God the trees are not migratory, else no doubt they too would have shunned our now unhallowed & pestilential neighborhood, but the horses are awkward & intractable."[45]

Cook himself was ill at the time and wrote he could scarcely hold his pen. That didn't stop him complaining about the inexperience of the men at Nelson Encampment. A few days later he wrote, "a Clerk came to the factory with his toes, as I am told, solidly frozen so that this fellow will be hauled back. I hope they won't send any more of these soft-toed gentry here. You see how they madly make free with this climate in not rigging themselves as they see old hands do."[46] This was Michael McDonell (no relation to Miles Macdonell) who had lost his way in white-out snow conditions and had staggered into York Factory late one night with one foot and two cheeks frozen. Macdonell complained that Cook had shown him no sympathy and had not even given him a blanket to keep him warm. Expelled from the fort the next day, McDonell arrived back at Nelson Encampment in the afternoon of Christmas Day, carried on a friend's back. He was *hors de combat* for the rest of the winter.

By early December, scurvy had arrived at Nelson Encampment. "What you so much dreaded, the Scurvy, has made its appearance here amongst us," Macdonell wrote, "but in the most favourable manner. Only one man has taken it as yet & he is mending…. None of the Essence of Malt, Cranberries, etc, which you intended to send by the return of your sledges from Churchill was left here with us."[47] It would get worse.

OMINOUS PORTENTS

The men at Nelson Encampment were surviving the winter. But beneath their struggle for food, deep divisions and resentments were bubbling up. A man called William Finlay whom Macdonell had hired at York Factory over Auld's advice that he was a trouble-maker was now proving Auld to have been right. "A report is likewise brought to me that Wm. Finlay is not obedient to the officer," Macdonell wrote on November 30, "& is forming a party among the men, giving out that they do not live so well as they should do, not as he has been accustomed when at the Factory."[48] A day or so later, Finlay had moved his tent a considerable distance up the creek and taken a long time to report for duty. "Find no direct charge against Finlay altho' there appeared strong grounds for suspicion," Macdonell wrote. "Exhort the party to obedience to their officer & good behaviour."[49] After a keg of rum had been broached on December 10, a "scuffle took place between Jn'n O'Rourke & Ja's Toomy, who cut O'Rourke's hand with a tin pot." The following day the two men boxed "by appointment with seconds [and] O'Rourke was the victor. Some others of the Irish prepared sticks for a combat."[50]

Although Father Bourke seemed to get on tolerably well with Macdonell, his feud with Hillier continued. They had quarrelled on board the *Edward and Ann* and had hardly spoken to each other since their arrival. Bourke recorded that the anti-Catholic feeling was running strong among the Scots. He cited the instance of O'Rourke, a most useful and helpful man, he said, who was given the poorest clothes and who lacked leather trousers. Consequently, he was frost-bitten. "This was done to vex me," Bourke wrote. "I knew it & do know it well, because he used to serve my Mass. In this state, the Doctor checked him, tho' it was impossible for him to work, being frostbitten in a tender place, which used to make the Doctor laugh heartily."[51]

Bourke recorded in his journal the aggravations of Hillier and his adherents. Three of the Irish men from his parish of Killala came to him and complained that their lives were in danger. Even in times when discipline was maintained by fists and sticks, Hillier was crossing the line. Bourke wrote that

> he used to bring them into his room & beat them with sticks & bloodgeons, knocking them down. Sometimes he beates them with his fists, dangerously. He beat Hart till the blood was gushing out of his mouth, nose & ears. Jordan was used alike. McEvee to save his life was forced to sleep out in the woods in the frost & snow, exposed to the Bears & wild animals & to the inclemency of the weather but less dangerous than Hillier's anger & passion. He another time tied McEvee to a tree & beat him severely.[52]

On December 29, Jordan complained to Macdonell and Bourke that Hillier had beaten him again severely with a stick, and blood was gushing from his mouth, nose and ears. On January 1, Hillier again beat up Hart.

By the end of 1811, the animosities between Macdonell and Hillier, Macdonell and Auld, Bourke and Hillier, and between the Irish and Scots were reaching a boiling point. The unreliability of the supply of provisions and the rising tide of illness only made matters worse. On New Year's Day, 1812, by way of celebration, both Macdonell and Hillier served out extra rounds of alcohol to their men, with disastrous consequences.

4

Mayhem and Mutiny

1812

"Having seen & spoken myself to your refractory people, I am now to observe that in my opinion a more determined set of mutinous, insolent miscreants at no time has appeared anywhere."

William Auld, April 30, 1812

In early 1812, all the discontent, national prejudices and complaints about bad treatment in the Nelson Encampment boiled over into two acts of insurrection. The first created the climate of insubordination and violence that led to the second. In the first, William Brown was not, as far as we know, involved; his complicity in the second brought him to the brink of personal disaster.

MAYHEM

On the night of January 1, 1812, a group of Irishmen led by Anthony Macdonell (no relation to Miles Macdonell) attacked the Orkney men as they were going to bed. "The Irish displayed their native propensity & prowess on the first night of the year," Macdonell wrote, "by unmercifully beating with sticks some Orkney men of Mr. Hillier's party. Too much liquor was the only incentive to this unwarrantable act."[53] Father Bourke suspected that Hillier, still angry that Macdonell had taken the best men for the Red River settlement, had given each of his men a pint of rum to start a fight. The Irish, he believed were merely retaliating. But then Bourke saw everything Hillier did in a bad light. Macdonell, Bourke added, then "could not well refrain from giving his men liquor in proportion as Mr. Hillier was giving it to his Men to avoid getting a bad name."[54] This one pint of rum they gave to each of the men to celebrate the new year undoubtedly contributed to the mayhem that followed.

The bloodshed started when Hugh Padden, a lad from Killala, somehow provoked Anthony Macdonell. His blood clearly up, Macdonell chased Padden into the Orkney men's cabin. On the way in, he knocked down William Loutit, who was standing in the doorway. Inside the cabin, they started to beat Padden up. Loutit tried to stop them. He told Macdonell that Padden, being a small boy, was not worth his time. James Taylor tried to calm tempers by inviting Macdonell to sit down and have a drink. Donald MacKay, one of the Irishmen, was about to sit on the stool someone brought up when Magnus Spence, one of the Orkney men, said "d—n you, you are not the man I asked to sit."[55] Macdonell then went for Spence, pulled his handkerchief around his neck and started to choke him.

A violent brawl broke out. James Hart assaulted Loutit with a stick while either Macdonell or McKay—Loutit was so beset he didn't know which—held his head. The Orkney men managed to pull Macdonell off Spence and pushed him and his violent companions out of the cabin, closing the door on them. A few moments later they were back, trying to break down the door with axes. John McLeod, the clerk from Lewis and a responsible officer, came up and tried to stop them. The Irish then went to the other door. They smashed that one down and started the fight again.

By now more help had arrived in the form of Hillier, Edwards (the surgeon) and others. When Edwards ordered Michael Higgins to go back to his own house, Higgins said he would be damned if he went home for him or any other like him. Eventually they did go back to their cabin, promising to get some sleep. Hillier assured the Orkney men that they could go to bed peacefully and in safety and that no further harm would come to them.

James Taylor for one was not so sure, and he lay on his bed in his clothes, unable to sleep. He was right to be worried. A short time later, the same group of Irishmen burst into the house again, armed with cudgels and bent on inflicting serious injury. They pounded on the men, and in particular on Taylor, who was trying to hide on his bed. Taylor declared he "fainted from a blow received on the side of his head & knows not what further took place."[56] Hart was heard saying that it was Taylor who had injured him and he would be revenged. Loutit lay stretched out on the floor and "appeared to move only one of his legs."[57] Someone had already gone for help. Hillier and McLeod, who had been dining together, came over in a hurry. When they arrived, they saw Loutit and Randall lying senseless on the floor and Higgins still mercilessly beating poor Taylor. They managed to stop the fighting and calm everyone down. The officers set a guard on the house for the rest of the night.

The next day Macdonell and Hillier convened a tribunal to investigate the assault. Converting the main hall into a courtroom, they set up a table with green cloth on it and brought up two chairs. In the following proceeding, they both acted as Justices of the Peace, although Hillier's claim to act as such was questionable. After listening to the evidence, which Bourke sourly noted was all against the Irish, they discharged a few of the culprits, with others going surety for them. Others they fined twenty shillings each.

They decided to hold the ringleaders as prisoners because they had beaten several of the Orkney men so severely their lives were still in danger. The savagery with which the Irish attacked the Orkney men suggests this was no mere alcohol-fueled brawl. With some of the wounds life-threatening, it was a full month before the doctor declared the victims out of danger.

When he heard about the affray, Auld sadly commented: "Merciful God! How our peaceful Service has thus been outraged. Crimes of the blackest dye committed in the short space of 6 weeks from 1st January to 12th Febr'y surmounting in number & enormity all the offences of all the Servants in these Territories since the Country was settled 140 years ago."[58] With the calmness of hindsight, Auld later suspected the affray was a consequence of the feud between Macdonell's men and Hillier's men, resulting in part at least from Macdonell's cherry-picking men for the Red River.

MUTINY

Scurvy was an ever-present menace. In January it arrived in full force at Nelson Encampment. By January 9, five men were sick with it. On January 13, Macdonell issued an order for the use of "the juice of spruce for the people for the Scurvy" and noted "they are very reluctant to drink it because they found it bitter, particularly the Orkney men by the advice of old hands who had been in the Country before. One of them, Wm. Finlay, refuses to drink the spruce juice & others following his example. I struck him off work."[59] The following day Macdonell ordered Finlay to resume work, but he refused, saying he would not work. On January 18, Hillier had to withdraw a work party because two of its members had scurvy, making a total of seven in his party suffering with it. Although nineteen of them were down with it by January 26, Finlay remained obdurate.

By early February, the men were drinking the spruce juice, albeit reluctantly, and were recovering "except one man, Robert Montgomery, who is reduced to the lowest extremity & whose life is despaired of by the surgeon."[60] Montgomery was one of the three men from Brown's own parish of Kilmaurs. At the end of February, Macdonell wrote, "at a time, our people were every day getting down in the Scurvy. Sixteen of my party & about an equal number of Mr. H's party were already seized with it. Regulations were established for the health of the people which Finlay refused to conform."[61] The men recovering from scurvy were given oakum (a tarred fibre, used to repair boats and weatherproof cabins) to pick, it being light work. Finlay refused to do even this, saying he could choose to do what he liked. Macdonell then read him the riot act, saying that he could not choose which work he wanted to do and which not. He had to do what he was told. Finlay still refused.

Miles Macdonell (1767–1828), who led the first party of settlers to the Red River and founded the Red River Settlement, of which he was the first governor.

Hillier, in his questionable role as a magistrate, found Finlay guilty of a number of misdemeanors and sentenced him to be struck off work for two or three days. Macdonell therefore ordered a few men to build a hut "in which I intended to put Finlay into to live by himself as a chastisement."[62] When Finlay wouldn't go, Macdonell had to interfere and drag him away, with Finlay loudly calling out to his associates to witness the manner in which he was treated.

That evening, February 12, Macdonell went out of his house and saw Finlay's hut burning. He heard loud hurrahs of joy from many voices around the blaze. Walking to the hut, he found thirteen of his men standing around watching.

> Two or three of whom I questioned as to this. They were silent. I then asked who had set fire to the Hut, what they meant by such conduct & asked one of them (Jn'n Walker), was it him? To which he made answer that they were all equally concerned.... The Hut was too far consumed to be an object worth saving. I directed Wm. Finlay to go into the people's House for that night.[63]

Since the mood of the men was now obviously mutinous, Macdonell ordered the officers to have their arms ready in case the insurgents attacked them, but the men were not prepared to use violence just yet.

Macdonell and Hillier spent the following day trying to take down evidence from witnesses to the burning of Finlay's hut. William Brown was one of the witnesses they examined. Daniel Campbell, another witness, objected to the proceedings and stalked out, followed by all the others. Brown's name now appears as an insurgent in many lists. He soon appears to have assumed a leadership role, thus making an appearance in this story as a mutineer.

The Orkney men among the insurgents appeared to have been simple, thoughtless boys that Macdonell considered nearly innocent followers. Auld approved of leniency towards them. In a note (not sent to Macdonell), though, he criticized Macdonell. He wrote: "I certainly disapprove of putting these Glasgow villains off duty. He should have never done this as that only drives them to worse conduct & in a manner shutting the door against future reconciliation or at least is a waste of means in this country & service."[64] He wrote to Macdonell on April 30.

> Having seen & spoken myself to your refractory people, I am now to observe that in my opinion a more determined set of mutinous, insolent miscreants at no time has appeared anywhere. Nor have they been individually able to offer the least shadow of apology for their flegetious [flagitious—heinous] conduct. It is true they allege that your putting the ringleader Finlay into a hut by himself as a temporary separation from his associates was inhuman at that season of the year tho' they

well knew that their fellow servants of all ranks were traveling thro' the country without even such a hut to shelter them from the Weather.… Your honorable anxiety to save the 4 Orkney lads and one other of the 14 Insurgents whom you declare misled & almost innocent I with great pleasure record.… Glasgow & its neighbourhood have long been notorious for the republican & leveling disposition of their inhabitants and these villains of yours prove the legitimacy of their descent.[65]

There was now general uproar and discontent among all the men—at least the Scots—at the Nelson Encampment. The insurgents, who were thought to be trying to stir up trouble with the other men, separated themselves from the main group and went to live in a cabin on their own. Macdonell sent a messenger to York Factory to warn them so that they could make any precautions they thought necessary. Auld and Macdonell breathed fire and fury and vowed to send them all home for severe punishment.

A strange standoff now developed at Nelson Encampment between Macdonell and Hillier, who were barely speaking to each other, on the one hand and the insurgents on the other. But what would the insurgents eat? Macdonell gave them some food—enough to live on—but refused to provide them with a sled to go to York Factory to obtain provisions there, leaving them no option but to walk there and back. Several of them did make the trek to York Factory on foot and, before the news of their mutiny was

Winter couriers of the North West Company.

widely known there, obtained not only provisions but also five guns, balls and powder.

On February 28, scurvy caused the only fatality at Nelson Encampment. Robert "Mongumry [Montgomery] one of the Glasgow lads died," Father Bourke wrote. "He was taken great care of & had all the medical & other assistance that was possible, wine, etc. He was much regretted, being a good lad." They buried him the following day. All the officers and men accompanied his corpse to the top of the hill, where he was buried beside the flag post. After the burial, Macdonell distributed a gallon of rum to the men. "The Surgeon read the Service of the Protestant Church for him," Father Bourke disapprovingly grumbled, "altho' he was a Presbyterian."[66]

With the coming of the first signs of spring, food became more plentiful. Indigenous hunters brought in more fresh venison. The men caught twenty-seven deer in their snares in the deer fence. Macdonell noted that in the first two weeks of May over 3,000 deer crossed the Nelson River below their camp, which not only alleviated the alleged food shortage considerably but also reduced the risk of scurvy. As far as food was concerned, the lives of the men at Nelson Encampment were improving.

Tempers cooled a little. The idea of sending the insurgents back to England to be tried began to lose its appeal. Auld wrote he was prepared to take them back into the HBC service, though he declared he would not negotiate with them. "But on no account," he wrote to Macdonell on May 10, "are they to prescribe terms of accommodation to us. I allude to the possibility of their demanding their wages for the interval they have been off duty or that they shall not be fined (The only mode we have to punish offenders by).... Everything will depend on future good behaviour."[67] In principle, therefore, if they agreed to his terms, he was prepared to forgive and forget. He instructed Macdonell to inform the insurgents of this. He also told Macdonell to make it clear to Brown, Carswell and Fisher, all three Glasgow clerks, that if they continued to visit and associate with the insurgents they would be dismissed and no longer continued on the books as officers in the service of the HBC.[68]

Macdonell sent for the insurgents. He read out Auld's terms to them and told them that if they refused to accept them, they would be sent back to England as prisoners to stand trial. They told him they wanted time to consider. At 11 o'clock, Macdonell sent an officer to find out what they were thinking. They then informed him of their terms. They told him they wanted oblivion—that is, amnesty—for what had happened before, after which they would serve the HBC again. After considering this, Auld sent Macdonell terms for the basis of a compromise. Macdonell summoned the insurgents to a negotiation on May 15 and announced he would read Auld's reply. Brown did not stop to listen. He stormed out and started back to his cabin. Macdonell then read out Auld's terms. The insurgents rejected them on the spot, saying they would not be dictated to.

On his way back to his cabin, Brown met three of Macdonell's officers coming towards him and realized they had been searching their cabins for the guns they had obtained at York Factory. The officers had not found them because they had been hidden in the woods. The insurgents were now furious at what they perceived as bad faith. They offered gross abuse and threats of violence to Macdonell and Hillier. "They are a most determined set of villains," Hillier wrote in disgust, "& I feel extremely sorry so many kind offers have been made to them."[69]

Auld and Macdonell's duplicity, as they saw it, enraged the insurgents. They sent their reply to Auld in writing. Brown, who signed this letter, may have had a hand in composing it because he was probably one of the few literate men among them. In part, it read:

> We have this day experienced the most cowardly usage from the Chiefs here [Macdonell and Hillier] which we understand was according to your orders. We were decoyed up for the purpose of agreeing [with] us. At the instant we arrived, they dispatched three Officers to rob the house in a most dastardly manner when we were all out but we timely interposed and prevented an action so base that no Gentleman who had any feelings of honour would ever have countenanced. We are happy, Sir, to find you all out in your true colours. This shews us what kind of men you are and we tell you once for all that we will never come to your terms. You mentioned in your letter that we would be sent home close prisoners on board the Company's ships to be delivered up to the civil power on our arrival.... We will never be intimidated with a menace so silly that we scarce think it worth answering.[70]

Two days later, exasperated, Macdonell wrote:

> The Glasgow clerks—Carswell, Fisher & Brown—have all along kept up a constant intercourse with these insurgents, of which I have ample proofs & the countenance thus given has been the means of keeping them hitherto closely linked together.... These Glasgow rascals have caused us both much trouble & uneasiness. A more stubborn, litigious & cross-grained set were never put under any person's care. I cannot think that any

liberality of rations or rum could have availed to stop their dissatisfaction. Army or Navy discipline is the only thing fit to manage such fierce spirits as theirs. I shall sign no more provision orders for them, but refer them to the Factory should they apply. Their late conduct has, I think, put them more completely in our power.[71]

In these comments, Macdonell was referring to all the insurgents, but he singled out Brown as one of the ringleaders. The insurgents went to York Factory for more provisions, but Auld refused to give them any until they surrendered their firearms and told him from whom they had got them. They wouldn't. He refused to negotiate and lowered what food rations he was allowing them.

On top of these troubles, Brown was responsible for a terrible accident on May 8. Hugh Padden, the Irish lad who had prompted the New Year's Day affray, told Father Bourke that Brown had called him over and loaded a blunderbuss for him. Brown then allowed Padden to fire it, whereupon it exploded and destroyed his hand. Padden alleged that Brown had put in too much powder to give him a shock. Unsurprisingly, Brown denied any such intention. To save Padden's life, the doctor decided to amputate his arm below the elbow. The injury was so serious that a couple of days later Father Bourke thought he had better give him the last rites. Padden survived, though, and returned to Ireland in the autumn.

Eventually, in mid-June, the lack of food forced the insurgents to surrender. Macdonell wrote to Auld on June 19.

> I was extremely well pleased to learn your success with the Insurgents. It was a fortunate move their going from here. They could never have been brought about while countenanced as they were with us. I trust you will now dispose of them as first intended by separation among the different posts. None of them of course go with me. They will notwithstanding, be the means of strengthening my party by leaving as many more men at your disposal. The Rascal Finlay & the two Irish scoundrels are yet on our hands. We shall dispose of them when we meet.
>
> The 3 Glasgow clerks, Carswell, Fisher & Brown, I imagine, can well be spared in the country & may be sent home. However, this is as you please hereafter. It is certain that should any of them be stationed at a post with any of these men, partiality & discontent will always exist.[72]

Father Bourke's feud with Hillier had not abated during these troubles. He learned that Hillier had been threatening to shoot him in the woods when he had been visiting Padden and was even preparing his firearms for the purpose. This warning persuaded Bourke to travel everywhere with his own loaded firearm close at hand. Perhaps to everyone's relief, Bourke now decided he wanted to return to England. By now, neither Auld nor Macdonell had a good opinion of Bourke and were glad to give him permission.

Although there was still ice in the river and frost in the morning, spring was finally arriving and everything was wet and splashy, with the earliest of green buds on bushes and trees and the arrival of birds not seen for six months. Macdonell began making preparations for his departure. On June 1, he wrote that the ice was expected to break in the Nelson River in the next few days and that floods were to be expected. By June 10 the river was open, although there was still much ice around. He was now sending the men around Marsh Point by sea to York Factory. On the way, one of the boats went missing. They feared it was lost in the ice, but they found it the next day. "All is completely wet," Macdonell wrote, "except a keg with some Powder in it, which escaped. Some dried meat, Oatmeal & Barley have got wet. All my Musical Instruments & music, etc, etc, has been laying in the water, but I shall recover them with little damage."[73] Father Bourke was not so lucky: his Mass book became sodden. They arrived back at York Factory on June 23, and looked to the parting of their ways.

CONSEQUENCES

Back at York Factory, Macdonell and Hillier prepared for their journeys southwards, the former to the Red River and the latter to the district east of Lake Winnipeg. Macdonell had written to Auld saying that of the persons coming with him to the Red River, fifteen were effective, two were felons, fourteen were mutineers and insurgents, and four were non-effective. Not an impressive group of men to establish a new colony! On July 1, Auld stepped in and readjusted the division of men. He assigned twenty-two of the forty-nine effectives to go with Macdonell to the Red River and the rest to Mr. Hillier and the HBC. He noted that the Orkney men did not want to go to Red River because they didn't want to have anything to do with the Irish.

Auld gives the impression that he would be heartily glad to see the backs of both Macdonell and Hillier when they went upriver. They had caused him nothing but headaches. Not that he had high hopes for the success of the Red River colony. "I'm afraid," he wrote, "Red River is not the country that will ever put a farthing of advantage into our concern.... Oh, how easy would my superintendence have been if I too had only one object to attend to!"[74]

Auld now had to decide what to do with the offenders.

First, he had to deal with the perpetrators of the New Year's Day attacks. As early as May, Auld had been expressing his inclination not to send the offenders back to Scotland. "Therefore," he wrote to Macdonell, "to promote your views of Settlement & to restrain these firebrands from reaching their country to counteract Lord Selkirk's recruiting for the Red River colony in Scotland, I agree, tho' with extreme reluctance, to dispose of them for the ensuing term of their engagements."[75] Auld accordingly allowed all or almost all of the offenders to remain in Rupert's Land.

Clearly the three Irish men in custody who had attacked the Orkney men on January 1—Macdonell, Hart and Higgins—had committed serious offences. Since Auld had no legal authority to hang them, his only practical recourse was to send the men back to Scotland or England and have the courts there deal with them. This was a time when men and boys were hanged for stealing handkerchiefs. These three he sent back to England, though there is a suggestion in the records that he allowed at least one of them, Hart, to remain.

And Brown and the other insurgents? What should he do with them? Miles Macdonell had no doubts: he wanted them also sent home for punishment. "The fourteen Insurgents here," he wrote, "will require to be disposed of till Ship time for I am determined with your concurrence to send them to London to answer for their conduct."[76] Macdonell, though, softened his views and said he was willing to forgive five of the least guilty. As for Brown, Macdonell made it absolutely clear that he was not going to take him to the Red River. So now Brown was back with the HBC, his fate hanging in the balance.

Let us consider Auld's dilemma.

On the one hand. Brown and other ringleaders had proved themselves to be troublemakers. The HBC certainly did not need any of these in Rupert's Land. Brown had become one of the leaders of the mutiny. By rights, as a mutineer, he and the other ringleaders should have been sent back to Scotland and tried there. If found guilty, they might have been punished severely. Auld would have thought they deserved punishment. Should not the law—or what was, for all practical purposes, more important, the authority of the HBC—be upheld? Not taking action against them would embolden other employees to disobey orders and think they could get away with it. Yes, he could hold them as prisoners all summer and then send them home on the autumn supply ship. Justice had to be done.

On the other hand, if he sent them back to Scotland for discipline or trial, he would also have to send back witnesses, dependable men he could not afford to lose. Furthermore, in Scotland the insurgents would be able to malign the HBC and the Red River Settlement at a time when the HBC would be trying to recruit more employees and settlers. Auld also had doubts about jurisdiction. He believed it was entirely possible that any trial in England or Scotland would not proceed on the technicality that only the courts of Canada had jurisdiction. The war that broke out that summer between Great Britain and the United States, however, could make it difficult to send them to Canada for trial.

To some extent, Auld blamed Macdonell's mismanagement, his conflict with Hillier, and in particular, his initial distribution of the men for what had happened that winter on Nelson River. "To this," he wrote, "is owing the 1st January massacre as well as the 12th February. Had union subsisted among the chiefs, Capt'n Macdonell's Irishmen would never have attempted Mr. Hillier's people. It is not even impossible but these monsters thought that their attack on the servants of a Rival would not be deemed other than a mark of devotion to their Master."[77] Auld was too fair a man to place all the blame on the men for what might, in part at least, be ascribed to their leaders. He did not want to be unduly harsh on men for offences for which their superiors, he suspected, bore part of the blame.

Auld then had to make the decision. What *should* he do with Brown and his comrades in crime? On the one hand, he needed men for the HBC service and Macdonell needed men for the Red River. On the other, these men were malefactors and deserved punishment. William Brown, in particular, singled out by name as a ringleader, certainly had cause to be worried. His adventures in Rupert's Land stood a fair chance of coming to an early and unhappy end.

Paradoxically, Auld was given a way out of his dilemma by another mutiny. A much more serious mutiny had occurred at the HBC post at Brandon Lake and the offenders were at that time at York Factory waiting for his disposition of them. To maintain its authority, the HBC had to punish mutineers. But discipline would not suffer if the mutineers from Brandon Lake were treated severely and the Nelson River insurgents more leniently. The affair at Brandon Lake may possibly have helped Auld make his decision: he would keep the three Glasgow ringleaders in Rupert's Land.

He therefore allowed Brown to stay with the HBC and work out his contract, sending him to be the clerk for the post at Reindeer Lake. Auld himself had been surgeon in charge there in 1808 and 1809 and knew it well. Established in 1798, Reindeer Lake was a quiet out-of-the-way place to give Brown a second chance.

Brown Proves His Worth at Reindeer Lake

1812-1815

> "The others tending the nets today killed only 2 fish.
> This is the most compleat starving that possibly can be.
> If we only had one Meal on the day it would not be bad,
> but at present we cannot afford anything near to it."

William Brown, April 17, 1813

So here he was. A clerk at the remote HBC post on Reindeer Lake. He had been given an opportunity to prove his worth to the HBC. Would he take it? He did. At Reindeer Lake he seems to have turned his life around. With something worthwhile to do, Brown settled down and became a valuable officer. In these three years Brown learnt his business as an HBC trader. They were quiet years, for which, after the turmoil at Nelson Encampment during the winter, he would probably have been profoundly grateful.

Trading with Indigenous people, finding food and hauling home firewood: these were what occupied Brown and the men at Reindeer Lake most, as they did at every HBC post. There was little in the way of fruit or vegetables. "There is no ground in Cultivation here," the District Report said, "The Quality of the Soil here is by no means adapted for cultivation, being too hard for the Spade."[78] The men were able to acquire some meat from the Indigenous hunters and this would have been welcome. For what it was worth, they had the consolation of knowing the Nor'Westers were in the same predicament. This, though, gave the Indigenous hunters and trappers bargaining power. With the Nor'Westers so close, Brown and Sutherland noted how often Indigenous people came to the HBC house and how many went to the French house.

Their main food was fish, which they had to catch themselves in the lake. Apart from keeping the accounts and trading in the store, Brown therefore spent much of his time at Reindeer Lake fishing and organizing the fisheries. Any conceptions he may have had of a lake teeming with fish, to be caught merely by dipping a net into the water, quickly evaporated. At that time, fish were not, the records indicate, plentiful in the lake. They had to catch enough not merely for their daily needs but also to preserve for winter. During the week of June 5, 1813, for example, they caught only thirty fish. On Monday, June 21, the post journal records "Our Fishing but very indifferent, having 10 Nets in the water & can barely get sufficient to serve us."[79] During the whole of February 1813, the men at the post caught only 164 fish.

They were close to the edge of hunger all too often, but somehow they always managed to pull through. "Very cold weather with strong gales of wind. Our fishing at the house failing considerably," Sutherland wrote, "so that I begin to be very apprehensive of want during the winter."[80] A few days later, the men brought in 196 fish and the following day 212. "The Men attending the Nets as formerly, but with very little success. Today got only 2 fish," Brown wrote on April 5, "& used the last of the froze ones we had in stock. Therefore, we have nothing to depend on now but what we get out of the Nets, unless Indians come to the House, which there are very little appearance of."[81] By April 17, he was writing, "the others attending the Nets today killed only 2 fish. This is the most compleat starving that possibly can be. If we only had one Meal on the day it would not be bad, but at present we cannot afford anything near to it."[82] On this occasion, once again, they managed to catch enough fish to survive.

Spring finally arrived. At the end of May 1813, after the ice had broken up on the lakes and rivers, Sutherland went downriver to Churchill with the winter's trade of nine packs of about ninety pounds each and a small keg of castoreum. He left Brown to manage the post and to keep the journal, and so, here, for the first time, we have Brown's own words. "This day," he wrote on May 29, "Mr. Sutherland embarked from this house for Churchill Factory, accompanied by 6 men, one of whom was to go to Nelson's House for a supply of Brandy & Return."[83]

Brown's entries in the post journal at this stage of his career were careful and matter-of-fact. His loquaciousness came later. June 26, 1813: "Nothing extraordinary taking place. Catching fish sufficient to serve us. During last week have caught 61 fish." The journal reveals that Brown's summer was one of quiet routines.

On September 16, Sutherland returned from Churchill and resumed writing the journal. "This day I arrived at this place from the Factory & everything safe," he wrote. "There was a band of Northern Indians at the house nigh chewing their own finger ends for want of Brandy & Tobacco. I gave each of them a small piece of Tobacco as soon as we got landed and in the evening gave them some Brandy to drink amongst them."[84]

Brown was continually sending out men to cut more firewood. The fort's need for wood was seemingly inexhaustible. Like fish, this was also necessary for survival. They seldom seemed to have enough of either. On September 20, 1813, Sutherland wrote: "This day 5 of the Men began cutting firewood & splitting it up in chords [cords] in the woods. Two Men attending the fishing but not catching nigh sufficient to serve us one man. Mr. Brown and self working new Nets. This evening I got one finished."[85]

Conflict on the Red River

While Brown was learning the trade and surviving at Reindeer Lake, momentous events had been taking place at Lord Selkirk's colony on the Red River. All was not going well.

Miles Macdonell and the eighteen men he had brought with him from Hudson Bay to establish the Red River Settlement had managed to live through their first winter, but not without the assistance of the Nor'Westers, who, not believing the settlement could possibly survive, had compassionately supplied them with food. The Indigenous Saulteaux people under Chief Peguis had also been supportive, helping the settlers find food and teaching them how to hunt. This happy relationship did not exist with the Métis, who, with good reason, believed the settlement was a threat to their way of life. The Métis depended on the buffalo and the Nor'Westers depended on the pemmican that the buffalo meat supplied. But as it became clear that the settlers on the Red River were determined to stay, their relations with both the Nor'Westers and the Métis deteriorated.

During 1812 and 1813, the settlers somehow survived. They were hardy folk who weren't going to give up easily, but they badly needed more sources of food. The sight of so much pemmican leaving their settlement irked them. On January 8, 1814, Miles Macdonell issued the famous Pemmican Proclamation. In it, he forbade the export of pemmican—indeed, all meat, grain and vegetables—from the whole 116,000 square miles of the Selkirk grant. He also forbade the hunting of buffalo there. This proclamation made conflict inevitable. Compliance with it would have quickly brought the North West Company to its knees as well as destroying the Métis way of life. The Nor'Westers therefore ignored the edict, leaving Macdonell with no option but to try to enforce it. He established blockades on rivers and highways used by the Nor'Westers and seized large amounts of their pemmican.

The Nor'Westers fought back, pledging to eradicate the Red River Settlement by encouraging settlers to desert and, if that failed, by inciting Indigenous people and Métis to destroy it. Under such threats, some settlers deserted the colony and a growing dissatisfaction, almost rebellion, grew in others. In the hot summer of 1815, the Nor'Westers and Métis moved aggressively against the settlement. They burnt houses, killed cows and trampled crops. In June alone, they attacked the settlement four times. The resolve of many settlers to stay weakened. In order to avoid further bloodshed and perhaps to obtain better terms, Macdonell surrendered. The

Nor'Westers sent him to Fort William and then to Montreal for trial. Apart from a few left behind to try to safeguard their interests, the settlers then abandoned the settlement. The Nor'Westers burnt most of the buildings. The settlers—now refugees—moved to the north end of Lake Winnipeg.

Colin Robertson now re-enters the story. It was Robertson who a few years earlier had tried to persuade the HBC Committee in London to move more aggressively against the North West Company. After a few years as a merchant in Liverpool, he had again proposed that the HBC challenge the Nor'Westers in Athabasca. This time the committee agreed and sent him to Montreal to recruit men for an expedition to open new posts in Athabasca. With 180 men and another ex-Nor'Wester named John Clarke, Robertson left Montreal with sixteen canoes on May 17, 1815. By chance he met the refugees from the Red River near Norway House. They persuaded him to help them re-establish the settlement. He sent John Clarke on ahead to Athabasca with a hundred men to begin the work there and then went to the Red River to re-establish the colony and rebuild Fort Douglas. There Robert Semple, the new governor of both the colony and the HBC, would join him.

Although the colony on the Red River had been re-established, the fundamentally different interests of the HBC on the one hand and the Nor'Westers and the Métis on the other meant that the conflict would soon resume in greater intensity.

BROWN IN CHARGE AT REINDEER LAKE

On June 6, 1814, Sutherland left Reindeer Lake to take the season's furs downriver to Fort Churchill and then on to York Factory, again leaving Brown at the post for the summer with two men and two boys to help him. This time Sutherland did not return, having been sent to another post where the factor was sick. For his last year at Reindeer Lake, Brown was in charge. Although his rank was now that of a trader, up from a clerk, he was in effect doing the work of the factor.

A few days later Brown recorded the arrival of the new chief of the Nor'Wester house: "This Forenoon Mr. England and his family, accompanied by three half Indian lads, arrived at the FH [French House] in a half canoe. They had a good deal of provisions but they did not appear to have any Trading Goods."[86] That afternoon, Brown went over to greet his new neighbour. He also wanted to talk about the desertion of Campbell and Anderson. He delivered a note from the superintendent to England about the two men. England prevaricated, saying he would certainly send it on but would not be able to do so until the following spring. Anyway, the deserters themselves had long gone on to another Nor'Wester post.

Peter Rindisbacher, *A Gentleman Travelling in a Dog Cariole in Hudson's Bay with an Indian Guide*, in about 1826.

There the matter ended and the two companies continued their cautious but civil competition. When one of the Nor'Westers had an argument about a gun with an Indigenous man and the man had threatened to kill a white man without ceremony, England came over to warn Brown. "Coming back," he wrote, "the French Master told me I would do well to be upon my guard as he had positive information that these Indians were coming in with the determination to take both houses."[87] Brown put his house on alert, stayed up until three in the morning for a month, but nothing untoward happened.

In the post journal, Brown recorded the constant comings and goings of the Indigenous people at both the HBC and the North West Company houses, and the constant struggle to find fish, meat and firewood. As the summer progressed, the trade goods in the fort began to run out. Brown recorded they were so low on tobacco and gunpowder to trade for furs or meat that once he had to take the blanket from his own bed to trade. He noted with relief the arrival of the boat with his supplies on September 16.

On occasion, Brown sent out a party at night to an Indigenous encampment. "Tonight after dayset 2 N'n [Northern] Indian Lads arrived at our house," he wrote. "None to the F.H. Had nothing with them. They are French Traders, besides several others at the same tent to whom I gave Credit in the fall & are come in slily for us to go to their Tents & get their hunts unknown to the Frenchmen. Today killed 18 fish." And the following day he wrote "Sent one of the above Indians off tonight about 9 o'clock to proceed to his Tent as fast as possible & secure the Furs until once my Men get there in case the French Men should hear them going off & go too."[88] He noted that the French had suspected but had not followed.

Measured civility between the two companies, though, was the usual behaviour, perhaps surprisingly so in view of the violence taking place between their companies not far to the south. On January 1, 1815, for example, the Nor'Westers came over to the HBC post and fired a couple of volleys in the air by way of wishing them happy new year. The HBC men went over to their fort and returned the good wishes in similar style.

GOING HOME

By mid-1815, Brown's contract was coming to an end and his thoughts would have turned to his return to Scotland. Now that the ice was out of the river, it was time for the annual journey to the coast with the year's collection of furs. This time it was Brown who took the boat down. On June 15, 1815, as Napoleon's troops were preparing to attack Wellington's army at Quatre Bras in the preliminary engagement that led three days later to the Battle of Waterloo, he left Reindeer Lake. He wrote: "This morning at Sun rising, I started off for the Factory, accompanied by 6 men, a woman & two boys. Have 8 Bundles of Furs, a Keg containing Castoreum lbs 14, gunstocks No.8, Hatchet helves N.18, & 298 lbs of pemmican."[89] The journey took twelve days. "This forenoon Messrs. Brown & Holmes," the Fort Churchill post journal recorded "arrived from the interior in their Batteaux with 19 men."[90] On August 1, he set off down the coast for York Factory.

Brown's contract with the HBC was now over. On September 22, he went on board the *Prince of Wales* to return to Scotland. The ill-fated new governor of the HBC, Robert Semple, had come out from England on the ship that took Brown home. On October 17, they met a brig from Copenhagen on its way to Canada and learned that Napoleon had been decisively beaten at Waterloo and had abdicated. Europe was finally at peace. Brown would have understood that European markets would soon re-open to the import of furs.

As he left Rupert's Land, he could reflect that he had done well. In the list of servants for 1813–1814, he was described as a young and enterprising young man. In 1814–1815, he is listed no longer as a mere clerk but as a trader. In the HBC, with its formal hierarchy of ranks, this was a promotion. Of course, in the staff of a small, isolated post, it still meant he had to keep the meticulous records the HBC required and do anything else that was needed. The record describes him as "an excellent trader. Fully qualified for the charge of a district. Active, courageous and highly deserving of promotion."[91] That is to say, he had arrived at Reindeer Lake as a clerk under the cloud of insubordination, mutiny even. He left three years later described as competent enough to manage a whole district, which would have several trading posts in it. A significant achievement indeed!

On November 3, William Brown ended his service with the HBC. He had left Scotland as a green and callow clerk. Now he was an experienced and well-respected HBC trader. The black clouds of Nelson River were well behind him. What would he do? Many HBC men who went home found they missed the open spaces, the freedom and relative absence of rules at the HBC posts. Unable to settle down, they often re-enlisted. What would Brown find in Kilmaurs when he arrived home? Were his parents still alive? Furthermore, would he renew his relationship with Elizabeth Armour? Their daughter would now be five years old, and he would be a stranger to her.

6

District Master and the Pemmican War

1818-1819

"Those 15 minutes at Seven Oaks changed everything.
No longer a commercial contest with the occasional
skirmish and post-burning, the struggle between the
Nor'Westers and Bay men had turned into a guerrilla
war."

Peter Newman, *Caesars of the Wilderness*

Back in Scotland, Brown went home to Kilmaurs to see his parents. He renewed his relationship with Elizabeth Armour and again she became pregnant. On August 17, 1816, they married. Their daughter Janet (Jenny) was born in October. In January 1817, the elders again disciplined Elizabeth for immorality before marriage and refused to pardon her until she showed signs of repentance. In March 1818, she must have shown the requisite signs because they rebuked and then absolved her. There is no available record that the elders took Brown to task.

For whatever reason, Brown decided to re-engage with the HBC. He picked up his pen on March 6, 1817, and wrote to the committee requesting readmission to the service. They replied nine days later, telling him to present himself in Stromness on the Orkney Islands on June 1. There he would take passage on the HBC ship to York Factory. He was not, however, on board when it sailed, for what reason we do not know. The following year, the HBC told him to be at Stromness at the end of May. Brown is said to have joined the ship in Inverness but since the *Prince of Wales* does not appear to have stopped there on its way north from Gravesend, it is more likely that he took another ship from there and boarded the *Prince of Wales* in Stromness.

The *Prince of Wales* would have been packed with trading goods for distribution to the HBC posts in Rupert's Land. It carried a fresh group of HBC men and settlers for the Red River colony as well as several officers returning to their posts after their furlough. Among those on board was the new HBC governor, William Williams. A naval man from Wales, he had reportedly been a captain on an East India Company ship. Sent to succeed the unfortunate Governor Semple, his job was to provide muscle to the HBC's

Peter Rindisbacher, *Cold Night Camp on the Inhospitable Shores of Lake Winnipeg, October 1821*. Brown would have spent many such nights on his travels.

challenge to the North West Company. And if that meant confrontation, even conflict—so be it. As an experienced trader, Brown would have been able to give him first-hand information about Rupert's Land and the people he would be dealing with. Williams was a useful person for Brown to be travelling back to Rupert's Land with.

THE MANITOBA DISTRICT

After his arrival at York Factory that summer, Governor Williams appointed Brown to be the master of the HBC's Manitoba District. Though there is no evidence for it, Brown's acquaintance with Williams may well have played a part in this appointment. By now, as an established officer of the HBC, Brown had no need to prove himself, unlike when he was at Reindeer Lake. Well aware of the routines of the fur trade, in the Manitoba District he was to show that he was a responsible, reliable pair of hands and also someone who could identify problems, propose solutions and implement them. But there had been changes in Rupert's Land since he had left three years earlier. Relations between the HBC and the North West Company had deteriorated even further, and Brown consequently had to be far more circumspect in his dealings with them.

The Manitoba District and its forts were west of Lake Winnipeg. Entirely within the bounds of the northern part of Selkirk's grant, this district was 163 miles wide and 157 miles from top to bottom. It was a region of lakes, rivers and streams, marshes and forests. There were four HBC posts in the district: Halkett's House, Williams House, Big Point House and Fort Dauphin, sometimes called Dauphin House. Brown's first task was to assess the state of affairs at these houses—whether they were well placed, what

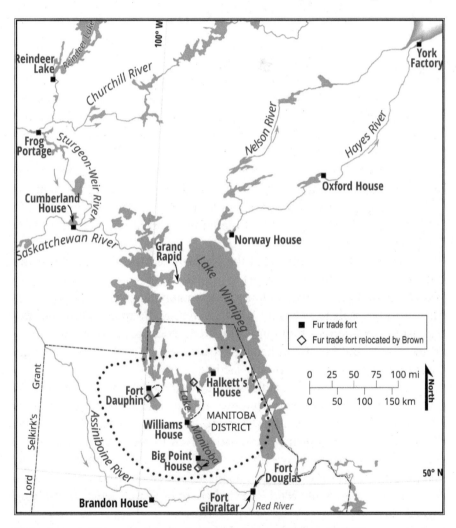

This map draws on Brown's district report and Peter Fidler's map and report on the Manitoba District. Fidler noted that the new Fort Dauphin was at latitude 51° 18' north. Brown closed Halkett's House, moved Big Point a few miles south, started the move of Williams House to the west end of Partridge Crop River (now named Fairford River), and moved Fort Dauphin a few miles south along the lakeshore.

condition they were in and how competent the employees were. Before he arrived, the district appears to have been in disarray, with dilapidated buildings and a general lack of attention to the trade. Brown attacked the problems decisively. In the short time he was there, he was like a spider newly come to a broken web, darting hither and thither to mend holes. Scurrying around by canoe, though, had its dangers. On one cold, calm day in November, he was in a canoe on a lake when the water suddenly froze, crushing in the sides. With water pouring in, he had to get himself to shore quickly.[92]

Halkett's House was a rundown collection of buildings on St. Martin's Lake. Brown described the buildings as being arranged in an oblong square and so low that he had to bend almost double to enter them. The master's room and cookhouse were useable, but the men's house and warehouse were dilapidated. The fort's garden of thirty-five square yards, the only ground under cultivation in the entire district, produced 120 kegs of potatoes. Although Halkett's House was a rewarding place for fishing—Brown noted that in one three-week period in the previous autumn two men had caught six thousand fish—it was badly situated, being surrounded by Nor'Wester posts, which were closer to Indigenous hunting grounds. He therefore closed this post and had the lumber and fittings carried to Fort Dauphin.

Williams House, situated at the Narrows of Manitoba Lake, was the only one close to a Nor'Wester fort. Originally known as Manitoba House, Brown renamed it Williams House, presumably after the new governor. There had been plans to extend it with a store and a man's house, but the bad fishing and derelict buildings suggested relocation. Now Brown wanted to close it and build another fort at the western end of the Partridge Crop River, where there was better fishing.

The house at Big Point at the southern end of Lake Manitoba was falling apart. It lacked doors and windows and most of its flooring had been taken up. When Brown arrived, he found, to his annoyance, that the men there had done nothing since they had arrived in September except cut a cord or two of wood. Moreover, the fort was badly placed for finding food. In February 1819, Brown closed it. In its place, he built a new fort close to the Nor'Wester fort at White Mud River, where the soil was better for growing vegetables.

Brown also thought that Fort Dauphin was badly placed. Although the buildings were in the best condition of any in the district, they still needed repairing. The fact that the river on which it was situated was full of rapids and not navigable by loaded boats tipped the balance into a decision to rebuild. He consequently built a new fort closer to the Nor'Westers, a place where the soil was more fertile.

Brown, it may be seen, was reorganizing the whole district. He was bringing fresh air and a sense of a fresh start that the apparently struggling district badly needed.

So how would the men there take all these changes? Including himself, the HBC had twenty-six men in the district, spread among the four houses. These men were of varying usefulness. Brown assessed their abilities in the blunt language of the age. He was crisp, critical and unsparing where necessary and laudatory where appropriate. William Duncan, he said, was slow and obedient but timid with the Indigenous people. Thomas Fidler was not fit for his situation as an interpreter, being disobedient, careless of property put in his charge and afraid of Indigenous people—but nonetheless handy and ingenious. Andrew McDermont was a good trader, could speak the language well and had the management of Fort Dauphin during the winter. He was active in learning about the Indigenous people, but "he has deceived them so often that they put no faith in his word."[93] On the other hand, William Sinclair was sober and honest, and Angus McIver was active, also honest and a good voyageur. Topesk was active in tracking and could be trusted in trading with Indigenous people.

Still only twenty-eight years old, Brown was decisive in giving orders. He seems to have had a no-nonsense approach that some resented. This caused problems. On occasion the men rebelled. In late December, for example, Brown sent Thomas Fidler and Thomas Swainey to visit nearby Indigenous encampments. They returned after an hour and Fidler announced he wouldn't go. After failing to persuade him to carry on with his duties as directed, Brown told him to pack his bags and leave the district. He left and went south to the HBC's fort at Brandon House. He returned on the last day of the year, however, asking to be accepted back. Brown consented, but told him that his wages would be dependent on his good behaviour.

INDIGENOUS PEOPLE

Brown noted that, except for a few Crees who visited Halkett's House, the Indigenous people around the forts were mainly the Saulteaux people. He wrote that

> the number of Males capable of hunting, I suppose, will amount to about two hundred, but a considerable number of these live in the plains where the Buffaloe are numerous and seldom or never procure any peltries [furs]. Of those who reside more in the tracks of country inhabited by the Fur-bearing animals, I suppose about one third of them may be reckoned as adherents to us, and the other two thirds to the N.W. Co. But in fact it does

> not much signify what party they pretend to adhere to,
> for whoever arrives first at their Lodges will very easily
> purchase either their Furs or Provisions, providing they
> have liquor.[94]

Both the HBC and the North West Company had been in the habit of giving credit to Indigenous hunters so they could acquire supplies, including ammunition, to enable them to hunt during the winter. In this way, many of them carried a considerable amount of debt on the HBC's books. The consequence of giving credit, Brown noted, was that Indigenous men were often afraid to come into the HBC post to offer their furs for trade because of the size of their debts. (This was a problem at many posts.) So they took them to the Nor'Wester fort, sometimes only a few hundred yards away. The North West Company had the same problem and, in turn, tried to prevent their Indigenous hunters from going to the HBC posts. Brown recommended that the HBC should not require Indigenous people to pay their debts and to be slow to give them any more credit.

The Pemmican War

While Brown was learning the fur trade at Reindeer Lake and also later while enjoying marital bliss with Elizabeth Armour in Scotland, momentous events had been happening at the Red River Settlement. The colony had been broken up and then, with Robertson's help, re-established. The Nor'Westers and Métis were still determined to destroy the re-established settlement and made plans accordingly. Both sides obtained arms, enlisted militia and continued skirmishing.

Under their charismatic leader Cuthbert Grant, the Métis burnt the HBC post at Brandon's House and moved on to attack Fort Douglas, the fort Robertson had rebuilt. On June 19, 1816, Governor Semple learned that Grant and a Nor'Wester force of approximately sixty men, mainly Métis with a few Canadians and Indigenous men, were approaching Fort Douglas. Accompanied by almost two dozen men, he rode out to a cluster of trees known as Seven Oaks. In the short engagement that followed, Semple and twenty-one of his men were killed. The Nor'Westers then took Fort Douglas and the remaining settlers fled.

For the second time in two years the Red River Settlement ended, and its inhabitants once again moved to temporary refuges on Lake Winnipeg. "Those fifteen minutes at Seven Oaks changed everything," Peter Newman wrote. "No longer a commercial contest with the occasional skirmish and post-burning, the struggle between the Nor'Westers and Bay men had turned into a guerrilla war, fought along a four-thousand mile front with unreliable troops and scheming generals.... Success would be determined by survival."[95]

Both companies continued to capture and burn each other's forts. Nor'Westers, for example, captured and destroyed the post at Reindeer Lake, where Brown had spent three quiet years. The most intense conflict took place in Athabasca. John Clarke had managed to establish five small forts there, including Fort Wedderburn on an island in Lake Athabasca opposite the Nor'Wester's Fort Chipewyan and also a fort on Great Slave Lake. The North West Company, under its aggressive leaders Samuel Black, William MacKintosh and John Stuart were relentless. When Clarke led fifty men into the Peace River region to establish HBC posts there, MacKintosh prevented them from finding food so successfully that sixteen of Clarke's men starved to death. In January 1817, the Nor'Westers invited Clarke to a meeting in Fort Chipewyan, arrested him and captured Fort Wedderburn. They held him, a young clerk named James Murray Yale and others as prisoners for six months. In December, the Nor'Westers expelled the HBC from Athabasca, on a promise not to return. They then burnt all their forts.

The HBC and the North West Company continued this strange war, at times in sporadic violence and at other times in civil competition. Much of the war settled down into attempts to arrest each other's leaders under claim of a legal warrant obtained in Upper or Lower Canada.

BROWN AND THE PEMMICAN WAR

In the Manitoba District, Brown was perilously close to the violence on the Red River. The North West Company had five trading posts in the district. Nevertheless, despite what had happened at Seven Oaks, he and Cuthbert Cumming, the Nor'Wester leader, managed to co-exist. Well aware of the developments not far to the south, both appear to have kept their heads down and stuck to their trade. Perhaps surprisingly, given the bloodshed elsewhere, they managed to maintain civil relations even as they competed strenuously for the furs and provisions the Indigenous people brought to them. Brown, for example, wrote that he had

> made the following agreement with Mr. Cumins [Cumming] of the N.W.C. "That neither party will give the Indians Liquor to drink at the House, nor send to their Encampments without giving the Other notice a day previous." The motive for entering into this arrangement with our opponents was twofold. 1st. To save expenses. 2nd. To prevent them from sending to the Indians till the season was further advanced, as at that time we neither have dogs nor provisions for that purpose.[96]

Civil coexistence, though, had its limits. Brown was active in his attempts to gain any advantage he could over his rival. He built HBC posts within yards of the Nor'Wester forts, something which the Nor'Westers would no doubt have resented. "Whenever the N.W.Co. settle an Out Post," he recommended, "be sure to oppose them and if possible have our house placed in such a manner as they cannot go from theirs without being observed and followed. By which means a great advantage will be derived from our Opponent's Superior Knowledge of the Country."[97] Both watched closely what the other was doing. Sometimes, when the Nor'Westers went out to find the Indigenous hunters to ascertain if they had furs to trade, Brown would send men to follow them and see where they were going. As did the Nor'Westers, when the HBC men went out.

There was an occasional incident, but not many. In the autumn of 1818, for instance, Brown had loaned a small, almost empty keg of rum to an Indigenous man, who had kept it. The Nor'Wester Will Delorme stole this keg from the man, and Brown was aggrieved.

> Understanding from an Indian that Delorme—who is Master for the N.W. at this place—stole a two Gallon Keg of mine from the Robber that I had lent him in the fall with some liquor, I sent over one of two Men to request him to deliver it up but he would not do it and returned an answer that he had traded it from the Indian for a fathom of Tobacco. And if I chose to give him the same quantity I would get it. Upon which I went over myself & pointed out the impropriety of him proposing to Keep it on the pretence of having traded it as he well knew the Keg belonged to me, the Initials of my name being upon the head of it. But this had no effect. I then requested him to shew me the Keg pretending that it perhaps was not the one belonging to me. Which he did & I immediately laid hold of it from him and one of his Men seized me to take it from me again, but I pulled out my pistol and told them that if they did not let me go I would fire upon them, the truth of which they did not appear to doubt for they let me go immediately.
>
> John Harper then came to my assistance, to whom I gave the Keg, which he went & secured. Seeing the Keg secured, I considered there would be no more about it & put my pistol in my pocket, but I was mistaken for whenever Delorme & his Man saw me put up my

pistol they both flew upon me & put me down in a short time. Harper came to my assistance a second time and I got up to my feet when the business ended in a Boxing match between Delorme & Me.

My Men behaved most shamefully bad. Not one offered to give me the least assistance except McLean & Harper. McKinnon in particular stood during the whole time with his hands in his Big Mits.[98]

Overall though, Brown had no complaints about the Nor'Westers. "Their Conduct during the winter could not be complained of," he wrote, "being nothing further than a fair competition of Trade. And save that trifling dispute I had with Delorme, there was no contest in the District during the season."[99]

Now that the Napoleonic wars were over, European markets had re-opened and the demand for beaver hats was rising. Writing the report on the district in April 1820, Brown made a number of recommendations on the ways to improve the trade. These were crisp and to the point. He outlined his ideas for rebuilding the district posts. Take more land under cultivation to reduce scarcity. Obtain more kettles for making maple sugar. Keep liquor on hand, it still being necessary. Give no credit to Indigenous hunters but turn the trade into a fair barter. Build posts near the Nor'Westers to observe and learn from them. His thoughtful advice would have only increased the good opinion his superiors had of him.

SPRING FINALLY ARRIVES

Spring began in early April in the Manitoba District. On April 5, 1819, Brown noted that the weather was warm and spring advancing rapidly. The leaves were on the trees by mid-May, particularly on the aspen, poplar and willow, though the oak came later. Snow was off the plains by April 8, though still lying deep in the woods and ice was still in the river. He saw the first goose on the 9th and on that same day he noticed the first buds on the thorn bushes. He also commented on the first maple sugar running. The marshes, streams and woods were full of melting snow.

The time came to take the furs collected during the year to York Factory for shipment to Europe. When Brown left the district on June 2, he set out with one boat and two canoes, taking with him ten packs of furs and thirty bags of pemmican. His destination was York Factory. The furs arrived. He didn't. Not yet anyway. Unbeknownst to him, he was heading straight into a violent confrontation at the Grand Rapid of the Saskatchewan River.

7

Arrest and Ambush

1819

"You are my prisoner, in the King's name."

William Brown, June 23, 1819

Governor Williams laid his ambush carefully. Below the Grand Rapid of the Saskatchewan River, about a mile before it entered Lake Winnipeg, was the perfect place. What the Nor'Westers had done to Colin Robertson in Athabasca deserved nothing less than an assertive response. Men primed their pistols. Soldiers prepared their muskets. Williams set a cannon on each side of the river. He placed Brown in command of the "capture" party. News arrived. Several Nor'Wester canoes were at that moment on their way down the rapids. Unsuspecting Nor'Westers were walking on the trail through the woods alongside it. Williams and his men waited. Ready.

THE PEMMICAN WAR HEATS UP

By 1818, the Pemmican War had become more intense. Although the HBC had a trading monopoly on the lands under their charter, the North West Company had a strong hold on Athabasca. Over the Rocky Mountains, the Nor'Westers also controlled the inland trade of New Caledonia. But the financial pressures on both companies were increasing. Events were dragging both companies into ever more aggressive measures, which were exhausting their men and their finances.

Both Athabasca and New Caledonia were rich in high-quality furs. Governor Williams and Colin Robertson understood that the HBC had to challenge the Nor'Westers first in Athabasca and then in New Caledonia. It was becoming a "them or us" struggle.

In 1815, John Clarke had established Fort Wedderburn on Potato Island (sometimes called Coal Island). This was a mere mile and a half away from Fort Chipewyan, the Nor'Wester headquarters in Athabasca. At one point, the HBC and the Nor'Westers had agreed to partition the land on Potato Island. The Nor'Westers had built a guardhouse on its part of the island, only a few yards to the east of the HBC post. The North West Company was not going to allow Clarke to remain there without a fight. As we have seen, they expelled him and burnt all the HBC forts.

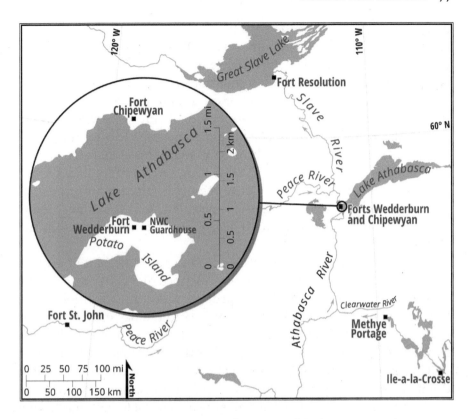

Athabasca, showing the location of Fort Wedderburn, Fort Chipewyan and the Nor'Wester guardhouse on Potato Island.

Fort Chipewyan, the most important Nor'Wester post after its headquarters at Fort William on Lake Superior, was at the hub of the numerous river and lake transportation systems in Athabasca. The way into New Caledonia at this time was to go from Fort Chipewyan up the Peace River, past Fort St. John, across the Rocky Mountain Portage and then down the Parsnip River to McLeod's Lake.

Because of its location and importance, Sir Alexander Mackenzie had called Fort Chipewyan the "Emporium of the North." Unlike Fort Wedderburn and its rundown buildings, Fort Chipewyan was grand, with buildings around three sides of a large courtyard, and with bastions, stockades and gates. It was also well supplied with provisions and books. A few years before, an erudite Nor'Wester named Robert Mackenzie of Terrebonne, Alexander Mackenzie's cousin, had brought in a library of two thousand books.

SIMON MCGILLIVRAY AND SAMUEL BLACK

In Simon McGillivray and Samuel Black, the North West Company had two particularly aggressive leaders. Both seemed to act independently of any particular post and seemed to have the objective of doing as much damage to the HBC as they could, whenever and wherever they came across them—something both did with delight and gusto.

Simon McGillivray had a significant heritage. He was the son of William McGillivray, the Montreal-based head of the North West Company. He was also the nephew of Simon McGillivray, who, writing as the Highlander, had tried to dissuade the emigrants from leaving Stornoway in July 1811. Sir Alexander Mackenzie was one of his godfathers. Whenever McGillivray clashed with the HBC men, he caused trouble. George Simpson wrote that he had been active in every nefarious transaction that had taken place in Athabasca and was notorious for his cunning. "Next to Black," he wrote, "he is more to be dreaded than any member of the N.W. Co'y."[100]

Samuel Black had the worst reputation of all. Like McGillivray, he was a known bully and fighter. Simpson described him as having a ghastly raw-boned and lanthorn (lantern-shaped) jaw with shrunken cheeks. "Unlike most of his fellow Nor'Westers, who treated the Bay men with either respect or contempt," Peter Newman wrote, "Black was a terrorist who took pleasure in his violent activities."[101] He wrote that Black enjoyed tormenting HBC men. Black reportedly "once placed a heavy piece of bark atop the chimney, nearly asphyxiating the snoozing occupants, and even killed and ate their pet dog."[102] He was a dangerous opponent. Not for nothing had the HBC taken out a warrant for his arrest.

The Imprisonment of Colin Robertson

Colin Robertson recruited another powerful force in Montreal to renew the challenge to the North West Company in Athabasca. In the summer of 1818, he took two hundred men back to rebuild the forts, including Fort Wedderburn on Potato Island on Lake Athabasca and a post on Great Slave Lake.

Robertson had come to Fort Wedderburn to challenge the North West Company on its own ground. This inevitably led to friction. On October 3, a leading Nor'Wester bully named Soucisse started a fight with one of the HBC men. When Robertson went to stop it, Black took hold of his shoulder, whereupon Robertson pulled out his pistol and pushed Black away, telling him he would not have his men abused. That same afternoon Black laid down a line on the beach and forbade anyone to cross it. When Alex McDonald, second in command at Fort Wedderburn, told him that by the law of the land all rivers, beaches and lakes were open to anyone up to the high-water mark, Black swore at him and said he did not give a damn for the law: the Nor'Westers would make their own.

These sparks ignited the explosion of the following weekend. On October 10, Nor'Westers, including Black, McGillivray and Soucisse, spotted an HBC canoe and attacked it, dragging out the Indigenous people who had been coming over to join the HBC. Black drew his sabre and threatened to cut off the head of an HBC man who was resisting. That evening, Joseph Boucher came across Soucisse on the beach and thrashed him.

Later that night, a party of HBC men arrived back at the fort bringing with them the body of a man who had been accidentally shot dead a few days before. Before dying, he had said he wanted to be buried close to his friends at the fort. McDonald gave immediate orders for a grave to be dug and a coffin made. For obvious reasons, haste was necessary.

Colin Robertson, the aggressive leader of the HBC in Athabasca. He later clashed with George Simpson, who wrote his most critical character sketch about him.

At ten the following morning, before the burial, Soucisse, accompanied by Black and McGillivray, came over to call Boucher out for a fight to get revenge for the beating of the previous day. McDonald went out to tell them to be more respectful. It was not Christian, he said, to continue a quarrel at such a time. And on a Sunday too! This did not stop the Nor'Wester abuse. Robertson then went out to Black and told him the conduct of his men was indecent.

Black's men then pounced on him. Robertson was not one to give up without a fight. The Nor'Westers dragged him into a canoe, which he tried to capsize so he could swim to freedom. But Robertson, struggling still, was not able to free himself and was carried exhausted and angry back to the Nor'Wester guardhouse, where he continued to struggle.[103] It all happened so fast that the other HBC men had been too stunned to give him assistance.

The Nor'Westers held Robertson prisoner in Fort Chipewyan for eight months. He spent much of his time reading and writing letters. Likely a prisoner from hell, he pestered the Nor'Wester chief in charge of the fort. On March 3, he admonished him, saying "Really, Mr. Keith, there is no pleasing you. Pray what puts you in such a fever? Command your temper and if you cannot be civil, be decent, or at least as decent as you can! Remember you are a partner of the North West Comp."[104] While a prisoner, Robertson read five volumes of Shakespeare's plays from the fort's library. He also found a way to communicate with McDonald, who was managing Fort Wedderburn in his absence. He devised a cipher and an ingenious way of getting his messages out, hidden in the bung of a barrel. In one of the letters that reached Governor Williams, Robertson pointed out that the HBC could—and should—ambush the Nor'Wester canoes at the Grand Rapid of the Saskatchewan River.[105]

The Nor'Wester partner John G. McTavish decided he would take Robertson back to Montreal for trial. His party, which included Simon McGillivray, Angus Shaw and William MacKintosh—all very senior officers of the company—together with Robertson, set off in canoes. After a narrow escape from drowning in Pin Rapids in which two Nor'Westers did die, Robertson suspected the Nor'Westers had been trying to murder him and make it look like an accident. Did he fear they would try again? The canoes arrived at Cumberland House on June 19, 1819. Several other Nor'Westers, including Benjamin Frobisher and William Connolly, had arrived there a few days before and left to go downstream on June 18. The others were going to follow a day or so later.

The Ambush

After hearing that the Nor'Westers had taken Robertson prisoner, Governor Williams plotted a powerful counterattack. "It is morally impossible human nature can bear such conduct without retaliating," he wrote to Selkirk. "Being too passive has given these barbarians a species of courage attached only to assassins."[106] To avenge the killings at Seven Oaks and also Robertson's imprisonment, he adopted Robertson's suggestion of an ambush at the Grand Rapid on the Saskatchewan River. "Finding passive measures no longer of any avail and the tardy progress of the Law so partially administered in Canada," he wrote, "and its lassitude likely to overwhelm us in difficulty made me resolve to retaliate on these Buccaneers."[107] In the autumn of 1818, he obtained arrest warrants for a number of his Nor'Wester adversaries. Additionally, he believed that if he blockaded the river to Nor'Wester canoes he could strangle the Nor'Wester trade with Athabasca.

The Saskatchewan River was the great highway to the West. The canoes of both companies carrying trade goods and furs to Athabasca arrived in Lake Winnipeg from two widely different starting points and headed upstream. Almost immediately, they came to the formidable barrier of the Grand Rapid. This was four or five miles of turbulent water that dropped seventy feet to

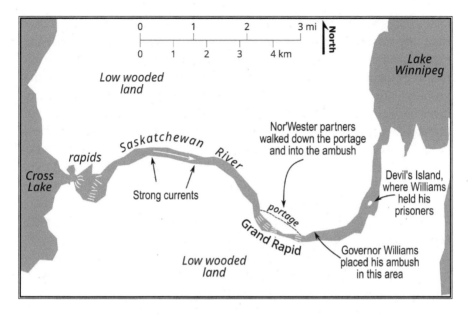

The Grand Rapid on the Saskatchewan River before the 1964 construction of the dam and consequent change in the landscape.

drain into the lake. For a century it had been a major obstacle for voyageurs. Loaded canoes could generally make their way over the rapids, although to lighten the load passengers often decided to walk down the portage track. The basin at the bottom of the rapids was a natural place for an ambush.

Williams assembled a small force of men and added to it twenty ex-soldiers of the De Meuron regiment to whom he promised land on the Red River. He took with him several swivel guns and several cannons, one of which was a brass 3-pounder. Leaving Norway House on June 17, 1819, he arrived at the Grand Rapid the following day and laid his ambush.

While on the way there, he met William Brown, his fellow traveller from the *Prince of Wales*, on his way to York Factory with his district's furs. He promptly swore in Brown as a special constable for Rupert's Land and attached him to his force. Williams also encountered John McLeod, another clerk from the voyage on the *Edward and Ann*, also on his way to York Factory. Usefully, McLeod could identify the Nor'Wester partners by sight. That morning of June 18, John Clarke arrived from Athabasca and told Williams that two Nor'Wester canoes had left Cumberland House and were not far behind him.

No sooner had Williams positioned his force near the basin below the rapids than he learned that several Nor'Westers were at that moment walking across the portage, leaving their canoes to run the rapids.

Brown saw the Nor'Westers approaching. William Connolly, one of the Nor'Wester party, wrote that Brown and a party of armed men suddenly attacked them. All the men Brown's party seized were unarmed except Benjamin Frobisher, who brandished a pistol at Brown and prepared to fire. Someone knocked the pistol out of his hand. Connolly wrote that Frobisher "on this account was treated in the most Cruel Manner, having received many violent blows with the butt end of muskets."[108] For his act of threatening Brown and putting up a resistance, Williams arrested Frobisher on his own authority as governor of Rupert's Land. Over vocal protests from their prisoners that their arrest was illegal, Williams imprisoned them all in a hut. When the prisoners looked through the door, the soldiers on guard threatened to beat them with their muskets and tie them up. Among those Brown captured were the alleged murderers of Governor Semple at Seven Oaks.

Later that day, Williams allowed those he had not arrested to continue on their journey. These included Connolly, who went to say goodbye to his imprisoned friends. "Mr. Frobisher," he recounted,

> was sitting on a cassette [personal box], where from the blows he had received & the paleness of his countenance plainly denoted the anguish of body and mind under which he laboured. Never before were my feelings so powerfully affected, but as it was impossible for me to render them any assistance, I therefore embarked at 9 o'clock and I proceeded to the entrance of the Lake, where we encamped.[109]

Unbeknownst to the HBC, Connolly then went back and took a position in the woods across the river from where he could watch what was happening. He sent a man to warn his Nor'Wester comrades upstream who, as he knew, would soon be coming down the rapids.

June 22 and 23, 1819, were action-packed days. Williams found out that

Lord Selkirk used retired soldiers from the De Meuron Regiment at the Grand Rapid ambush. After being discharged in 1816, many had kept their uniforms.

the Nor'Westers upstream probably had learnt about the ambush. He might have thought, that's it. No more canoes will come down the rapids. He sent his prisoners downstream to York Factory and moved his force to a redoubt overlooking the river in case the Nor'Westers did try to come down. There they waited. They were in luck. That day they stopped eight more Nor'Wester canoes. After arresting four of the men in those canoes for robbery and burglary, Williams let the canoes with their packs of furs proceed on their way. All the while, Connolly was watching helplessly from his vantage point across the river.

The Nor'Westers upstream had indeed learned about the HBC ambush. Three canoes with a number of senior Nor'Westers on board, including Angus Shaw, William MacKintosh, John G. McTavish, John Stuart and Simon McGillivray, encountered Connolly's messenger on Cedar Lake, which was to the west of Cross Lake. Colin Robertson, ominously, was not with them. Where was he? Had something sinister happened to him? They learned that the HBC had seized Frobisher and others at the Grand Rapid. They deliberated about what to do. Not having any arms, McTavish said "it is possible they may take us also, but we cannot help it if they do."[110] They did, though, decide to split up. While Shaw, McTavish and MacKintosh took the canoes downriver on the intended route—and towards the HBC ambush—Stuart and McGillivray "were appointed to pass by a very circuitous and rarely frequented road, thereby to find additional security to someone reaching the general rendezvous at Fort William should the Hudson's Bay people be so very forgetful of all moderation as to stop the others."[111] Above the rapids, Shaw, McTavish and eight others decided to walk down the portage. "William MacKintosh," McTavish wrote, "being in a bad state of health and unable to endure the fatigue of walking, remained to pass the Rapid in his canoe."[112]

At approximately 6:00 a.m. on June 23, "Mr. Brown, the Constable," Governor Williams wrote, "perceived some persons coming thro' the bushes along shore."[113] Accounts differ about exactly what happened next. The Nor'Westers later claimed that the HBC were sleeping and taken by surprise. "Aux armes, aux armes," the soldiers were said to have shouted when they saw the Nor'Westers approaching. "The noise of their approach awoke the HBC people, who were fast asleep," a group of six voyageurs said in a combined statement. "Among the first we saw was Mr. John Clarke, who started naked out of his tent, and observing our party called to the Meurons, who as soon as they could arm themselves came and seized McTavish and put an armed man on each side of him to keep him prisoner."[114]

McTavish swore they appeared armed with "muskets, fusils [a light flintlock musket], pistols, swords, daggers and lances," and surrounded the Nor'Westers, taking them all prisoners.[115] According to the Nor'Westers' understandably self-serving accounts, the HBC men handled their prisoners roughly. Shaw went to the group surrounding them and asked which one of them was Governor Williams.

"I am Governor Williams, I command here," William Brown said. "What do you want with him?"

"Why do you stop the King's highway in this manner with armed men?" Shaw asked. "Where are your warrants against us?"

Brown replied, "I have warrants to execute."

"If so, shew your warrants peaceably," Shaw demanded.

Governor Williams now came up, announced who he was and declared, "I have something to say to Mr. McTavish." Brown then placed his hand on McTavish's shoulder and said, "You are my prisoner in the King's name."

Shaw again asked to see the warrants and alleged that Brown replied that he had no warrants. Apoplectic with anger, Shaw protested belligerently about the illegality of the proceedings and that Williams was ignoring the recent proclamation of the Prince Regent to keep the peace. "I do not care a curse for the Prince Regent's Proclamation," Williams said. "Lord Bathurst and Sir John Sherbrooke, by whom it was framed, are damned rascals. I act upon the Charter of the Hudson's Bay Company and as a Governor and as a Magistrate I have sufficient authority, and shall act as I think proper."[116]

With undying indignation, Shaw related that he and McTavish were physically attacked and beaten. One soldier, he declared, used his musket as a club and another pointed a musket at his heart and was about to shoot when he was stopped by another soldier. He swore he would bring 250 men with him and teach the HBC to respect them by spreading carnage and bloodshed throughout the country. Williams, his patience now exhausted, arrested Shaw for breach of peace and put him with the other prisoners.

By this time the Nor'Wester canoes had navigated the rapids and were in sight. Compelled by the menace of the HBC cannon, they came towards shore, MacKintosh with them. Brown would have recalled that it was MacKintosh who had been instrumental in starving sixteen HBC men to death in Athabasca a couple of years before. Nor would Clarke, whose men they had been, have forgotten. "If the Rascal makes resistance," Governor Williams called out, "shoot him."[117] Brown waded into the river, seized the canoe and pulled MacKintosh out of it onto the bank, where one of the soldiers struck him. Complaints to Williams about this treatment were, Shaw alleged, met with a torrent of abuse and invective. "We shall act independently of the rascally Canada government," Williams declared. "Lord Bathurst will be turned out of office by Lord Selkirk as soon as he gets to England, which is doubtless done ere now, and I shall make use of the colonists and every other means in my power to drive out of this country every

Grand Rapid, Saskatchewan River, head of the Old York Boat Portage, 1890. It was at such a place that Governor Williams laid his ambush in 1819 and stopped the Nor'Wester canoes.

damned Northwester or perish in the attempt."[118]

Williams then opened the Nor'Westers' cassettes. In McTavish's, he found sealed papers and a sabre, all of which, except for a few unimportant memoranda, he kept. Williams wrote he found in these papers "a chain of premeditated Villainy against the Concerns of the Company."[119] He wrote that he hoped this would be a death blow to a group of unprincipled robbers who had "committed such repeated acts of barbarism which already has made mankind shudder with horror and even made a savage blush."[120]

Williams now learned that the biggest prize, Simon McGillivray, son of the head of the North West Company and a brigand in his own right, had slipped through his fingers. He ordered his men to take all the prisoners to the island to join Frobisher and the others. They stayed there as prisoners for eight days. On June 30, they spotted another canoe coming down the rapid. With their cannon and over fifty men prepared to receive it, the HBC men were eager to take more prisoners. The arrival, though, turned out to be Colin Robertson, who had broken the parole he had been allowed at Cumberland House and escaped.

The following day, Williams heard that "a party of Half breeds and Indians was mustering to remove his blockade and release his prisoners."[121] He therefore decided to move his force to a safer position closer to York Factory.

Brown took MacKintosh in one canoe, and McTavish went in another.

The Nor'Wester William MacKintosh was sick. Brown and Clarke, who were his guards, compassionately prepared his bed and built a fire for him. While they were doing that, MacKintosh seized his opportunity and escaped into the woods. Brown found a note written by him in a book that said he had decided to commit suicide. Governor Williams didn't believe this and organized a search. They tracked him to the edge of the lake and saw his footprints going out into the water. On the shore, they found a piece of bark on which MacKintosh had written "I have drowned myself, having tied a Stone round my Neck to keep me at the Bottom."[122] Since the lake was only eighteen inches deep for about a mile out, Williams didn't believe this story either. Sure enough, they found MacKintosh's footprints coming out of the lake not far away. MacKintosh escaped and made his way to the North West Company headquarters at Fort William. Brown was furious at being duped and swore revenge.

While at the HBC post of Rock Depot, on their way downstream from the Grand Rapid to York Factory, Robertson held long discussions with Williams about the future of the HBC. "The extension of trade was the next point," Robertson wrote,

> and I stated to Mr. Williams my intentions of estab-
> lishing New Caledonia and McKenzie's River.... I then
> began to arrange the appointments of Athabasca. First,
> I intended Mr. [Alex] McDonald to winter at his old
> quarters, Fort Wedderburn, Mr. Brown to proceed to
> Great Slave Lake, act as second to Mr. McVicar, but to
> devote his principal attention to the collecting of in-
> formation relative to McKenzie's river and Great Bear
> Lake, a district where he was to winter in 1821. As to
> myself, as soon as the outfits for the posts in the vicinity
> of Fort Wedderburn were made out, I was to proceed
> to Peace River, and put in execution the arrangements
> entered into by Mr. Clarke to establish New Caledonia,
> a country, according to all reports, rich in furs and the
> natives perfectly independent.[123]

Brown was now on his way to Athabasca, ground zero for the con-
flict between the two warring companies. As far as the Nor'Westers were concerned, he was now a marked man. Soon they would obtain a warrant for his arrest.

Privations at Fort Resolution

1819-1820

"In regard to Mr. Brown, I must beg leave to inform you that there are very few in the North that are more Conversant in the nature of the Indian Trade than he is. And I am of opinion that he may be considered as an Indian Trader, one of the most enterprising men in Athabasca."

Chief Factor Robert McVicar, May 1820

Athabasca. The fur-rich Eldorado beyond the boundaries of Rupert's Land. The most contentious territory in the fur-trading lands of the North. The place where the HBC had to challenge and defeat the North West Company if it was going to survive as a profitable company. The HBC forts there were at the end of a long road from York Factory. With its long, harsh winters and short mosquito-thick summers, it was a rugged land of hills, rocky outcrops and stunted forests of spruce, pine and birch. The northern lights filled the winter sky with spectacles of magic and wonder. Athabasca was a frontier, a place to send exploring parties into, a place to throw down the fur-trading gauntlet and fight to the finish.

Following Robertson's advice, Governor Williams sent William Brown to the HBC fort on Great Slave Lake, the tenth largest lake in the world and the deepest in North America. Brown's mission, in addition to assisting Robert McVicar, the chief factor there, was to open a new fort and district at Mountain Island. He was also to gather information about the MacKenzie River, which flowed from Great Slave Lake to the Arctic Ocean. By now, Brown was seen as an intelligent officer. Clearly a man with a future in the HBC, he was decisive and demonstrably capable of taking the initiative and making decisions. With the brain he had shown in the Manitoba district and the brawn he had shown at the Grand Rapid, he was a useful man to have around.

JOURNEY THERE

After the affair at Grand Rapid, it is likely that Brown went downriver to the HBC headquarters at York Factory. Then, after seeing to the delivery of

Peter Rindisbacher, *Extremely Wearisome Journeys at the Portage*, 1821. This painting shows the men carrying the canoes and loads around difficult rapids near Norway House.

his district's furs, he turned around and started back across Rupert's Land to Athabasca. Colin Robertson, the superintendent of the Athabasca Department, and his lieutenant John Clarke set out a few days after them in two light canoes.

Brown reached Cumberland House on August 20, where, a couple of days later, Robertson caught up with them. Five days later they all set out and headed to the HBC fort of Île à la Crosse. There they learned that two loaded Nor'Wester canoes had arrived at the 380-yards-long Frog Portage (Porte du Traite). This party included John Stuart and William MacKintosh, the Nor'Wester who had slipped through Brown's fingers after the Grand Rapid affair. Still smarting about how MacKintosh had tricked him, Brown was eager to take him prisoner. The other officers were not so sure. They thought this might put them in legal jeopardy because they did not have a warrant for his arrest. Collectively, they decided to leave MacKintosh alone.

That was not the end of the matter. The next day they met the Nor'Wester canoes at the western end of the portage. Robertson wrote that

> Mr. Brown, one of the gentlemen I received from Governor Williams and who had charge of Mr. MacKintosh when he made his escape, swore he would seize him wherever he found him. This happened in one of the

Portages of the English River where Mr. Brown, with a man of the name of Harper, went up to MacKintosh surrounded by his people, and, although armed with pistols and hanger [a Scottish hunting sword], he dragged him from a bush and brought him to our tent. Although I did not approve of the measure, I could not help admiring the cool and determined courage of Brown.[124]

Robert McVicar added detail and an ending to this story. He confirmed that when they learned that MacKintosh was in the Nor'Wester party, Brown had indeed proposed arresting him, but the others, fearful of the consequences, were reluctant. McVicar wrote:

Under such circumstances, Mr. B had the mortification to give MacKintosh his liberty. When he began to expostulate with some of our Gentlemen on the impropriety of such violent proceedings, one of our Gentlemen answered him, "That for his part he was not concerned in the business, neither would he implicate himself by advancing any illegal measure and if Mr. B. was so headstrong as to embark in the affair, of course, he alone was responsible for the consequences."[125]

When they arrived at Portage des Espangles (Pin Portage) on the morning of September 8, MacKintosh, through an intermediary, demanded that Brown apologize. Brown refused. MacKintosh then demanded the satisfaction of a gentleman, that is to say, a duel. Brown said, fine, name the time and place. MacKintosh kept silent and no duel ensued. Once again, though, MacKintosh had escaped.

THE OBSTRUCTIONS OF ALEXANDER McDONALD

Brown's mission was to establish and manage a new fort at Mountain Island in the Great Slave District. This was a strategic move to outflank the North West Company by enticing the Indigenous hunters to come to them there. To accomplish this, Brown and McVicar were to go to Fort Wedderburn, draw the necessary supplies for the HBC fort on Great Slave Lake and also for the proposed new fort at Mountain Island. Brown would then take these supplies north to Great Slave Lake. Meanwhile, Robertson made his base at St. Mary's Fort in the Peace River country.

In charge of Fort Wedderburn at the time was Alexander McDonald. Second in command when Robertson had been there in 1818, he had been in charge while Robertson was a prisoner in Fort Chipewyan, not far away across the lake. Robertson wrote him many "Dear Mac" letters while held

Fighting up rapids such as these was hard, grinding work but an inevitable part of travel in Rupert's Land and Athabasca.

a prisoner and left him in charge after McTavish and the Nor'Westers took him away for trial in Montreal.

Brown and McVicar arrived at Fort Wedderburn with nine canoes on September 28. A few days later, McVicar left to go north on the Slave River to Great Slave Lake to take charge of the HBC fort there. He wanted to lose no time in convincing the Indigenous people at the lake that the HBC was not abandoning them. "It being considered absolutely necessary," Brown wrote, "for him to proceed there with all dispatch in order to prepare the Indians, and if possible to prevail on some of the leading characters amongst them to espouse our cause before the arrival of the North West Canoes in that quarter."[126]

Brown stayed behind at Fort Wedderburn to obtain provisions and supplies. Intending to follow McVicar a few days later, he drew up the lists of what he needed and submitted them to McDonald. He now met a significant obstacle. McDonald was ill in bed with rheumatism, and he refused to give Brown the supplies he requested. Brown wrote:

> I drew out a list of the different Goods I thought would
> be required for the District ... and presented the list
> to Mr. McDonald for his consideration. Who did not

even condescend to take it out of my hand but being in bed at the time, he leaped out with all the appearance of a maniac and told me, "That I neither knew nor had anything to do with the business, and that he would be Damned if my Indent was paid any attention to," and at same time desired Mr. Miles just to give me what he pleased.

His frantic mien, with the strange and inconsiderate assertion that I neither knew nor had anything to do with the very business I remained purposely to transact, was so novel to any thing I had ever seen before and at the same time was so truly ludicrous that I would not have been able to refrain from laughing in his face had I not been kept in awe by the formidable manner he all the while kept brandishing his tremendous crutches. Which convinced me that it was not a time for mirth, as it appeared I was in a place where neither justice nor civility was to be expected. Therefore I contented myself with informing him that I had done my duty by laying an Indent before him, and if he did not choose to pay any attention to it, he might act as he pleased. But to recollect that he must be answerable for the consequences.[127]

When McDonald finally did allocate supplies among the posts he did so in secret, behind the closed and barred doors of the storeroom. Brown wrote of his allocation,

It is far short of every article—but principally Ammunition, Rum, Tobacco and Twine—for accomplishing the plans that Mr. McVicar and I had agreed to act upon during the winter.... Such being the case, I remonstrated with Mr. McDonald on the impropriety of curtailing our outfit so much, particularly in those articles the want of which may be of the most fatal consequence to the concern. But I reaped no other advantage from my remonstrance than a string of incoherent curses.[128]

Brown also objected in writing but to no avail.

Twine was necessary for making and mending fishing nets. The equations were brutally simple. No twine, no nets. No nets, no fish. No fish, starvation. Brown found he was also short of axes, which were necessary for the acquisition of firewood and lumber to make boards for the houses, as well as snowshoes and traineaux. No axes: no wood for fires. The axe heads he did have were of poor quality and so brittle they quickly broke. Furthermore, he was also short of trading goods, including the essential tobacco and liquor. Without these they would not be able to acquire furs or food from the local Indigenous people.

Brown realized that these shortages would have serious, perhaps fatal, consequences for them all. "It is truly galling," he wrote,

> to reflect that such a Man as Mr. Alexander McDonald, who is destitute of every ability to render him of any service to the Company in this Quarter should have it in his power to carry his Caprice so far as not only to deprive us of the means to enable us to follow up (and effect) the Instructions of our Superior but also (in a great measure) of the means of Subsistence, which may tend to the most fatal consequence to the concern.[129]

Why McDonald did this is not clear. Robertson noted that he had rheumatism and that it wasn't getting any better. There could also, perhaps, have been other reasons deep in the politics and personalities of the HBC that caused McDonald to be so obstructive.

After a delay while the blacksmith made 100 nails for him (Brown had asked for 300) and two axes (he had asked for four), Brown left for Great Slave Lake with men and canoes on October 7. McVicar was anxious to have him arrive because the Nor'Westers at Fort Providence, their fort on Great Slave Lake, had been telling the Indigenous people that the HBC was not bothering to send a canoe with supplies.

Brown's journey down the Slave River to Great Slave Lake took almost a week, downstream but against the wind. It was cold and at times snowing. He had to make seven portages around rapids. When he arrived at Great Slave Lake, winter was closing in fast. He wrote, "Wind South and very cold, particularly in the Morning, with a great deal of Ice about the shore & sides of the Canoe. The Trees and Bushes are now entirely stripped of their leaves. The Birds of passage are all gone—if it is not a chance one that has lazed behind—and every thing prognosticates the speedy approach of winter."[130]

When Brown unpacked the supplies and trade goods he had brought with him, his gravest misgivings were confirmed. He was deeply disappointed to conclude he would have to give up any idea of establishing the new post at Mountain Island until at least the following year:

> The Establishing of that Post this year would have been productive of the greatest advantages to the Company....

> By not establishing Mountain Island the Company not only sustains the loss of the Trade of that part but also gives the North West Co. many advantages over us at this place. It would not be in their power to harass us so much had we been opposing them at both places.[131]

One other unfortunate consequence of the inability to establish the new post was that the men who were meant to go there with Brown would have to remain at the fort all winter, putting an additional strain on its food supplies.

Food shortage during the harsh winter at Great Slave Lake was a real possibility. McVicar and Brown had to use their trade goods to persuade local Indigenous men to hunt for meat, rather than for furs. Trading for meat—not that caribou and other meat sources were plentiful at that time of year anyway—meant that the Indigenous people would not trap the fur-bearing animals that justified the existence of the fort. If there weren't any furs, what was the need for a fort?

On October 20, McVicar and Brown erected a flagstaff and christened the post "Fort Resolution." As was customary, they then fired several volleys to celebrate the event.

Winter was now moving in fast. On October 28, the surface of the lake as far as the eye could see was covered with ice, though the wind during the day broke it open again. Driving ice destroyed nine of the nets

George Back, *Mountain Fall Rapid on the Slave River*, painted while on the Franklin Expedition, July 27, 1825. This was one of the rapids Brown had to navigate on his way to Fort Resolution.

they had put in the water, which, not having the necessary twine, they were unable to repair. Even by late October, Brown was writing, "We are taking so few fish owing to the small number of nets we have that we are obliged to reduce our Men's allowance."[132] On November 16, they considered the ice thick and safe enough to put nets below it. They were wrong. The wind broke up the ice and drove it out into the lake, taking fifty scarce lines and hooks with it. Winter settled in with strong winds, intense cold, snow and rain and with the occasional mild day to cheer their spirits.

McVicar was as exasperated with McDonald as Brown was. He told Governor Williams that if Fort Resolution was to continue to receive its supplies from Fort Wedderburn while McDonald was still in charge, he would not take charge of it. After describing how McDonald had refused to give them the supplies they had requested and how short they were, McVicar went on to predict, "So that we may rely upon suffering many privations ere spring."[133]

His complaints to McDonald himself did not seem to make any difference. Writing on behalf of McDonald, William Todd (no relation to John Tod) replied to McVicar:

> Mr. McDonald requests that should you have any real or imaginary grievance to complain of, you will address yourself on that subject to Gov. Williams or Mr. Robertson in whose power alone it is to do you justice, recommending you at the same time to avoid, if possible, these aerial flights with which you are so fond of embellishing most of your Narratives, as nothing looks more despicable than official falsehood.[134]

Such a communication through a subordinate could have done nothing to improve either McVicar's or Brown's opinion of him.

McVicar replied testily on February 5. "On perusing its contents, some parts made me smile while others were beyond the reach of my comprehension," he wrote, and

> in answer to that sublime paragraph—Aerial flights—Embellishing narratives—Official falsehoods, I have only to say I am unacquainted with the first two figures and if you can bring forward a single instance where I have set my hand to "an Official falsehood" I will not only thank you, but will immediately retract it and make all the necessary reparation in my power. If you cannot do so, you will certainly not feel hurt at being branded with the name of a Defamer.[135]

For the moment, though, McDonald had the last word. In the list of employees in the account books, someone scrawled out Robert McVicar's name and wrote "alias Baron Münchhausen," adding that he was resident in China. Münchhausen was an eighteenth-century storyteller from Hanover whose stories were so far-fetched that his name had already become a by-word for tall stories and lies. No one else but McDonald would have dared write this in an official journal, and the fact that he did so suggests some kind of instability.

By now Brown was fed up. McVicar had already written to Governor Williams complaining about McDonald's conduct and informing him that Brown had made clear his intention to leave Athabasca in the spring "which will be a serious loss to this Expedition."[136]

TRADE AND LIQUOR

There were twenty-three men at the fort. Nineteen were from Canada and had come up from Montreal with either Clarke or Robertson, and three—Brown, McVicar and Aulay McAulay, the clerk—were from Scotland. Their names reflect their origins: Raymond Mastas, the interpreter, aged 36; Joseph Piché, aged 26; Antoine St. Denny, aged 23; and Joseph Hyacinthe Thibault, aged 34. This may have presented Brown, whose French was rudimentary, with communication problems.

The Indigenous people around Forts Resolution and Wedderburn were Chipewyans (Denesuline). The North West Company was well established in the region, with large supplies of liquor, tobacco and trade goods. They were able to offer the Indigenous people more than the HBC, and this gave them a substantial advantage. Both companies had Indigenous trappers and hunters who brought them food and furs, whom the traders labelled the "English Indians" and the "French Indians." The groups were not well defined and perhaps existed more in the minds of the traders than in reality. Both companies thought they were entitled to the exclusive loyalty of "its" hunters and, as at most posts, each tried to poach from the other. Wise and experienced traders, the Indigenous people did what anyone would have done in such a situation and played the companies off against each other to their own advantage.

When the Indigenous people saw that Brown had arrived with a supply of trade goods, tobacco and liquor (although, thanks to McDonald, far less than requested or necessary), they started moving their trade loyalties from the North West Company to the HBC. The Nor'Westers tried to keep them loyal. McVicar wrote that soon after Brown arrived with supplies they "changed their measures and commenced lavishing liquor toward a degree of extravagance almost incredible so that the Indians were in a state of intoxication for 12 days without intermission, at the end of which time the N.W., seeing they were gaining no advantage from their prodigality, put an end to their foolish experiments."[137]

If Brown was annoyed by how lavishly the Nor'Westers distributed liquor to "its" Indigenous men, this was partly because the HBC, with its limited supplies, could not compete. He wrote:

> It is really surprising the enormous quantity of property the N.W. are squandering away amongst the Indians. The most insignificant of those belonging to them are Equipped with Capots, Trousers, Shirts and Blankets and their principal Hunters have in addition to that Hats, feathery Waistcoats, English shoes, Stockings etc. This extravagance cannot be with a view simply to debauch those Indians who have joined our concern, for they must be well aware that if they should, we will have a supply of Goods before them, and of course will have an opportunity of drawing them back.... It would appear from their proceedings, and some hints we have received from their people, that their intention is to ruin the trade of the place for a year or two, hoping that if the H. B. Co. receives only triffling returns during that time, that they will become disgusted, and abandon the Country.[138]

PRIVATIONS

The ice on the lake was now thick. Snow drifted across it in the wind. Men were trying to catch fish with nets lowered below the ice and others were at the endless task of cutting firewood and hauling it home. At the fort they lacked almost everything they needed to survive. Even if McDonald had given them all the supplies they had requested, they would still have been short. As it was, they approached starvation. Furthermore, measles swept through the local Indigenous communities, causing great suffering and many deaths. This meant the HBC men could not rely on them to provide meat. Not only did this reduce the number of hunters and trappers, but it also stopped their relatives from hunting during their time of mourning.

The men at Fort Resolution came close to starvation that winter. They depended on fishing for their survival, but the fisheries had collapsed. The lack of nets and their inability to mend broken nets for want of twine severely hampered their efforts. On December 16, Brown wrote in the post journal, "Had all the froze fish in the store counted today. There are only

George Back, *Southeast View of Great Slave Lake from Fort Providence, the Nor'Wester Fort*, November 30, 1820.

1,200 of them, of every kind that is fit for eating. So that there is almost a moral certainty of us suffering severely before spring."[139] By Christmas they had enough "froze fish" to feed them for only twenty-five days even at their reduced allowance, which, Brown wrote, rendered their prospects gloomy and distressing in the extreme. Furthermore, they were critically short of dogs, without which they could not bring home meat or fish caught far from the fort.

"Wind W. and very cold," Brown wrote as 1819 ticked over into 1820. "None of the Men employed, they being celebrating the return of another New Year."[140] On January 9, the first promise of better weather arrived: "Wind S. E. and the finest day we have had in the season. The sun is beginning to shew itself over the top of the hill at the back of the House, which it has not done for this month past, not being high enough above the horizon for that purpose."[141] The next day the woodcutters broke the only axe they had left, giving them the option of having no fire (unthinkable) or asking their rivals for one (also unthinkable).

On February 1, Brown recorded that St. Denny had returned from Isle de Prière (another fishing ground) with twenty-two fish, but that they were taking very few there. The men, he said, had been on half allowance since the beginning of the year. A few days later one of the Nor'Westers told them that Edward Smith, their chief, was surprised that lack of provisions had not caused them to surrender. On February 8, Brown wrote: "Sent Plomondeau to the Ile de Prière to order Lapoint to come to the Fort with all

George Back, *Winter Travelling on Great Slave Lake.*

the fish at that place. He arrived at 12 o'clock but in place of fish, brought the report that they were starving there. Our prospects in regard to living are becoming really alarming. We have been obliged to make a further reduction in our own and Men's allowance."[142]

But the end of winter was coming. The snow started melting on the houses early in March, though it would be a long time before it was all gone. The ice on the lake, which had been eight feet thick, was thawing rapidly. Joseph Perrault, who arrived one morning with thirteen fish, was then sent off on a journey to find more but had to turn back because there was too much water on top of the ice. Their hopes that the worst was over were increasing every day. On March 7, their hunters killed a moose and a caribou, which was a welcome supply of fresh meat. They were still, though, dangerously short. They were even running out of paper to maintain the accounts, letters and the post journal. And they had little left in the way of goods to trade with Indigenous people.

They were living on hopes, but these were not yet matched by reality. By March 17, Brown was writing that they were still badly off for provisions. What fish they did catch didn't go far among the men at the fort. Then on April 15, he wrote,

> Wind E. Blowing fresh with the weather thick and
> snowing a little. Thawed very triffling about the Fort,
> but I understand the snow is dissolving much quicker

in the woods. The exposed situation to the cold from the Lake prevents it greatly here. The Gooseberry bushes, where they are sheltered from the North wind and open to the influences of the sun, are beginning to bud. Cadian Sappient informs me that he saw an Eagle upon the 11th Inst, and that the snow in the woods is covered in a number of places with the little black flies, which are always the forerunner of spring.[143]

Spring did finally arrive. The ice on the lake became thin, honey-combed and unsafe to walk on, after which it started to break up. Channels opened in the lake. The ice in the lake melted. The frogs recovered from their torpid state and began making extraordinary noises in the swamps. Geese were now flying overhead. Mosquitoes were becoming more numerous and a nuisance in the evenings. And then on May 22, Brown saw his first swallow of spring. They had survived the winter. No one had died from scurvy, violence or starvation. That in itself after such a winter was an accomplishment.

HOT AND COLD WITH THE NORTH WEST COMPANY

In September 1819, the veteran Nor'Wester John Stuart had arrived as *Tête des affaires de Athabasca*. Stuart knew the territory. He had been active in Athabasca in the conflict with the HBC in the years 1815 to 1817. He was a man Brown would become very well acquainted with. "This looks well!!," Robertson wrote. "Stuart is a poor body, that has all the inclination but not the ability to do mischief. The Canadians, when speaking of this Gentleman, have an excellent double entendre. He has the misfortune to have very long heels, and they distinguish him from another Stuart by the appellation of Mons' Stuart la grande 'talent', in place of 'talon.'"[144]

As at Reindeer Lake and in the Manitoba District, relations between the HBC and the North West Company were competitive but co-operative, with the occasional flash of confrontation and risk of violence. In his instructions to McVicar, Robertson had written: "With respect to your opponents, keep them at a respectable distance. Be firm & decisive with them. At the same time avoid all kinds of menace or irritating language, but do not upon any consideration permit them to acquire a footing over you so as to intimidate the Indians. Keep a respectful distance but a bold front."[145] Robertson did not want to promote conflict largely because he knew that the North West Company had more men and was more powerful.

On one occasion, McVicar learned that a Nor'Wester had robbed two of the HBC Indigenous trappers of eight marten skins. He complained to

Edward Smith, who replied that the two men in question were in debt to the North West Company and they were merely taking what was theirs. Smith declared, "You appear to take things very heinously when the Game goes against you. You have sanctioned and supported your men in acts of violence and aggression on the property of the N.W. Co. in possession of the Indians when unprotected." Brown commented that it was

> an established maxim with them [the Nor'Westers] to term any fair competition of trade wherein their rivals are more successful than they would wish "Acts of violence and aggression." It is certain that we have received a considerable number of skins in the course of the winter from the Indians they equipped in the fall, but the whole was procured by fair barter.[146]

And so the game, as Smith called it, went on.

On the one hand, as elsewhere, the two companies competed vigorously to persuade Indigenous hunters to bring their furs to them, using alcohol, tobacco and trade goods, all of which the Nor'Westers had more of, as inducements. On the other hand, on several occasions the HBC was the beneficiary of Nor'Wester generosity. Without a serviceable axe, the HBC men could not cut the wood needed to light fires, light the darkness or cook food. When he had no unbroken axes left, McVicar asked the Nor'Westers for assistance. He wrote to Smith:

> If a Barter a/c is allowable, when not interfering with the principle of trade, I would esteem it a particular favour—besides payment—if you would allow your Blacksmith to repair one axe & make a few nails.

To this, Smith graciously replied:

> Your Note lies before me and in answering I have only to Mention if an axe arranged by our Blacksmith—or more—can give Satisfaction to Mr. McVicar, I will get them repaired. In so doing I expect no payment. The axe and Iron for the Nails may be sent tomorrow Morning.[147]

McVicar took advantage of this to have two hatchets repaired and fifty nails made out of an old chisel. Several times Smith, having heard the men at the HBC fort were short of salt, sent part of his own supply to relieve their deficiency. On one such occasion, McVicar sent the following note to Smith: "Yesterday I was informed of your generous offer of Salt, for which I feel very grateful and now send Whitman in hopes that you may be able to let me have the loan of 4 Gallons until the latter end June, when I will return it twofold." Smith replied, "According to your request I send you 16 quarts Salt, which you please return when convenient. No interest is required."[148]

BROWN DECIDES TO LEAVE

As early as November 1819, Brown decided he had had enough of McDonald and his erratic behaviour. Additionally, he may have felt demoted or at least undervalued. Having been a district master in Manitoba, here he now was second in command of a small fort at the edge of the HBC world, with no prospects and deprived of command of a new district at Mountain Island. He decided to leave Athabasca and return to Europe. This alarmed Robertson, who wrote to him from Fort St. Mary on February 3, 1820:

> I am extremely sorry to learn by your letter of the 25th Nov'r last that you have determined on visiting Europe the ensuing summer. I hope that circumstances and the happy change the Company's affairs have taken in Athabasca will induce you to change that resolution. I presume you are aware that Messrs MacDonald & Thomas retire from the service in the spring and allow me to observe that, independent of these vacancies, I had promised you a District in the Outfit of 1820, which I will still adhere to, should your knowledge of the French language enable you to arrange with the Canadian servants of the Company.[149]

Robertson wanted to persuade Brown to stay. Having told him that McDonald was soon going to be retiring, he wrote a little mysteriously to McVicar on February 5: "May I request you to be very communicative with Mr. Brown regarding your District. I have particular motives for this request, which I will state more fully in my spring correspondence."[150] Clearly, the HBC had a high opinion of Brown and didn't want to lose him. McVicar agreed with Robertson and wrote: "In regard to Mr. Brown, I must beg leave to inform you that there are very few in the North that are more Conversant in the nature of the Indian Trade than he is. And I am of opinion that he may be considered as an Indian Trader, one of the most enterprising men in Athabasca. Mr. B. has made out a report of this District, by which you will perceive that he is perfectly acquainted with its resources."[151]

That February, Robertson wrote to Governor Williams telling him that Brown had sent in his resignation on account of his disputes with McDonald: "I know not what promises have been made this gentleman, but he seems much disappointed with his prospects in this country; I have offered him a District the ensuing summer, which I hope he will not be so imprudent as to refuse."[152]

Robertson came up to Fort Wedderburn to see for himself. Arriving on Wednesday, May 23, 1820, he found the situation there far worse than he had imagined. He took a good look around and saw that McDonald had totally lost his grip. He wrote that "Mr. McDonald has made dreadful work at this place. He has quarreled with all his people."[153] He also wrote:

> Had some conversation with Mr. McDonald, rather of an unpleasant nature. This person has very much deranged the Company's business at this place. No returns! No remains! And no work done!!! Not even a morsel of gum for the Canoes. No subordination. His Clerks and Interpreters have all left his table, and refused to do their duty. The reason they assign for this conduct is that Mr. McDonald had not given them their allowance of the little luxuries the Company allotted them. At all events the business of this place is in a most awkward situation. The deficiency in the returns is owing entirely to the unfortunate state the natives were reduced to by sickness, but there is no excuse for Mr. McDonald's throwing away the Company's property, when he was perfectly aware that our summer establishments depended solely on the Spring remains of Fort Wedderburn.[154]

Robertson also found that the food supplies at the fort had been badly mismanaged and that the men there were starving. He related one incident in which one of the men had caught McDonald taking a basin of flour from the store, hidden under his coat. Another man went into McDonald's room and pulled a dish full of cakes from under his bed. Hoarding food, even if you are the chief—perhaps especially if you are the chief—does not endear men to you. Robertson commented sourly not only on the insolence of the men but also on McDonald's lack of management. This wouldn't do. On the following Saturday, he removed McDonald and sent him down to another fort, ostensibly to obtain provisions.

William Brown left Fort Resolution on May 27. His intention was to take the eight packs of furs to the depot and then go on to York Factory. When Brown arrived at Fort Wedderburn a few days later, Robertson sat down with him for an important conversation.

9

Fort Wedderburn—George Simpson and Simon McGillivray

1820

"They have killed my father! They have killed my father! There he lies!"

Four-year-old Edward McGillivray on November 21, 1820

Colin Robertson intended to send an expedition over the Rocky Mountains into New Caledonia to challenge the North West Company's monopoly. When Brown arrived at Fort Wedderburn from Fort Resolution, Robertson made him a proposal. Needing a man with both brawn and brains to lead the expedition, he offered the job to Brown, who accepted.

Then Robertson left. On June 6, 1820, Brown wrote in the fort's post journal: "In the afternoon Mr. Robertson with ten men embarked in a Light Canoe for the Depot, when in compliance with his orders I took charge of the District until the 1st of August, when Canoes are to be here, with which I am to embark for the New Caledonia. He left no instructions further than I was to 'have all the roots taken up that are inside the Fort and the place put in better order.'"[155]

Brown's instructions, therefore, were clear. Stay in Fort Wedderburn until his replacement arrived. Clean the place up. Restore order among the men. Then head to New Caledonia in August to challenge the North West Company. Like so many plans of mice and men, this did not survive contact with reality.

When Brown took charge of Fort Wedderburn, he expected he would be leaving in August to establish a post in New Caledonia in the autumn. Robertson had already been putting out exploratory feelers. In October 1819, he had engaged a man named Ignace Giasson and had sent him on an exploratory mission to the Rocky Mountains. The following April, Giasson crossed the Rockies and moved cautiously into New Caledonia. His mission was to find out whether the Indigenous communities there would be willing to trade with the HBC and to locate good places to establish the first HBC fort. The Nor'Westers in New Caledonia learned about his presence and were greatly concerned.

Brown found Fort Wedderburn in a mess. Clearly a strong hand was needed to take charge. McDonald had already left after several years of neglect and mishandling. The buildings were in severe disrepair. The provisions were at starvation levels and the local Indigenous hunters were in danger of defecting to the Nor'Westers. The men had a forge but little iron to make anything with, meaning that the blacksmith had to make their own nails—always a necessary but scarce item—out of scraps of old metal. McDonald's mismanagement had resulted in a discontented, recalcitrant workforce. Fort Chipewyan, on the mainland only a mile and a half away, was bigger, more powerful, and much better supplied with men, food, liquor and ammunition. The Nor'Westers had every intention of eradicating Fort Wedderburn if they could, and they had the means to do it. Could the HBC survive these dangers?

Brown was not the man merely to follow Robertson's instructions—tear out the roots, clean up the yard—and leave it at that. He saw the need for more extensive renovations, both major and minor, and he started them right away. His first task was to set men to dig up the roots in the fort. Two other men then started to clean up the garbage in the yard. Then he ordered men to cut and square wood for the houses he was planning to build and others to clean and level the canoe yard, dig trenches and repair the gates. He had two men in the forge making more nails. One additional need was the right type of mud to bind stones together. They then had to haul this to the fort. Mud was important for the construction of chimneys because with the weak mud that served as mortar the chimneys had a distressing tendency to fall down.

By mid-August, Brown was wondering where the brigade of canoes bringing the supplies and his replacement was. Until it arrived, he could not leave for New Caledonia, and it was already starting to grow late in the season. He couldn't know it, but one of the reasons for the delay was that the canoe men of the brigade went on a drinking spree at Norway House and were drunk for three days.

On August 27, Brown received the bad news that the Nor'Westers had taken Colin Robertson prisoner again, this time at the Grand Rapid, which Brown would have remembered so well. (Robertson later escaped and made his way to England.) Without the trade goods necessary for his expedition to New Caledonia and without instructions, Brown could only continue what he was doing. Houses, bastions, stockades—the building continued apace. He had 104 logs squared, sufficient for a new bastion. By September the men were putting roofs on the new house and installing partitions. The following day, five men started to erect the Bastion "which they have got as high as the first beams. It is 14 feet beyond the former stockade bastion but still a considerable way within the boundary line."[156]

The Nor'Westers disagreed with this and would cause trouble. Brown was also having an ice house made to preserve fish. Under his drive and direction, Fort Wedderburn was a busy place.

The North West Company

Brown was at the exact point where the conflict with the Nor'Westers was more intense than anywhere else in Rupert's Land and Athabasca. The threat from the more powerful and better provisioned North West Company was never far away, both literally and metaphorically. The Pemmican War became more vicious as the competition more intense. Fears of attack and opportunistic arrests grew. This was a strange war, though, with a surface level of civility and frequent fraternization. But it was fraught with the existence of arrest warrants that seemed to be merely pretexts for the capture of an opponent. Civility was declining and the possibility of violence increasing. Simon McGillivray and Samuel Black, the well-known Nor'Wester troublemakers, were present at Fort Chipewyan. If the North West Company was to maintain its monopoly in Athabasca, it would have to expel the HBC again. The men at both forts knew this.

Tension between the two forts was rising fast. George Spence, a constable from Montreal, arrived with a warrant for the arrest of Black. The following day the HBC men saw an opportunity to arrest him, but fumbled the execution. Black was on the shore near the Nor'Wester guardhouse and about to go over the lake to Fort Chipewyan. When he saw the constable approaching, he brought out his pistol, whereupon the constable lost his nerve and did nothing. Black made his escape in a canoe. Soon after he left Fort Chipewyan and went to New Caledonia. He would be back.

Not long after Spence arrived, Brown received unsettling news. "Received private letters," he wrote, "desiring me to be upon my guard as the N.W. had a warrant for me on account of the part I took at the Grand Rapid in the spring of 1819."[157] On August 30, he noted in the post journal he had heard that the Nor'Westers were boasting they would take him prisoner before the HBC canoes arrived. He expected daily that he would be a victim of Nor'Wester violence and was determined, it was recorded, to die hard.

Shows of bellicosity did not stop the two parties from civil behaviour when tempers were not aroused. William Todd, the doctor, recorded that one night an HBC man had become lost on the lake in a snowstorm and had spent the night rambling about on the ice between the two forts. A Nor'Wester from Fort Chipewyan found him and escorted him back to where he could see his own fort well enough to find his own way home. Such politeness, though, did not deter Brown from continuing with the erection of a stronger bastion.

On September 6, after several Nor'Wester canoes had arrived at Fort Chipewyan, the Nor'Wester leader Edward Smith informed two HBC men that King George III had died, Lord Selkirk was seriously ill and had gone to France for his health, and "a new governor of the name of Mr. Simpson has come out by the way of Canada."[158]

On September 16, the HBC canoes finally started arriving and this eased the fort's acute shortages. By this time, they had no twine left. They also brought a letter from Governor Williams telling Brown that he should proceed to New Caledonia with every dispatch as soon as his replacement arrived but only if he would have time to reach the Rocky Mountain Portage (the way through the mountains into New Caledonia) by September 20. Clearly it was now too late for him to do this. Brown also learned, perhaps to his consternation, that George Simpson would soon be arriving at Fort Wedderburn.

George Simpson

George Simpson was never one to waste time. He arrived at Fort Wedderburn four days later, on September 20.

Although the exact date of Simpson's birth is not clearly established, in 1820 he was likely thirty-three years old and therefore older than Brown by only two or three years. Born in Scotland, illegitimate, Simpson had been working as a manager in the London sugar-broking business of Graham, Simpson and Wedderburn. The important HBC Committee member, Andrew Colvile, who had changed his name from Wedderburn in 1814, was the Wedderburn of the firm and he recognized Simpson's abilities. He sent Simpson to assist Williams in Rupert's Land. As far as is known, Simpson had never been to North America before and knew little of the fur business when he sailed from Liverpool on March 4, 1820. When he arrived, people at first saw him as a lightweight. But only at first. He was, in fact, a man of iron, with all its metallic charms.

Simpson had arrived *locum tenens*—on a temporary basis—to take over should the Nor'Westers succeed in arresting Governor Williams. Simpson wrote that his original intention had been to return to England in the autumn of 1820. After the Nor'Westers had captured Robertson for the second time, the HBC had no leader in Athabasca. Williams decided that Simpson's services were now necessary there and sent him to take charge.

Simpson intended to spend the winter at Fort Wedderburn to learn all he could about the fur trade. In 1826, the HBC would appoint him head of its entire operations in North America, and he would become the autocratic governor of an area covering one-twelfth of the world's land surface, a position he held until his death in 1860. He would earn a controversial

Sir George Simpson later in life. In 1820, he was most likely approximately thirty-three years old.

reputation, then and now. Peter Newman called him a "bastard by birth and by persuasion." He was undoubtedly a hard man, but arguably the necessary man at that time to head the HBC.

Meanwhile, here he was, making his first trip across Rupert's Land and intending to spend the winter with Brown at Fort Wedderburn. While there, he wrote a daily journal, later published as *Journal of Occurrences in the Athabasca Department by George Simpson, 1820 and 1821, and Report.*

The presence of Simpson must have been daunting for Brown. There would have been no room to hide. It all seemed to start well. But would it continue?

On September 20, 1820, Simpson wrote:

> Arrived here at twelve a.m., where I found Messrs Brown, [Duncan] Finlayson, [Joseph] Roy, McBean & [Louis Dennis de La Ronde] Laronde, who welcomed me in Athabasca with every mark of respect and attention. Mr. Brown has had charge of the District during the summer, and seems to have been very attentive to the duties of his situation; the people have undergone some hardships from the scarcity of provisions, and I regret to observe that there is a great want of subordination amongst them.... had Mr. Brown gone from hence previous to my arrival, I intended having given the charge of the District to Mr. McAulay, but as the former Gentleman remains here during the winter, and has conducted the business very much to my satisfaction, I have continued him in charge.[159]

A few days later Simpson described Brown as a gentleman of considerable talent who, with slender means, had done wonders in the fort during the summer. So far, then, so good.

Notwithstanding Simpson's presence, Brown was in charge of the fort, and he had to deal with its daily problems. Even though the canoes had brought some supplies with them from the east, the fort was still not adequately provisioned. One of the consequences was that Brown did not have enough goods to trade with the Indigenous hunters for furs or meat. Nor indeed were there sufficient supplies of tobacco, rum or ammunition. Nor of twine to repair and make nets. Brown reckoned he needed at least

Peter Rindisbacher, *Two of the Companies Officers Travelling in a Canoe made of Birchwood Manned by Canadians*, ca. 1824.

120 fish each day to feed the people of the fort. The fisheries, though, were not producing nearly enough.

On occasion, the men actually did come close to starvation, and Brown had to send men away from their settlements to find their own subsistence. Furthermore, Indigenous people were often also starving and came to the fort asking for help. On December 9, Brown wrote, "the English Chief arrived, had nothing. His family is about a day's march from this [place], all starving, and he has come before them for fish to subsist them until they reach the fort." The next day he continued, "gave the English Chief 20 fish with which he went off to meet his family. To supply the above we were obliged to reduce our men's allowance."[160]

TROUBLES WITH THE MEN

Ever since his arrival at the fort, Brown had been having problems with the men. McDonald had let them have their own way far too often, not to mention his hoarding of food, and Brown, still a relatively young man, had difficulty asserting his authority. His brusque manner of dealing with them did not help. He levied fines for insolence and disobedience to his orders in the hope this would end the pernicious idea, as he put it, that orders did not have to be obeyed. This may or may not have been a successful strategy. He was a straight-speaking Scot—uncourteous in his address was how Simpson called it. He said what he thought, and at times, this rubbed people the wrong way. Undoubtedly part of the problem lay in the cultural differences. He was Scottish, English-speaking, probably Presbyterian and driven to achieve the HBC's objectives. Although there were a few Scots among them, most of the men at the fort were French-speaking Catholic Canadians and often defiant. Brown was sometimes too blunt and direct when tact and diplomacy might have worked better.

In his report on the district, Brown gave succinct assessments of the employees. He did not, he wrote, have a high opinion of Amable Grignon. Although employed as a clerk, he could not read or write. Brown thought he was not worth the provisions he ate or the tobacco he smoked. Robert Miles, on the other hand, was a very steady and knowledgeable servant, being an excellent accountant and thoroughly dependable. Jonas Oxley, a Scotsman and a clerk, was unacquainted with the business and not possessed of enough perseverance to acquire it. Worse, he joined in all the intrigues and cabals. Robert Clouston, Brown asserted, was a reliable Orkneyman—sober, steady and active. He was also a good, and therefore valuable, blacksmith.

Although Simpson had a high opinion of Brown, rating him as one of the two officers of competence at the fort, he did criticize his blunt handling of insubordinate employees. After Simpson arrived at the fort, even he, a no-nonsense hard driver, found that on occasion he had to moderate Brown's discipline. Simpson shared Brown's views about almost all of them, but, wiser perhaps, he knew there was more than one way to handle men. Simpson wrote that as long as provisions were low they had to submit to the men's misconduct and coax them into a better mood. He was also aware that with the Nor'Wester guardhouse so close, an unhappy employee could desert at any time. This, though, didn't stop Simpson from authorizing a beating to a ringleader of a group of men who were refusing to embark in a canoe on a voyage.

On several occasions, employees flatly refused to obey Brown's orders. One of the few tools he had to enforce discipline was to levy a fine. For example, he fined one man 200 livres for losing a dog he had been told not to take with him on a journey. He put another off duty and on half allowance for refusing to carry fish to the fort from a fishery. But he had to be careful. If he was too harsh, a disgruntled employee might defect or spread rumours among the Indigenous communities about HBC problems. This might easily lead them to take their furs to the Nor'Westers. Once he learned that McVicar at Fort Resolution had no fishermen, Brown decided to send

George Back, *Fort Chipewyan, May 27, 1820*. Back's depiction was a little fanciful. The hill is not that high. Possibly the island in the distance was Potato Island, where the HBC's Fort Wedderburn was situated.

three men to help him. They refused to go, citing a vague promise they asserted Robertson had given them in the spring that they didn't have to leave the fort.

In September, hearing that the Nor'Westers had gone to debauch Indigenous men and women—that is to say, ply them with liquor and persuade them to trade—Brown told Amable Grignon and La Mallice to go and do what they could to prevent it. La Mallice refused to go, maintaining he was engaged for the Peace River and didn't have to obey orders given at Fort Wedderburn. Brown told him he would report his insolence to Simpson when he arrived. To which La Mallice replied that "he cared as little for the Governor as he did for me," and then stalked out of the room.[161] Brown fined him 500 livres. When he arrived, Simpson confirmed the fine and gave La Mallice a severe lecture.

A few days after Simpson arrived, Brown wrote to him explaining his problems with the men and seeking his support. He complained to Simpson that

> in the discharge of my duty during the summer at this place, I met with a great deal of opposition from the insubordination that prevailed amongst the men. It being such that they would cavil at every trifle and when ordered to do anything that did not suit with themselves, they would either refuse to do it altogether or else perform it in such a slow & slovenly manner that it was disgusting to see them.[162]

Brown, seemingly a little insecure, offered to resign if Simpson did not approve his conduct. Simpson did approve, calmed him down and wrote, "permit me now to remark that the zeal you have uniformly manifested in the service merits the highest encomiums [praise] and it is extremely satisfactory to me that the charge of Fort Wedderburn District is in such competent hands."[163]

The Capture of Simon McGillivray

The drama with the North West Company continued throughout October 1820. The Fort Wedderburn post journal contains a litany of alarms, warnings and provocations. The HBC heard all too often that the Nor'Westers were about to attack them or that they were going to arrest one or more of them. On numerous occasions, Simpson and Brown had to put the men in the fort on watch all night with their firearms beside them. They were well aware that the Nor'Westers had more men and more arms, and so did not want to provide them with an excuse to use them.

The presence of the Nor'Wester guardhouse so close was a constant annoyance. Simpson wrote that it was approximately twelve yards from the HBC's corner bastion and projected five yards beyond the front of their fort towards the lake, "so that from their back windows they command a full view of all our proceedings, which is extremely unpleasant."[164] On October 18, to remove this eyesore, Simpson ordered the erection of a new stockade from the corner of the bastion to the water's edge. Simon McGillivray and several Nor'Wester bullies, all armed, came out and ordered them to stop. He maintained the HBC men were building over the boundary line and were on Nor'Wester property. HBC men, also armed, came out of the fort to defend their ground. The two groups of men faced each other tensely.

Simpson came out and met McGillivray for the first time. "My name is Simpson," he said. "I presume yours is McGillivray."

"It is," McGillivray replied.

Simpson then told McGillivray he was determined to maintain the HBC's rights. "I intend," he said, "erecting these Stockades from the corner of the Bastion in a direct line to that stump…. Pray, Sir, what are your objections?" He added he had no intention to encroach on Nor'Wester property, to which McGillivray replied sullenly, "Time will show."

Simpson wrote that during this conversation, his

> Tarrier Dog Boxer (a very playful fellow) was amusing himself with a stick close to Soucisse's feet, and while the Bully was regaling him with an ill-natured look, as if about to give him a kick, I with a smile addressed the dog, "Come here Boxer, you do not seem to be aware that you are committing a trespass." McGillivray with a good deal of asperity observed "We have no intention to molest your dog, Sir." To which I replied, "Nor shall you his Master with impunity."[165]

The Nor'Westers, not wanting to start a fight at this time, backed off and the HBC men completed the stockade.

The following day, Brown wrote "at half past 7 o'clock a.m., word was brought to me that the N.W. had commenced to dig a trench within two feet of our Bastion, and about the same distance upon our side of the Boundary line for the purpose of building a Bastion right opposite to ours. I therefore went out and desired Mr. McGillivray to desist as they would on no account be permitted to build within the line of demarcation."[166] McGillivray, he said, treated this request with contempt.

Simpson, Brown and the other officers then held a meeting to decide what to do. At this point, Grignon, the illiterate clerk who was also a constable, joined them and announced he possessed a warrant for the arrest of

Simon McGillivray. Should he take McGillivray prisoner? Simpson cannily—or was this merely what he wanted the record to show?—answered this was a legal matter, quite separate from the affairs of the HBC, and he could not interfere. If, however, Grignon arrested McGillivray and called for help then, of course, he would be obliged to give assistance.

They all went out to stop McGillivray and his men from building. Simpson recorded what happened next.

> I then proceeded to the spot where the North West workman were employed attended by several of our people stationed in such situations as to defend me in the event of my being attacked; on my approach Mr. McGillivray came out and I addressed him: "Mr McGillivray, I should be glad to have some further explanation with you on the subject of this boundary line."
>
> He was about to reply when Mr. Grignon came up and collaring him said: "I arrest you in the King's name." He resisted and Mr. Grignon called on [Joseph] Boucher & Latondre, two of our people, to assist him in the King's name, who immediately laid hold of and conveyed him into Fort Wedderburne. His party cocked their pistols, but seeing us prepared they withdrew in confusion, and the villain Soucisse took refuge in the woods.
>
> On my return into the Fort, I found Mr. McGillivray venting his spleen in a torrent of abuse; he inveighed against me with much warmth, declared that the arrest was illegal and that he would have warrants against the whole party without loss of time. I replied that the Officer had acted on his own responsibility, and could alone be liable for the consequences.[167]

In the diary he kept during his imprisonment, McGillivray wrote that he had heard Simpson cry out, "Seize him. Seize him," and that the HBC men—he mentioned Brown by name—dragged him into the fort.

Brown feared the Nor'Westers might launch an armed attack to rescue McGillivray and made his arrangements accordingly. He set a strong watch of three men, including one officer. The men were to be relieved every three hours. The officer, though, was to be on duty all night. He stationed one man in the bastion and one at the door of McGillivray's room. If an approaching person did not reply to a challenge, the guard had instructions to fire. Brown wanted to send McGillivray to a stronger HBC post at once, but he was overruled. All the others thought they could not reach it by open water and that it was better to keep him at the fort.

Inside, McGillivray complained loudly and at length about the illegality of his arrest. He demanded to see the warrant. Simpson referred him to Brown, who went and got it from his room and read it to him. Although it did indeed set out his name, McGillivray immediately saw that it was an old warrant for the arrest of his father (William) and namesake uncle.[168] This warrant, he protested, was no more than waste paper, merely an excuse to kidnap him. Simpson told him it was in retaliation for what the Nor'Westers had done to Colin Robertson and then paid no more attention to his complaints.

Brown took McGillivray into the ten-foot-square room in a three-room house that was to be his prison. His room was sandwiched between the guardroom occupied by his keeper and one occupied by a party of HBC Canadians. McGillivray complained about the obscenities and ribaldry of the Canadians on his left and of the rough treatment by his keeper and Grignon on his right. The Canadians, he believed, took great pleasure in taunting him. His keeper was a man he called Canute or Knight, but was in fact an ex-Meuron soldier called Johann Knipe. Knipe guarded him closely, locking and unlocking the door to his room. He always followed McGillivray to the privy armed with two pistols and a sword, having first locked all the doors to the fort. There were iron bars on the window. Brown's sentinel paced outside.

McGillivray had to ask for everything he needed, including a chair, paper—they bought him one sheet at a time—four blankets because he was cold at night, and eventually a poker for the fire. He complained to Simpson, who promised to find him what he needed, but somehow Simpson's instructions never reached Knipe. He noted that Simpson, taking no chances, always came to see him with two pocket pistols. Simpson's journal, no doubt as partial as McGillivray's, records civil, almost convivial, conversations about trade conditions, the death of Lord Selkirk and negotiations between the two companies in London. Then McGillivray correctly realized that Simpson was pumping him for information and ended the discussions. McGillivray complained of the holes in the plaster and the door that allowed the Canadians and Knipe to peer through. When he complained to Simpson, they were filled in, but soon uncovered. "My room was plaistered yesterday and my next door neighbours found ways & means to unplaister it. I found two new holes this morning newly made."[169]

The arrest of McGillivray naturally incensed the Nor'Westers. Simpson and Keith exchanged angry letters, with Keith complaining that the arrest was utterly illegal. Simpson innocently replied it was nothing to do with him: the constable Grignon was merely executing an outstanding arrest warrant. Meanwhile, the Nor'Westers continued to build their own bastion on their side of the boundary line, only a few yards from the HBC fort. When completed, this would command a view of the front gate of the HBC fort, which of course would be intolerable to the HBC. In reply, Brown started to build another bastion on top of the rock behind the fort.

McGillivray never ceased to complain about the illegality of his arrest and how he would have justice in the courts in Montreal. He singled out Brown for prosecution on account of his prominent part in the Grand Rapid affair in 1819.

A couple of days after the arrest, Brown told McGillivray that his wife, Teuse, wanted to visit him, but this could only be allowed if at least two witnesses were present. Moreover, they were not to talk about his confinement and had to speak in the Cree language. McGillivray would not agree to these conditions. Eventually, though, a deal was worked out. Simpson wrote that McGillivray agreed not to communicate secretly with his Nor'Wester colleagues and not to attempt to escape. Teuse and their two children came to live with McGillivray in his room. Simpson had a door cut in the wall of his room into the fort, called T's door, so that she did not have to go through the Canadians' room. She brought fresh clothes for him and Keith sent some supplies. Brown put these in a separate room and went through them item by item looking for concealed weapons before he allowed McGillivray to have them. The women of the fort searched Teuse.

Although Teuse and the children were not meant to be prisoners, Knipe's reluctance to lock and unlock Teuse's door meant, in effect, that they were. Teuse was ill for much of the time, which did not stop Knipe or Grignon from following her armed with pistols whenever she went to the privy. McGillivray's four-and-a-half-year-old son, Edward, was the eldest of the children. His sister was almost two. Knipe, grumbling, would let Edward out in the morning to play but would not let him back in the room for four or five hours at a time. "I have several times," McGillivray wrote, "seen this inhuman jailer tell the Child to go away and play in order to save himself the trouble to open the door and attend to him."[170] Since this was mid-winter and dark for much of the day, playing outside for long periods would not have been pleasant for the little boy.

On November 21, Edward came running to his parents, crying and saying that Knipe and Grignon had told him they had instructions to shoot his father if he tried to escape. This greatly alarmed McGillivray and Teuse, especially when the news was confirmed not only by two other children but also by Knipe himself. "*Je vous tuerai,*" McGillivray quoted him as saying. "*Je ne vous manquerai pas.*"[171] McGillivray complained to Simpson, saying that if his intention was to murder him, he should do it quickly and not in the slow way by inches as he was doing at present.

Certainly, Knipe and the other guards kept close watch on them. They carried their pistols and swords at all times, evidencing every intention of wanting an opportunity to use them. "I am afraid to be murdered by my Keeper Canute [Knipe]," he wrote, "for he always carries a Pistol or two whenever I go out of my prison, which happens once & sometimes twice a day."[172] Neither he nor Teuse trusted the word of Simpson and feared the worst. "Mean wretches!... Mr. Simpson must be privy to all of this. He can not be without knowing it.... Horrid brutes!"[173] Simpson angrily denied this. "The insinuation," he wrote, "is so foul, iniquitous & false that I could not pass it unnoticed." He wrote to Keith in protest: "The accusation is fabricated in the mind of one who is accustomed to cool and deliberate plans of assassination."[174]

On December 2, Edward woke from a nightmare. "The people of the Fort," McGillivray wrote, have "too much frightened my Boy Edward about Killing me that he got up in his sleep at about 7 p.m. and calling out violently, 'They have killed my father. They have killed my father.' There he lies! Pointing to where his little sister slept."[175]

The routines of the fort continued—excursions to find firewood, the constant search for more fish and provisions, attempts to persuade Indigenous men to bring furs to the HBC rather than to their rivals, dog problems and the completion of the fort's own bastion. Meanwhile, the Nor'Westers, furious at McGillivray's imprisonment, were watching and waiting for their opportunity. Simpson received a warning they were planning desperate measures to free him. Everyone was on high alert—or should have been.

10

Fort Wedderburn—Conflict Rising

1820–1821

"'Well, then,' the Nor'Wester said, 'he danced with us too, and we have taken care of him.'"

Quoted by George Simpson, December 4, 1820

With McGillivray in his prison fearing the HBC would murder him and with Simpson and Brown fearing the Nor'Westers would attempt a rescue, tensions between the two fur-trading companies on Athabasca Lake were high. Each side watched the other carefully to see where they went and whom they met. Both sides watched for an opportunity to arrest the other's leaders. Since the Nor'Wester guardhouse on Potato Island was only a few yards away from the HBC fort and Nor'Westers manned it constantly, the threat was real and ever-present.

At ten to one on the night of December 4, Brown, on watch, learned that men were walking about in the Nor'Wester guardhouse. Afraid they were preparing to launch an attack to rescue McGillivray, he woke up Simpson, who put the fort on high alert. Brown assembled twenty men under arms and, because the night was so cold, gave each a dram of liquor to keep them warm. These men he stationed strategically around the fort to repel any attempt at rescue. Simpson sent La Mallice to go and see what he could find out. La Mallice crept over to the Nor'Wester guardhouse and pressed his ear to the wall. When he heard someone inside the guardhouse say that the English were up and one of them was listening to their conversation, he beat a hasty retreat.

"The morning being bitterly cold," Simpson wrote, "I gave the people a second dram and they danced a few Reels in the Hall for the sake of Exercise as it was impossible to remain inactive on account of the severity of the weather. The noise about the Fort I conceived had roused the prisoner as there was a fire in his room, and his Woman and Children were heard walking about."[176] At about three o'clock, with every man under arms, it appeared that if the Nor'Westers had any intention to attack, they had changed their minds.

The fort calmed down. Brown remained on his watch until 7:00 a.m. and then went to bed for a couple of hours' sleep. Early that morning, two men went down to the lake for a bucket of water. There they met a Nor'Wester who asked if Mr. McGillivray had joined in the dancing. Yes, he had, they replied. "Well, then," the Nor'Wester said, "he danced with us too and we have taken care of him."[177] On their return to the fort with their buckets of water, they mentioned the conversation to Jonas Oxley, one of the clerks. His suspicions instantly raised, Oxley hurried to check McGillivray's room and found him gone. His wife, Teuse, though, was still there. At first, she declared that her husband had escaped up the chimney. No one believed this because the chimney was too narrow. Might someone inside the fort have helped him?

Suspicion fell on Knipe, McGillivray's keeper. When they questioned Teuse about the escape, she

> with much hesitation confessed that McGillivray had bribed the man and that he was conducted out by him between the hours of 8 and 9 o'clock last night; that the plan had been concerted several days, but they had no opportunity of carrying it into effect until last night, when Knipe opened the door and said to Mr. McGillivray, "If you promise faithfully to meet me in Montreal and keep your word I shall now permit you to escape as the Night is dark and there are no people moving about the Fort."[178]

When interrogated by Simpson in English, French, Italian and Spanish, all languages he was believed to know, Knipe professed not to understand the questions, and could they ask him in German, a language no one in the fort could speak. As far as they could get anything out of him, Knipe seemed to deny all knowledge of what had happened.

Astoundingly, two Nor'Westers arrived at the fort later in the day asking if they could collect McGillivray's clothes and possessions, which were politely handed over. One of these men, Picque (Julien Tavernour dit St. Picquè), said that McGillivray had arrived back in their guardhouse at eight or nine the previous evening. He related that McGillivray had said he had put on one of his wife's dresses and then asked Knipe to escort him to the privy, leaving the door to the fort open, through which he had escaped. Simpson and Brown thought this was merely a way to try to take the blame off Knipe. If so, it didn't work.

Simpson allowed Teuse to leave the fort with the children and rejoin her husband. A day or so later, McGillivray returned a towel and a tobacco box that Teuse had taken with her by mistake. Brown wrote back politely, returning the towel and saying that it did not belong to any of them. Even this excess of politeness did not end. McGillivray replied that he had borrowed a towel from one of the gentlemen of the HBC, had been unable to find it and so was sending this one back to repay his debt.

A few days before Christmas, Brown learned from Picque that the Nor'Westers had been planning to attack Fort Wedderburn for a long time but were waiting for reinforcements. Picque said that the Nor'Westers had sent an express canoe for Samuel Black and that when he arrived, they would strike. On Christmas Day—it was clear and cold—McGillivray appeared at the Nor'Wester guardhouse, having returned from Fort Chipewyan. Brown suspected a trick and put eight men on watch that night. But nothing untoward happened. Simpson recorded that on December 25 he gave the men a "holyday" and an extra dram. The gentlemen, he wrote, sat down to the most sumptuous dinner of English fare—roast beef and plum pudding, followed by a "temperate kettle of punch."

1821

The dark days of mid-winter ticked over into 1821. "At 6 o'clock a.m.," Brown wrote, "our men gave us the usual salute of firing that is customary in the Indian country on the Commencement of the New Year, after which we brought them into the Hall and treated them with cakes, rum etc."[179]

Simpson wrote in his journal that

> the whole Inmates of our Garrison assembled in the hall dressed out in their best clothes, and were regaled in a suitable manner with a few flaggon's Rum and some Cakes; a full allowance of Buffaloe meat was served out to them and a pint of Spirits for each man; the Women were also entertained to the utmost of our ability. In the course of the day St. Picque & Rondeau, contrary to Mr. Keith's instructions, paid us a visit, the object thereof was to guard me against a plan that the N.W. have in contemplation of apprehending me and the principal Officers of this establishment.... Black, he says, is expected in a few days, and is to commence open hostilities immediately on his arrival. Messrs Keith and Mc-Gillivray, also Soucisse, are endeavouring to excite their people to attack our Fort. In short, he assures me that our destruction is resolved upon without much delay.[180]

This visit to the HBC fort got Picque into trouble. When he returned to the Nor'Wester guardhouse, McGillivray berated him for visiting Fort Wedderburn and threatened him with all manner of violent punishments. Picque then decided to desert. Later that night he arrived back at Fort Wedderburn "as he was resolved no longer to serve such a band of Robbers &

Assassins as the N.W. for they were always pushing him on to attack some of our party and he was afraid that thro' liquor or bad example he might be induced to do something which would endanger his life."[181]

Simpson had a spy in the Nor'Wester guardhouse named Thomas O' Hara, a former sergeant in the De Meuron regiment. He had come to Fort Wedderburn for protection in early January because McGillivray had threatened to shoot him. Simpson announced that he did not trust O'Hara and sent him back. Perhaps, though, there was an understanding between them, because O'Hara secretly continued to provide Simpson with information about the Nor'Westers. "Met O'Hara in the Bastion at 4 o'clock a.m.," Brown wrote,

> according to an appointment I made with him yesterday. Offered him a handsome reward by Mr. Simpson's orders if he will give such information as will enable us to take Black prisoner without risking lives. This he readily consented to do but said "That it would not be safe to attempt taking him in his House as they are so well prepared that some one would be sure to fall before he could be secured. Each of their men has a Gun and a Pistole. Besides they have 14 stand of arms in their Hall and Rooms all ready for action." The best plan, he thinks, to take him will be upon the Lake, he being in the habit of going over to their Big Fort in the evening, and returning at a late hour, when he might be taken in the traverse.[182]

Sometimes O'Hara slipped a note through a chink in the wall of the HBC bastion in the middle of the night. In one such note he informed them that McGillivray was going out in the spring to prosecute Simpson for taking him prisoner and intended to include Brown in the charges for his part in the affair. Picque also gave credible warnings. "Mr. Simpson, pardon me for putting you on your guard," one such warning went, "You are going to be attacked subsequent to Mr. Back's departure."[183]

During the first three months of 1821, the men at Fort Wedderburn expected an attack daily. All the signs indicated the Nor'Westers were making the necessary preparations. They were much stronger than the HBC, having seven officers, four interpreters and sixty-five men. O'Hara told them that McGillivray had been plying his men with liquor to stiffen their courage. Simpson, afraid the Nor'Westers would shoot him in his bed, went so far as to have a second shutter put up over the window in his bedroom. Although he said he had little confidence in his officers except for Brown, Simpson resolutely made as much of a show of force as he could and exuded fiery defiance.

This show of resolute defence apparently succeeded. On March 29, O'Hara told Simpson the Nor'Westers had abandoned their project of attacking Fort Wedderburn and were now on the defensive, fearing an attack themselves. Black and McGillivray, he said, were sleeping with bolted and barred doors to their rooms. "As they never appeared," Brown wrote "but loaded with arms, and when they took their meals, they invariably had two or three pair of pistols lying upon the table."[184] They returned across the lake to Fort Chipewyan, seemingly afraid to stay in their guardhouse on Potato Island. Eventually—and probably to everyone in Fort Wedderburn's great relief—both men left Fort Chipewyan to carry on the battle against the HBC elsewhere.

Routines—Life Must Go On

All this time the usual business of the fort continued—trading with Indigenous hunters and trappers, finding provisions, hauling home firewood, and building and repairing the structures at the fort. Quite often, Brown sent men out on derouines, which was the practice of visiting Indigenous villages and lodges to trade there.

Brown had a pleasant surprise in early January. During renovation work in his room, he lifted up a floorboard and found a most useful hidden cache. This consisted of a small keg of gunpowder, six falling hatchets, nineteen trading hatchets, an augur (broken), a beaver trap (part thereof) and iron hoops. The hoops were a most useful source of iron, always in short supply, for reworking into nails. The hatchets were also welcome. Most of the ones they had been using had been reforged so often they had become too brittle to cut frozen wood. Brown was not only pleased but also lucky. A few weeks before, a small fire had broken out in his room a mere two feet from the hidden gunpowder.

Building work continued through the winter. By January 22, they had started to build a stable for their horse. "Delonie squaring posts for the Door of a stable that we intend to have built," Brown noted, "as it is both inconvenient & disagreeable to have the horse standing in the Cook Room. Besides, we intend to have it repaired for the servant to live & cook in, in place of the Hall."[185] The men had the stable, ten feet by six feet, finished and mudded by the end of the month.

Simpson's Assessment of Brown

Simpson approved of Brown in such warm, lofty terms that it is easy to forget that he was only a couple of years older and that Brown was vastly more experienced in the fur trade than he was. On September 22, barely ten days

George Back, *Lake Athabasca, with Fort Chipewyan on the Bluff on the Right,* 1832. By this time Fort Wedderburn would have been derelict and the wood rotting.

after he had arrived, Simpson wrote "Mr. Brown seems to have been most attentive to his charge; the Fort is in tolerable repair; all our Indians are staunch."[186] He was never, though, one to withhold criticism. In October he was writing "the general routine business of the Fort is now conducted with some method, and there is still room for improvement: Mr. Brown is very zealous and active, but unfortunately has little system in his arrangement."[187] And again, "Mr. Brown is a most attentive zealous Servant but unfortunately harsh and uncourteous in his address: he grants his favours with a bad grace, and his manner is by no means prepossessing, so that I have much difficulty in maintaining Peace and quietness between him and some of the Officers and Men."[188]

Simpson knew that Brown was keeping a private journal in addition to the post journal. Always obsessed with secrecy, the HBC had a long-standing policy that it owned all journals written by HBC traders, clerks and men, both public and private. He made it clear to Brown that he would eventually have to surrender his private journal.

Country Wives

Many HBC men entered into relationships with Indigenous and Métis women. Such a relationship was known as marriage *à la façon du pays* or country marriage. This was a long-standing institution both for the HBC and the North West Company. The country wives were essential links between the European and Indigenous cultures. Although these relationships were often transactional and all parties generally benefitted from them, many of them were long and happy. Despite occasional—and futile—attempts to limit them, the HBC saw these country marriages as valuable because they provided stability in its relationship with local Indigenous people. Through them, the company obtained Indigenous goodwill and a solid entrée into their economic trading networks.

Little was written at the time in the post journals, district reports or correspondence about these women and their importance to the HBC. Company documents were for business: they were not for recording the social life of a fort. They rarely mention the women, what they did or the children who must have been playing and working around each fort. In April 1821, for example, there were thirty-one women and forty-nine children living at Fort Chipewyan, but we hear nothing about them. When listing who went where in canoes, the writers of the post journals rarely included the presence, let alone the names, of the women and children.

When it comes to Brown's women in Athabasca and later in New Caledonia, we have enough information to ask questions but not enough to provide answers. The existence of a wife in Scotland did not, in any event, appear to be any impediment. Simpson noted in his journal at Fort Wedderburn that a woman had placed herself under Brown's protection. Joseph Greill, under whose protection she had previously been, then made a four-day journey in two and a half days to reclaim her. Greill and Brown appealed to Simpson for adjudication. He wisely ruled that the woman herself should decide which of the two protectors she wanted. Alas for Brown, she did not choose him.[189] That evening Greill gave the treat customary on such occasions. The following day, consequently, everybody was too drunk to work. Brown did not hold any grudge against Greill. He described him as a "very steady, careful, interested servant who is capable of undergoing the Hardships of the Country."[190]

ON TO NEW CALEDONIA

On June 10, 1820, the Nor'Wester James McDougall, stationed at Stuart's Lake in New Caledonia, wrote in the post journal that he had received

> a report of there being at the Forks of the Fraser's River one of the H. B. Co. Clerks [this was Ignace Giasson] and 3 men with the Iroquois, distributing out Goods & Tobacco gratis with promises of their coming in force early in the Summer, but I can hardly credit them as certainly our Gentlemen in Peace River would have

> sent us notice of it. If such is the case, they certainly
> will play the deuce with the Natives and all their Furs
> without my having it in my power to prevent them for
> I have neither the means nor men to send to ascertain
> the truth.[191]

Alerted to the coming challenge, McDougall issued orders that a watch should be kept for further incursions and every obstacle placed in their way.

After much anxiety and fears that the Nor'Westers in New Caledonia had murdered Giasson and his party—which, reportedly, they had tried to persuade Indigenous people to do— Giasson surfaced, to general relief, on February 20, 1821. His journey had been arduous but successful. He had found the Indigenous people in New Caledonia welcoming and eager to trade with the HBC. He had also located two places where HBC posts could be set up profitably. In short, New Caledonia beckoned.

Governor Williams decided that Brown was to continue with the original plan of leading an expedition into New Caledonia in the summer of 1821. Simpson agreed. "I highly approve of your choice of Mr. Brown as a Leader of the party," he wrote. "He is intelligent, active, zealous, and brave, but I suspect they [the Nor'Westers] have a Warrant against him."[192] Brown had been organizing for this expedition all winter, engaging men and gathering supplies. On February 9, Brown wrote to Greill, one of the men he wanted to take with him, that he was "very happy to learn you have no objections to crossing the Rocky Mountain in the spring. The pistols, sword and belt, I will have in readiness for you.... It is intended at present that we start with two Canoes & a small appointment of Goods in the beginning of June, and there are 4 Canoes to be dispatched after us from Norway House, with a full outfit of everything necessary for the trade of that Quarter."[193]

Brown's opponent in New Caledonia would be the redoubtable John Stuart—le grand talon—newly arrived back in the land he knew best. Based at the Stuart's Lake post, Stuart was aware of the coming threat from the HBC and determined to stop it. On February 25, he wrote to James McDougall, who was then at the Nor'Wester post at McLeod's Lake: "A strict watch ought to be kept night & day on the Parsnip River to prevent a possibility of their arriving or passing unknown to you and if a person from Athabasca [by which Stuart probably meant Black] do attend them and the Iroquois, you will furnish that person with the necessary supplies and leave him to act as he thinks fit."[194] Stuart, it was clear, was prepared to fight. When Brown left Fort Wedderburn, on his way to attack the Nor'Wester monopoly in New Caledonia, he likely knew he would meet fierce and probably violent opposition when he arrived.

Governor George Simpson on a tour of inspection. In the summer of 1821, Brown travelled with Simpson in such a canoe from Fort Wedderburn to York Factory on Hudson Bay.

The time came when Simpson and Brown were ready to leave Fort Wedderburn, the former to report in person to Governor Williams, the latter to complete his preparations for challenging the Nor'Westers in New Caledonia. On May 5, while Simpson and Brown were preparing their cassettes and the men were pressing and packing the furs for the coming journey, Napoleon Bonaparte, emperor of the French, died in exile on a far-away island in the South Atlantic. In his library at his death was a copy of Alexander Mackenzie's book about his journey to the Pacific Ocean. George Simpson, an illegitimate Scot, would in time become de facto governor of a territory larger than any Napoleon had ever ruled over.

With twenty men in two canoes, Simpson and Brown left Fort Wedderburn at 2:00 a.m. on May 23, 1821. "Mr. Brown has this day given up charge of the District to Mr. McVicar," Simpson wrote, "and I am glad it has fallen into such competent hands. It is, however, but justice to say that Mr. Brown's steady, careful and judicious management, together with his firmness and activity under all our difficulties merits my warmest acknowledgements, and I do not know that the Hon'ble Coy have a more faithful servant in their employ."[195]

The route back to Norway House was familiar. The landmarks ticked by as they paddled, glided and portaged eastward. They reached Cumberland House on June 15. The weather was hot, the flies troublesome, and the danger of an ambush mounting.

They approached the Grand Rapid, site of the ambush of the Nor'Wester canoes in June 1819. They would have been apprehensive. They knew the Nor'Westers badly wanted to arrest them both. As Brown knew well from his personal experience, the Grand Rapid was the perfect place for such an ambush. "I fully calculated on meeting the N.W. at the Foot of the Rapid this morning," Simpson wrote, "and therefore made the necessary defensive preparations."[196] Sure enough, they spotted a group of Nor'Westers waiting on the bank below the rapids.

Soon Brown and Simpson would hear news that would turn both their worlds upside down.

11

Fort St. James and Fort Kilmaurs

1821–1822

"But what pleases myself is to have our old rivals, if not foes, into staunch friends."

John Stuart, November 11, 1821

The Nor'Westers at the base of the rapids waved them over, indicating they wanted to tell them something. Simpson, Brown and their canoes approached warily. Not without reason, they suspected a trap. Cautiously, they approached within speaking distance. "Mr. McLeod, a N.W. Clerk," Simpson wrote, "hailed me by name and intimated that a coalition had taken place between the Coy's."[197] McLeod showed Simpson letters that purportedly proved what he was saying, but Simpson was still suspicious it might be a ruse. He and Brown continued their journey to Norway House, where they arrived on June 19. Here Governor Williams confirmed the news. The mighty Hudson's Bay Company and the North West Company had agreed to merge. The Pemmican War was over.

Complicated merger negotiations had taken place in London. Both companies had been exhausting themselves in the struggle and the need to unite had become obvious. Moreover, the British government had been putting pressure on both companies to end their war. Parliament ratified their agreement on July 2, 1821.

"This is, indeed, a Message of Peace," the *Canadian Courant* in Montreal pronounced, "to carry pacific intelligence to contending parties and dispel that discord which has hitherto existed amongst them, blending their interests and exertions into one channel, and promoting among opponents friendship."[198] News of the merger spread up the rivers to the forts of both companies. It arrived at Fort Chipewyan on August 1. "It is needless to say," the fort's post journal recorded, "that we greeted this news with heartfelt pleasure and satisfaction. The majority of the men partook of the general joy, but the Indians heard it with sullen silence."[199] As well they might. They would have realized at once they could no longer play the two companies off against each other.

The HBC appointed George Simpson to be the governor of the Northern Department and William Williams governor of the Southern Department. The Northern Council met at Norway House for the first time on August 12, 1821. The council laid down the new organization, deciding which forts were to be abandoned, which maintained and who would be chief factors and traders. Unsurprisingly, it closed Fort Wedderburn and moved its Athabasca base to Fort Chipewyan. It appointed John Stuart to be the chief factor and William Brown to be the chief trader for New Caledonia.

NEW CALEDONIA

By then, however, Brown was already on his way. He had arrived at Cumberland House on August 10 with four loaded canoes. A few days before, a windstorm had shattered the flagstaff and everyone was busy erecting a new one, fifty-six feet high. (Did anyone comment on the symbolism of this?) Leaving in the early morning a few days later, Brown arrived at Fort Chipewyan on September 16 and left soon after. The Rocky Mountains were formidable barriers, but there were ways through them. Brown took the tried-and-true route of the Rocky Mountain Portage, which had been Alexander Mackenzie's original passage. This route went from Fort Chipewyan up the Peace River, over the gruelling twelve-mile portage, then down the Peace and Parsnip Rivers to McLeod's Lake in New Caledonia. He and his party arrived there in mid-October.

Brown was now in territory which both for him and the HBC was new. With the few exceptions of the HBC men he had brought with him, he would now be working with those who, only a month or so before, had been his enemies, with warrants for his arrest in their pockets. John Stuart, for example, the new superintendent and chief factor, had previously been an opponent in Athabasca. Many of the Nor'Westers resented losing their identity in the new HBC. How well would they accept the HBC men coming into what had been their jealously guarded territory? Friendly acceptance or resentment and resistance?

New Caledonia was a land of long, thin lakes, of wide rolling prairies, of mountains and thick forests. Though the climate was milder than at Fort Wedderburn, it was never reliable, and it rained a lot. Eagles watched from tall trees. Unseen cougars spied on travellers from the woods. There was always a risk of meeting a grizzly bear when journeying from one fort to another. The Indigenous people who lived there—the Dakelh, Sekani and Atnah Nations—spoke different languages, wore different clothes and had different customs. But, above all, it was the sense of being over the barrier of the mountains and isolated from Rupert's Land and Athabasca that made New Caledonia feel so different from any place Brown had ever been before.

Brown came this way through the Rocky Mountains in 1821 and went out this way in 1826. Until 1827, this was the usual way out from New Caledonia.

John Stuart himself had helped establish the forts in New Caledonia: McLeod's Lake in 1805, Stuart's Lake and Fraser's Lake in 1806, and Fort George in 1807. The North West Company's main fort—now the HBC's—was at the southern end of Stuart's Lake. After February 1822, it became known as Fort St. James.

Babine Lake, the largest in New Caledonia, was a long lake to the west of Stuart's Lake, to which it was connected by a twelve-mile portage, but by a track yet to be cleared. The Babine River (also known as McDougall's River) flowed north out of Babine Lake and joined a big river (today named the Skeena). The merged river then flowed west, joined Simpson's River (today named the Bulkley River) at the Forks and then flowed one hundred and eighty miles to the Pacific coast. The flat land opposite the point at the Forks (today known as Mission Flats or Anderson Flats Provincial Park) was a place where for many centuries the Indigenous coastal nations and the interior nations had met to trade. As far as is known, at this time no non-Indigenous people had ever visited the Forks.

There were several main groupings of Indigenous people in New Caledonia. Those around the lakes and forts of the central interior were the Dakelh peoples, or the Carrier as they were also known. The word Dakelh appropriately means "people who travel upon water." Another nation, the Sekani (Tse'khene) people lay mainly to the north and northeast. The Wet'suwet'en (Wit'suwit'en) village of Hotset, or Witset as it became known (and later still as Moricetown), was on Simpson's River where it enters the Hagwilget Canyon, approximately twenty-five miles upriver from the Forks. At the Forks, a few miles from the western end of the canyon, lived an entirely different people. These were the Atnah, as the Gitxsan people were then called by the Dakelh. The closest Atnah villages to Babine Lake, though, were Need Chip, Weep Sim and Chil do cal, which were on the Babine River near where it joined what is now the Skeena River. A branch of the coastal Tsimshian peoples, the Atnah people were a people with a different language and different ways.

Until Brown's arrival, the Nor'Westers had a trading monopoly in the interior of New Caledonia. But they were not entirely undisturbed. On the coast, Russians, Americans (known as Boston men), and the British (known as King George's men), had been trading with the coastal Indigenous people since the early 1790s. Alaska was still Russian territory, and the Russians had settlements up the coast. These ship-based traders had a flourishing business with China, where the demand for furs and sea otter pelts was high. They traded with coastal Indigenous people, who in turn came upriver and traded with the interior Indigenous people at the Forks.

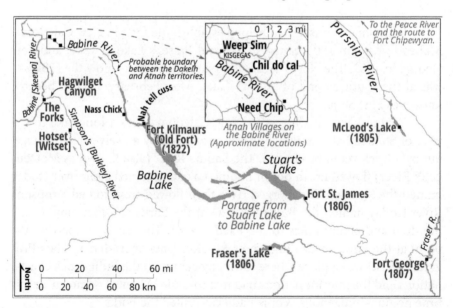

The HBC forts in New Caledonia. The Dakelh people around Fort St. James called the Gitxsan people Atnahs, meaning "strangers." The central Atnah/Gitxsan village was at the Forks.

OLD ADVERSARIES, NEW COLLEAGUES

On July 17, 1821, William McGillivray and his brother Simon wrote a joint letter to John Stuart, informing him not only about the merger but also that he had been appointed chief factor for New Caledonia. Stuart, who did not receive this letter until November, then accepted what was obviously a *fait accompli* and wrote that he was not surprised. "The more strenuous I was in opposing the H.B.Co. while their interest was opposed to mine," he wrote, "the more effectually I can promote theirs, now that our interest is one."[200] Though there is no reason to believe he was dissembling, he would have been aware that everything he put down on paper would be read at York Factory and, if it so desired, by the committee in London. It would have behooved him to be seen to be happy with the changes. Later he wrote, a little wistfully, that he was noticing the distinction between being a partner in an independent concern and that of being an employee, albeit a chief factor in charge of a district: "The one was *something*, but the other is a name without substance and, being no Stockholder, is nothing more than a Servant of the Company, whose orders he is bound implicitly to follow."[201]

Stuart and Brown now met as new colleagues and seemed to get along well together. Stuart declared,

> our present Establishments are well provided for, and Mr. Brown, whom I am happy to find a Gentleman of respectability, possessed of considerable talents and great application is well calculated for a Post in the Babine country, which I intend to get established next fall previous to the return of the people from the Depot, for then it would be too late. In not one material instance does our opinion differ and the more he is getting acquainted with the Country the more our Ideas coincide.[202]

Stuart sent Brown to take charge of the Fraser's Lake post for the winter, graciously saying, "But I beg that in your communications with me you will no longer mention the word *orders*. Advice you may, and welcome, for it never shall be withholden."[203]

Then there were the McDougall brothers, James and George. James had been third-in-command of Simon Fraser's expedition downriver to the coast and had made several explorations of the lakes in New Caledonia. Stuart called him "the Father of New Caledonia."[204] This was a title that could have been applied to Stuart himself with equal justice.

One of the most valuable and respected employees in New Caledonia was Jean Baptiste Boucher, usually called Waccan. With a Canadian father and a Cree mother, he was a Métis. Born in about 1789, he had come into

John Stuart as an older man. In 1821, he was forty-one years old. He was Brown's adversary before 1821 and his colleague and superior officer afterwards. He died in 1847.

New Caledonia with Simon Fraser in 1806 and accompanied him on his epic journeys. On those voyages, Waccan had become well acquainted with Stuart and the McDougall brothers. His second marriage was to James McDougall's daughter Nancy, with whom he had no less than seventeen children. He was often called an interpreter because he spoke numerous Indigenous languages, but he was, in truth, good at almost everything he turned his hand to, including making canoes, sledges and snowshoes. He was also at times put in charge of a fort. Additionally, and most usefully, he was a fearless enforcer of HBC discipline. Wherever there was a problem, Waccan was there helping to solve it. Brown noted his abilities early: "Waccan," he wrote in December, "is a most excellent man, whose services are of most infinite Value at this place."[205]

Not long after Brown arrived in New Caledonia, he is reported as having a country wife named Josette Bolieu, as Brown spelled her name. Who she was remains a mystery. With few available facts—but enough to tantalize—we can only speculate. He may have brought her from Fort Chipewyan. Though there is no evidence to support it, it is at least possible she was one of the many children of François Beaulieu, whose named Brown spelled in the post journals as Bolieu. In 1820, Beaulieu was at Fort Chipewyan. He had at least three concurrent wives, many liaisons and many children. Was Josette one of them? Would Brown have had any opportunity of consorting with the daughter of one of the Nor'Wester guides? Josette, though, may have been brought up by her mother in another location, less tied to the North West Company. Beaulieu had been with the North West Company since his journeys with Alexander Mackenzie and had spent time in New Caledonia, possibly with unsurprising consequences. Or Josette might just have been a girl from New Caledonia, as John Stuart hinted at, with no connection to Beaulieu at all. Perhaps Brown was merely following Simpson's injunction to take a country wife from a local Indigenous community as soon as he arrived in New Caledonia. With so little information, we just don't know.

A little unfeelingly, Brown wrote to Stuart in December that "my Dame amuses me with a serenade of crying once or twice after I left Stuart's Lake, but I threatened to send her back to her mother, since which time I have had no more of her moans."[206] He later sent to Stuart a little "smoking weed which my Dame arranged.... It will not serve you long, but I will employ her ladyship in procuring more against [for when] another opportunity offers of sending to your place."[207] For whatever reason, the following summer Josette appears to have left Brown and returned to live with Indigenous people, which suggests a local connection. Stuart hinted that Brown then entered into a liaison with another Indigenous woman.

Nicholas Garry was president of the Council of the Northern Department, having come over from London to implement the merger of the two companies. Stuart wrote to him about the difficulties of the fur business in New Caledonia. "This part of the Country lies under many disadvantages," he said,

> and its distance from any Port of entry and the difficulty of getting the necessary supplies will continue to operate against it. The number of people required will be more than in proportion to the returns, and such as expect a rapid increase of returns will be disappointed.... Another matter not unworthy of consideration is the bad living in this quarter. It is no more to be compared to the East side of the Mountains than Tripe de Roche [Rock tripe—an edible lichen commonly used as emergency food] is to Turtle Soup.[208]

Indeed, New Caledonia soon acquired the reputation of being the Siberia of the HBC's territories. Over the mountains and far away. Simpson sent difficult employees there to punish them or toughen them up.

BUILDING FORT KILMAURS

Stuart wanted to extend the trade from Stuart's Lake into the still relatively unknown Babine Lake district. He therefore proposed establishing a new fort on Babine Lake. As early as January 1822, he was mentioning the possibility of making an exploratory expedition, which he and Brown did in late July. In April, he wrote that Brown and twelve men would establish the post in the fall.

On October 10, 1822—a stormy, boisterous day that delayed their departure until the evening—Brown and his party set out from Fort St. James. He intended to canoe up Stuart's Lake to the narrow crossing to Babine Lake, clear the portage and then canoe up the lake to search for a suitable site for the new post. Among those he took with him were the ever-useful Waccan and O'Doherty, a French-speaking clerk. Most of the men of the party were Canadians. Stuart loaned Waccan to Brown to help him because, he said, he could not establish the new post without half the advantages he would have if Waccan was with him. But Brown was told to send him back to Fort St. James in the spring.

When he reached the portage between Stuart's Lake and Babine Lake, Brown had to cut the new portage track through the fallen timber. Even with the fifteen Dakelh men and women he hired to help, this took approximately ten days. Most of the porters carried two packs weighing ninety pounds each across the portage. When the portage was finished, Brown wrote that he had the satisfaction of knowing that they had done a good job that would endure. Then he continued up the lake and started to look for a site to build the fort on. With the help of Chief Caupin (sometimes spelled Casepin) and local Dakelh people, Brown selected a site. The site he chose was close to the village of Nah tell cuss, on an island a quarter of a mile away, where twenty-four families lived. It was approximately eighty miles from the portage across to Stuart's Lake and thirty-five miles to the entrance to the Babine River. On October 25, Brown wrote:

> I therefore after breakfast took Waccan, the Chief and six men in the Canoe, and made a tour of part of the Bay to examine the advantages and disadvantages of the different places the Natives have been pointing out, when I pitched upon the Point which juts out between the summer Village and the entrance of the Narrows. This place being the best situated for the different stations the Indians mention for fishing. Besides the soil is good and well calculated for cultivation, the most of the Point having been burnt and is at present a kind of Prairie. The wood behind is strong and well adapted for building, but it will be [necessary] to carry for about two hundred yards and some of it perhaps for more. However I thought it was better to put up with this inconvenience than to build either upon the right or left as the ground is uneven, low and swampy.

Having chosen the site, he brought up his supplies and, accompanied by most of the villagers, took possession. The next day they commenced the work of planning what buildings to set up and where. Waccan arranged a place for himself and his family, along with the crew of his canoe. The weather was worsening and it was blowing and raining all day. The following day, Brown continued,

Canoe on Babine Lake, looking west, 1891.

the fisherman arranged a Net for setting, but it was blowing too fresh to put it in the water.... I much doubt it will be few Nets we will be able to procure from the Indians for this some time unless we give an extravagant price for them as they see we are in want of these articles and seem inclined to take all the advantage they can. So I am dubious the fishing season will be over before we will have the means to reap any advantage from it. Received in the course of the day 1 Marten, 3 Musquashes, 1 old Net, 28 large and 25 Small Salmon.[209]

Brown and his men started work. They started to cut trees and make boards, but soon found their saw was bad. The men complained of not being able to cut a straight line with it. When questioned, Waccan stated that "he saw Hudson [Thomas Hodgson, the blacksmith at Fort St. James] examine the New Ones and finding them good they were put part for St. James and the Old one which was known to be of little worth was laid aside for this place."[210] But they persevered. They somehow cut sixty-six logs of different lengths to build a store of twenty feet by sixteen feet, thirty-seven of which they carried home with the assistance of the local Dakelh villagers from Nah tell cuss.

Brown now faced the problem of finding food. The promise of good fishing was not, it now seemed, to be fulfilled. On the first Monday, the fishermen only caught one white fish. But salmon have their own timetables and eventually they did arrive. Generally, when the salmon came upriver, they arrived at Babine Lake a month before they found their way into Stuart's Lake. Because of this, the salmon fishery on Babine Lake became of considerable importance as the provider of food for the other forts in the district. As Brown was finding out, neither the time of the salmon's arrival nor the quantity that arrived was predictable. In some years there was feast and in others famine: 1821 had been a good year; but in 1823 not only the salmon but also the white fish failed. That winter was the coldest on record and there was much hardship. During the winter they ate dried salmon. The daily ration was four per day in summer and twice that in winter. Not for nothing was New Caledonia called a hardship post.

By now snow was falling and winter was heavy upon them. Undaunted, they continued with their building. On October 31, they took a break to christen the new fort. Brown wrote that

> the people all employed the same as yesterday. After the work of the day was over, they brought home a Flagstaff and put it up, when the Fort was named "Kilmaurs." Gave them a dram to drink success to the New Establishment, which they did, and afterwards fired a few Volleys at the Flagstaff, which so alarmed the natives that I understand the most of them took to the Woods for refuge under the impression that Indians had arrived from below [that is, Atnah men coming up the Babine River from Need Chip] and we were killing them and would serve them in the same manner. Baptiste Arionga got his arm severely cut in putting up the Flagstaff.[211]

No one worked on November 1, it being All Saints Day. Most of the Canadians were Catholic and they observed their feast days, especially if it came with a holiday. The following day they were back at work gumming canoes and working on the roof for the store.

On November 5, Brown wrote in the post journal: "Weather blowing with some rain in the Morning. 3 men putting flooring in the store and earth upon the roof of it. Delonie making a Door for the store. Taylor employed at the Nets. Waccan with four men commenced to square wood for a House of 40 feet by 24 feet. Cut & squared 8 pieces, consisting of poles, beams etc, 4 of which the Indians carried home."[212] In the morning, the mountains were covered with snow. This would have been a trying time for

Brown, with worries about the houses, the poor fishing and the lack of furs being brought to the new post by Dakelh hunters and trappers.

On November 12, he reported on progress to Stuart, noting his shortage of axes and door hinges and asked Stuart to have some made: "In fact the first cannot be dispensed with without injuring the Establishment. However the last are only required as a matter of convenience and of course must give way to anything that is of more importance."[213]

Brown decided he should go down the lakes to Fort St. James to discuss company business with Stuart. He left on November 17 and was back at Kilmaurs on December 21. His journey back was nightmarish. The party's sleds, loads and dogs went through the ice on the lake numerous times and had to be pulled out. On shore they froze in the freezing temperature and solid masses of ice festooned the loads. When he arrived back at Kilmaurs, he found

> all hands well, but [I was] extremely sorry to observe that during my absence my orders had been neglected, the plan of the buildings entirely abandoned and to say the least everything in state of confusion. In place of building a men's House on the East Wing of the Main House, they have built one in the Rear of 20 feet by 16 feet and have all the Men Lodging in it and the Hall. Owing to the Bad earth the Chimneys have been built with, they have fallen repeatedly and are all on the point of doing so again.[214]

More agreeably, he also arrived back to the news that on December 8 his wife Josette, who had by now returned to him, had given birth to a son. They named him Daniel, undoubtedly after Brown's father in faraway Scotland. Perhaps Brown was more expressive in his private journal, but he makes no mention of the happy event in the fort's post journal.

The men had a difficult time building chimneys and keeping them standing. The mud they were using to bind the stones together seemed to be ineffective, and the chimneys kept falling down. On Christmas day, Brown wrote

> Pierre & Baptiste pulled down the Hall fireplace and commenced another, it being all broke and on the point of falling. So that the place was constantly full of smoke and every moment in danger of taking fire. Taylor and Lancteau hauling home Mud. Vandalle and the other three men completed the square of the House and put on part of the Roof.[215]

By December 27, Pierre and Baptiste had rebuilt the fireplace. That same day, alas, the chimney fell down again. On the 28 he wrote: "In the morning set six men to rebuild my Chimney and to haul Mud. I was in hopes of getting it finished today, but when it was as high as the [roof] it fell down again, and it was quite dark before they got it the same length a second time. So it remains in that state."[216]

They also had continuing troubles with axes. Sharp, well-tempered axes were essential for the fort's survival. Without them, no wood could be cut. By January 9, the men could not even cut one board. As with the saws, he suspected that the blacksmith at Fort St. James had given him a bad one on purpose, but he could not prove it. Since he was entirely dependent on Fort St. James for essential supplies, such as axes, nails and twine, he had to take what they would give him.

They celebrated the arrival of 1823 on January 13. This was partly because Brown was away for a week visiting Dakelh villages on the Babine River to the north and partly because he had no special food to offer them but dried salmon. And he thought they deserved something better to celebrate the new year. While away he had purchased thirty Indigenous dogs, thirteen of which were for hauling and breeding and seventeen for eating as a New Year's celebration feast. "This being the day appointed for holding in place of the New Year," Brown wrote, "the men, as usual, fired three rounds a little before daylight. Came in and partook of a breakfast which was prepared for them, and consisted of roasted Dogs, a Beaver, Cakes and Cheese, with as much Rum as they chused to drink. Had a few songs with a very pleasant morning's amusement."[217]

Still worrying about the axes, Brown wrote to Stuart in mid-January:

> The Pit saw I return as we can do nothing with it here. I have tried every man at the place who knows anything of sawing, both with green and dry wood. And all my attempts have proved unsuccessful. So that what boards have been required of late for the building had to be split and chopped. It is possible that some of the men at St. James will be able to saw with it as they are much better acquainted with that business than those here. If it is possible to dispense with one of the New Ones I hope it will be sent, as it is much required here, there being Pickets, flooring, ceiling, etc, to saw in the course of the spring for arranging the buildings in the summer. If a hand saw could be spared it would also be of great service.[218]

Outside, the weather was thick and cold, with falling snow. Inside, Baptiste Arionga put up a bookcase and made a rack for muskets. Pierre started to square wood for the extension to the main house that was to be twenty feet long and twenty-four feet wide. Brown was finding his room too small and needed somewhere larger to transact business with the Indigenous hunters coming to the fort to trade. All seemed to be going well until heavy rain one night started to pour in through the roof. He then had to have the property in the store quickly covered up and secured. Work continued on the chimneys. Pierre persevered in trying to cut and square more wood. The lack of good axes, though, severely impeded progress. Nevertheless, they got the work done.

Fort Kilmaurs was now substantially finished. In the nature of HBC forts, it would never be totally completed. There would always be a need for a new building—a separate house for the men, a forge, an icehouse, a necessary repair, a stockade and perhaps a stable if they could acquire a horse. But it was now fully functional as an HBC fort. If only the chimneys would stay up!

THE THREAT TO THE HBC MONOPOLY

To Brown, the threat to the HBC monopoly in New Caledonia from traders on the coast was clear and pressing. Daniel Harmon, who had been in charge of the Stuart's Lake post between 1810 and 1816, had recorded in his journal on June 16, 1811, the presence at the post of Indigenous traders from the Babine River. These were probably Atnah traders. They had told him that every year a group of white men came from the coast to the Forks to trade with the Atnah there. Harmon thought these were Americans, but they could just as easily have been British or Russians. Others have written they were merely Indigenous traders from the coast. There is no written or independent confirmation of any such visits. Either way, though, it shows that the reach of the trading ships on the coast was coming closer. Dakelh people told Brown that a party of non-Indigenous people had an establishment at the Forks, but he thought they were merely trying to improve their bargaining power by magnifying the threat of rival traders. He made discreet inquiries and proved to his satisfaction their story was untrue.

Brown strongly believed that when the Indigenous traders on the coast came up to the Babine River they would turn south to trade with the Atnah at Weep Sim. Then they would continue upriver to Babine Lake and on to Stuart's Lake. The local Dakelh people would then be able to play the HBC off against the coastal traders, thus breaking the HBC monopoly. Indeed, the Dakelh were already using this threat as a negotiating tactic. It was only a matter of time. Already Indigenous people from the coast were bringing trade goods from the ships on the coast higher upriver than the Forks on a regular basis.

Brown discusses the problem and his solution.

> It does not appear to me that we are able to cope with
> these people by making derouines into the Countries
> they are in the habit of visiting unless we sell our prop-
> erty so cheap as to prove prejudicial to the trade of
> Western Caledonia and even then we will not be able to
> secure one half of the trade. For we do not meet on an
> equal footing, as they receive goods at a low rate from
> the Vessels which frequent the coast. And though their
> articles generally speaking are old and little worth, par-
> ticularly the arms, still while compared with any thing
> we can give at the same price, they appear great in the
> eyes of Indians who have no knowledge of the intrinsic
> value of property.
>
> To which may be added they work their own Crafts
> coming up the River, understand the language and are
> at no expenses for provisions nor anything else. Con-
> sequently can afford to give a high price for what Furs
> they receive, and then have what will appear to them
> handsome profits. Besides they have recourse to means
> which would not do with us. For instance, on their ar-
> rival at a Village they ascertain, if they do not Know
> previously, who have Furs and the amount of them.
> On which they go to the person's Lodge, blow a par-
> cel of Swan's down upon his head, which is marked a
> great honour, both amongst the Carriers and Atnahs,
> and then commence dancing and singing a song in his
> praise. After which they make him a present and treat
> him with something to eat. When he, according to the
> Custom of his Country, makes them in return a present
> of his Furs, which if not equal to what he has received,
> he adds siffler [marmot] Robes, and dressed skins to
> make up the Value....
>
> While at the same time the traders from the coast seem
> as if they intended to extend their trading excursions as
> they seldom used to come higher than the Forks of the
> Babine and Simpson's River, and very frequently not so
> high. But last fall they came as far up as the upper At-
> nah Village [possibly Chil do cal] and traded the whole
> of the Furs and siffler Robes the Natives had to dispose

of. So that when I was there in March, all that I could collect amongst them was only thirty Martens and a little Beaver coating, and that at a very high rate, which induced me to return from Chil do cal in place of going to the Forks as was my intention.

It appears to me that the only effectual method to put a stop to this traffic, to protect Western Caledonia from the Inroads of these people and to secure the trade of both Rivers to the Concern is to form an Establishment at the Forks of the Babine and Simpson's River, by which such Furs as are not procured there will be got at either Kilmaurs or Fraser's Lake. If some such measure is not adopted to check them, the evil will ere long become of a serious Nature. For they are yearly extending their Voyages and there is not a doubt but they will continue to do so, while they can procure Furs and are not opposed. They have now made their way as high as the Upper Atnah Village and have only to make one stretch more to reach this Lake. As to Simpson's River they have had the greatest part of the Furs of that Quarter for these some years past, which they either procured by these Indians, meeting them at the Forks, or by the means of the Atnahs, who act as agents for them, going there and trading them.[219]

Brown therefore took a strategic view. When he was at Fort St. James at the end of November, he wrote to Stuart and argued there was a need to explore the Babine River to the sea. He offered to lead such an expedition. A couple of days later, Stuart in a long, reasoned letter turned his proposal down, partly because it would cost too much and partly because he did not have men to spare. He reminded Brown that such an expedition might also be dangerous. The Russians on the coast he wrote "can scarcely keep them [the coastal Indigenous people] in subjection, though the heads of sometimes sixty of a morning are placed upon poles as a warning to others."[220] Moreover, he estimated the cost of such an expedition would be as high as £430. Since retrenchment and economy was the order of the day in the HBC, he claimed that Simpson and the council would not approve, though he did reluctantly say he would find out.

Brown replied to Stuart the following day and argued his case more fully. He discussed the threat from the traders on the coast. "It being reasonable to conclude," he wrote, that if they are allowed quietly to collect the Furs along the Sea Coast, they will ere long extend their Views to the Interior and if we do not go to meet them, they will come to meet us. The consequence of which will be the ruin of the whole Trade of this quarter. In fact if any reliance is to be placed on Indian reports, they have already Establishments in the Interior and every year ascend the Babine or McDougall's River to a considerable distance for the purpose of Trade.[221]

With some irritation, Stuart replied on December 2, again turning down Brown's proposal. "I would have been pleased" he wrote, "to find the Idea of keeping additional people inland for the special purpose of discovery had been abandoned."[222] He was also afraid to taunt what he called the Russian bear: "If you show the Russians on the North West Coast of America the way to the interior, you will not be able to stand before them."[223]

The following day, December 3, in a flagrant case of a subordinate going over his superior officer's head, Brown wrote to Simpson, but not without invitation. "Such documents are highly interesting," Simpson had written to Brown on July 27, 1822, "and I have to request the favour of your communicating from time to time the result of your enquiries in regard to the Country and Trade, as information on these topics are very important to the Interests of the Concern."[224] Brown was merely taking Simpson up on his invitation. What could be wrong with that? "Finding that it would be impossible this winter," Brown wrote to Simpson, "to extend our knowledge of the Babine Country and the adjacent tribes further than from such information that can be collected from those Indians who visit the Fort, I formed the Idea of descending the River in the course of the Summer to the Sea or as far as it deemed prudent or any advantage to be gained."[225] Though Stuart had turned him down, he did not know Simpson. Brown did. He had spent the winter with him at Fort Wedderburn and may have had more accurate reading of Simpson's thoughts than Stuart.

If Stuart knew about this correspondence—and he probably did because all mail went through his hands—he may have seen it as a threat. No one likes a subordinate to have a direct and private correspondence with his superior officer. The suspicion alone can be poisonous.

Differences not only of opinion but also of personality were opening up between the two men. Stuart was thinking of his resources, the number of men he had and the cost of such an expedition. His eyes were on today's problems and today's horizons. Brown was thinking ahead to the heavy damage competition from the coast would do to the HBC's trade in the interior. His horizons were tomorrow's and the future.

12

Alarms and Excursions

1823-1824

"No greater misfortune could have befallen the Company."

John Stuart, October 24, 1823

A coolness grew in the hitherto warm relationship between William Brown and John Stuart. This resulted in part from Brown's insistence that the trade would be ruined if they did not reach the Forks and establish a post there. He wanted to fight to protect the HBC's monopoly of the interior. But there was probably more. Although Brown was number two man in New Caledonia, Stuart felt the difference between being a partner in the North West Company and an employee of the HBC. Perhaps he also felt that Brown, with his personal connection with Governor Simpson, was being preferred. Despite self-serving warm words in post journals, many Nor'Westers may well have resented the union. The cultures of the two companies may not have merged as smoothly as it sometime appears.

The quarrel between the two men, as with many such quarrels, began with something small. In January 1823, Brown had written to Stuart complaining about the pit saw and other items Fort St. James had supplied him. He implied—or Stuart may have thought he implied—that this was the deliberate act of the St. James blacksmith. Stuart replied ten days later:

> Your letter lies before me and, having observed the contents of it, you cannot, I imagine, think the worse of me if I answer it in the same strain in which I conceive it to be written.... With regard to the Pit Saw, the first article mentioned, no one that saw it can doubt that it was in every respect as good as new and in perfect good order when delivered to you.[226]

Stuart then complained that Brown was asking for too much. Brown answered Stuart's complaints to his own satisfaction and added a few more of his own. Such is the way quarrels grow.

Two weeks later, Stuart complained that the quantity of furs received from Fort Kilmaurs did not agree with the itemized list of what Brown said he had sent, and that part of what he had sent was defective anyway. Brown defended himself with spirit on February 10. "Though an Enemy of Cavaling [caviling] and altercation," he wrote, "I am fully of opinion that in Public business it is always best to be Explicit and come to the Point."[227] He said he had counted the skins several times and had also asked one of his men to check the numbers. Some skins must, he asserted, have been stolen en route to Fort St. James.

One other cause of contention was that, in addition to the official post journals, correspondence books and accounts, Brown kept a personal journal. Governor Simpson had complained of Brown's writing this at Fort Wedderburn and warned him he would have to give it up. Stuart reminded him that such a journal was the property of the HBC. Brown stated that he had made available all official documents for his inspection: "but in regard to the Private Memorandums or Journal (if it may be so called) which I kept at other times, it was solely written for my own use and as such is altogether unfit for Public inspection. I am therefore sorry that I cannot comply with your Request by sending it."[228] Stuart, a stickler for the rules, did not approve.

On March 1, Stuart sat down and wrote to Brown:

> I know you have had your share of troubles and that there is no one who is more desirous to forward the general Interest. Such you always appeared to me and such I represented you and however much we may differ in opinion on some points and whatever you may think of me, I have too much respect for myself ever to stoop to the means of acquiring either fame or fortune by misrepresenting others.[229]

Brown replied a few days later that

> nothing but a sincere wish to avoid every kind of altercation prevents me from answering them at present. For a continuation of such a correspondence can be of no advantage to the business, whereas it may be very detrimental by forwarding the views of the intriguing and designing, who for this length of time have been endeavouring to embroil the Department by sowing dissension amongst the Gentlemen. I therefore take this opportunity of stating that I will take no notice of any Letters addressed to me, further than what is necessary for forwarding the business.[230]

And there, for the time being, their relations remained. Business-like, courteous, but decidedly cool.

A pair of fishermen standing alongside a salmon trap at the outlet of Stuart Lake. A bushfire can be seen in the distance.

Dogs were an essential part of life in an HBC fort in New Caledonia. They were used primarily as working animals, each being able to pull a sled with a load weighing 180 pounds. Simpson wrote that three active dogs could run ten miles an hour drawing a cariole (light vehicle), a passenger, a driver behind and fifty pounds of luggage. "At this place, where so much hauling is to be done," Stuart wrote in agreement, "it is more Dogs than Men that are required. One man with good Dogs will perform more labour than three with bad ones."[231] Dogs, though, were often in short supply. When Stuart arrived back at McLeod's Lake in the autumn of 1823, he brought with him in the canoes thirty-three much-needed fully grown dogs, four young ones and two bitches. When the men were short of food, they could spare little to feed their dogs, who sometimes starved to death. Any man who killed and ate a dog while on the trail, as some did, ran the risk of a heavy fine. One of the men once broke the leg of Brown's white dog coming downhill, and then killed and ate it. Brown was not pleased and fined him.

Brown bred dogs. In the winter of 1823, he mentioned that he had kept five bitches for breeding and bemoaned the fact that Waccan was taking his large dog back to Fort St. James. This meant he had to trade precious trade goods with the local Dakelh people to acquire more of their dogs. Moreover, as the New Year's celebrations showed, dogs ran the risk of being eaten. Canadians in particular saw them as delicacies, likening them to mutton, and they ate them gleefully on festive occasions. Sentiment did not seem to play any part in their dealings with man's best friend.

Saturday, February 1, 1823. The weather was clear and cold, though good for travelling. The fort was busy, with Pierre and Baptiste squaring logs and others procuring firewood. Waccan and a party arrived with 400 medium-sized white fish, approximately 6 per man per day.

Then, suddenly a crisis erupted. A group of Dakelh men from the nearby village of Nah tell cuss came into the main building of the fort. Several pushed their way into Brown's own room. This vexed him, not only because he was about to sit down to supper but also because, his room being small, he had repeatedly asked Indigenous traders to stay in the hall when they visited the fort. He asked them to leave. When they didn't, he took one of them by the arm and led him out of the room. Then he shut the door. The man banged it open again into Brown's face and barged back in. Brown tried to push him out again. The man's father then stepped into the room, seized Brown's capot, pulled out his knife and was about to stab him when Waccan moved in and took away the knife. Brown broke the handle of a broom and used it to defend himself. A fist and kick fight ensued, which ended with Brown and Waccan subduing their attackers, pushing them out of the room and calming everyone down.

Brown then gave the Dakelh men in the hall a lecture saying that the HBC

> did not come amongst them for the purpose of quarrel-
> ing, but to supply them with such Articles as they were
> in need of, that them [they] and their families might
> live more comfortable than they have been in the habit
> of doing. However, though our intentions were of the
> most friendly nature, still we could not allow any Indian
> to insult us or dare us with impunity.[232]

The men then went away, threatening to return that night and attack the fort with arms. Brown placed two men on guard all night and gave each of the men a musket or a gun so as to be ready for any trouble that might arise. The night, though, remained quiet.

The next afternoon, Brown sent for Caupin, the Chief at Nah tell cuss, to find out what had been behind this affray. The Chief told him to calm down. The men had been village troublemakers and had indeed tried to stir up an attack by making false statements about what had happened. The Chief told Brown he had given a true account of the affair to the village.

"Those Indians," Brown wrote, "who are not related to them seem particularly pleased at what has happened, as that family is in the habit of threatening the whole Village with arms when the least dispute takes place."[233]

STUART LEAVES THE DISTRICT, AND RETURNS

In the summer of 1823, Stuart left the district to go east to York Factory. It was not clear whether he would be returning. He was tired and perhaps disenchanted with the new order. He thought, perhaps hoped, he would be going somewhere calmer. Before leaving, he repeated his disapproval of liaisons between HBC men and Indigenous women. He also had made it clear to the officers that he did not want them to leave their forts without good reason. But would they obey? Perhaps some of them were quietly pleased he was leaving. Stuart left Brown in charge and told the other traders to follow his instructions. Many, perhaps even Brown himself, believed he would succeed Stuart as superintendent. Stuart sent James Murray Yale back to Fort George and Baptiste Beignoit and Belonie Duplanté to go with him as labourers, joining the two Dakelh men already there.

Both Stuart and Brown were courteous to each other when he left. Brown wrote to him on May 6, "Did I think that any thing that I could write would have any influence with you, I would endeavour to prevail upon you to return again to New Caledonia, but I am doubtful my efforts would have any effect."[234] Stuart was no less gracious. "I am now leaving New Caledonia," he replied to Brown a few days later,

> perhaps never to return, but whether I do or not I will ever feel a kind of fatherly affection for the place as a child of my own rearing and though I have both last winter and Summer met with rebuffs I little expected, I will on leaving the Department forget that any difference, even of opinion, ever existed. I have not the vanity to think myself always in the right for experience often convinces me of the contrary.... And now, wishing you health & prosperity, I will beg leave to conclude.[235]

After crossing Athabasca and Rupert's Land, Stuart met Simpson for the first time at Norway House and was immediately impressed by him. He went on to York Factory, where Simpson persuaded—or directed—him to return to New Caledonia.

Stuart left York Factory with heavily laden canoes for his return to New Caledonia on July 23, 1823. Joining Stuart was John Tod, Brown's shipmate from the *Edward and Ann*. Simpson was reportedly sending Tod to New Caledonia because he considered him indolent and self-satisfied in his previous post and he thought that the rigours of New Caledonia would smarten him up. Simpson didn't like Tod, a feeling Tod fully reciprocated.

STUART RESUMES COMMAND

After leaving the Rocky Mountain Portage, Stuart and his party moved up (that is to say, southwards) the Parsnip River towards McLeod's Lake. Brown went to meet him at the Thorn River on October 24 and brought terrible news. Thinking there was not much for him to do at Fort George, Yale had left his post there on August 3, leaving behind his country wife, as well as Beignoit, Duplanté and the two Dakelh men. When he returned, he found to his horror that the two Dakelh men had murdered Beignoit and Duplanté, leaving their hacked-up bodies for dogs to eat, stolen a little property and then fled. This crime—the first murder of white men in New Caledonia—shocked the entire HBC community. Stuart was appalled and deeply shaken. Showing his anxiety, he wrote a number of times that "no greater misfortune could have befallen the Department."[236] Stuart saw the murders as a major disaster for the HBC's trade.

Grumbling about how matters had deteriorated since he had left in the spring, Stuart now set about reasserting his control. He reallocated the officers and men among the various posts. He confirmed Brown at Fort Kilmaurs and authorized him to make a trading expedition to Simpson's River though only if he could do this without leaving "the other Establishments to perdition [utter destruction]—without an Outfit—without provisions.… It would be equally unfair to sacrifice the other Posts for the sake of any one particular Post as it would be to sacrifice one Post for the sake of the others."[237] (So did Brown have permission or not?)

Stuart sent George McDougall to take charge of the fort at Alexandria, farther south. On the way, he was to make a thorough investigation of the Fort George murders and take appropriate action. Yale and others wanted a pre-emptive attack on the Dakelh people to teach them a lesson. Stuart was not so sure. If the murders were premeditated, he asked, why did they strike while Yale was away and just before he was due back at the fort? And why was so little property stolen? He had no wish, he declared, to punish the innocent together with the guilty. McDougall reported back that he found no evidence of any involvement of Dakelh people other than the two murderers themselves. He lectured them severely and told them they could prove their innocence by executing the murderers, who had long fled, themselves. He could not, though, find out why the murders had been committed. Stuart suspected a more personal explanation, and he was right.

But he didn't find out the reason until the following February. He then learned from several sources that while Yale had been away, his country wife had conducted a liaison with one of the Dakelh men at the fort, a former lover. Beignoit had found out and threatened to tell Yale. The man had then persuaded the other to join him and together they killed Beignoit and Duplanté to silence them. Stuart had not authorized Yale to leave his post and held him indirectly responsible for the murders. Whatever Stuart thought, Yale was perhaps too useful a trader to be dispensed with and was allowed to remain. But this murder, as Stuart had feared, unsettled relations between Indigenous and non-Indigenous people.

Stuart clearly thought the management of New Caledonia had deteriorated while he had been away. He blamed Brown, without absolving the others. He wrote to James McDougall:

> I found that during my short absence my views had been thwarted in every Instance while a disregard to my instructions, though the only one authorized by the Company to issue any, had very nigh ruined the Department, and now happen what will! Three years of the best management will not replace it in as favourable a situation as I left it last May. And to have rather obeyed the directions of Mr. Brown than [me] I consider to be more criminal in you than in any other, for you knew that he had but the nominal superintendence while the responsibility remained with me. And that when I referred you to him, it could not be to obey any directions that might be in contradiction to my own but in the event of Circumstances occurring that I had not either foreseen or thought unnecessary to mention.[238]

This was perhaps a "while the cat's away, the mice will play" situation. Moreover, Stuart had indeed put Brown in charge of the district and was now blaming him for what he thought was going wrong. More likely, the dispute may have reflected a difference of management style between the old Nor'Wester and the HBC cultures. Then, as now, the merging of two cultures after a takeover brings its problems.

Since the murders at Fort George had happened when the officer in charge was absent, Stuart became even more nervous about officers leaving their posts. He complained about Brown's having left his post and the consequences he saw resulting from it. Perhaps Stuart was worrying too much. Whenever a messenger from Kilmaurs was overdue, he feared that Brown had gone off again to Simpson's River or, worse, that the fort had been destroyed and everyone there had been slaughtered. Happily, though, all was well. His subordinates, even if they were not always obedient, knew what they were doing.

Then Stuart addressed the vexing problem of country wives. When he arrived back, he found that his instructions on this subject had also been disobeyed. The HBC had a tradition of allowing men to take country wives. The North West Company, at least in New Caledonia under Stuart, had not. He wrote that he always believed that liaisons with Indigenous women would lead to trouble and ruin the trade. He attributed the murder of the two men at Fort George to Yale's taking a country wife, which confirmed his thinking. In October 1823, without banning it outright, Stuart explicitly restated his rule. He laid down that "All Gentlemen in Charge Keeping Native Women not the wife of a Servant or allowing others to do it, under the pretense of their doing the Work of the Fort" pay for their board at double the usual rate that is to be charged for the wife of a servant.[239] He also stated that any woman, the reputed wife of a servant, who left her country husband's bed and went to live with Indigenous people should not be allowed back into a fort.

In February 1824, Stuart wrote in the post journal:

> It is long since I apprehended that too free Intercourse with the Carrier Women would be the ruin of the Company's affairs in this quarter. The North West Company provided in a great measure against it by prohibiting any of them from being taken into keeping or suffered to reside in the Company Forts, and on my being transformed into a Chief Factor of the Honourable Hudson's Bay in the very first letter I ever wrote to the Governor and Council of the Northern Factory I apprized them of the evil tendency of sending people into this quarter who had no women of their own, and without presuming to say that the prevalent custom lately introduced into Western Caledonia, not only in opposition to my orders but altogether unknown to me, of taking Native Women into keeping, is owing the Murder of their Servants and the almost total ruin of their trade.
>
> I would fain [be pleased to] hope that the Governor & Council of the Northern Factory will publish a law prohibiting the admission of Native Women into their Forts. Mr. Yale has already discarded of himself the one he had and so has Mr. McBean. But there are still two at Kilmaurs who in 1821 [1822] deserted their husbands' beds & left the Company's Fort [one of them was Josette] but was afterwards admitted in direct opposition to my wishes.[240]

Brown was living by HBC customs, though not perhaps by Stuart's. Josette gave birth to a daughter, whom Brown named Margaret. Stuart tolerated the presence of the women at a fort to perform their necessary work, but seemed to think he could also forbid, or at least limit, country marriages. In his report on Western Caledonia in August 1824, Stuart wrote that the number of women maintained in the district was never great but rather too few for the labor required for them. During the previous winter, he wrote, they "amounted to five half breeds and two native women and six children. Of those Mr. Brown has a half breed woman, and a native woman (presumably Josette) and child that in 1821 lived with him and still remains at the Fort under his protection."[241] Is Stuart hinting that Brown may have been conducting a relationship with a woman other than Josette? The 1825 district report stated that nine officers, one of whom was Brown, had wives. Together, they had two boys over seven and eleven children under seven, eight of whom were girls.

John Tod

Stuart sent Tod to work as a clerk in Fort George under Yale. While at York Factory, he had been warned about Tod, probably by Simpson, and advised to be cautious of him. As Simpson had observed, Tod, though able, was not altogether a model employee. He had a violent streak in him, perhaps not surprising in an age when fists and boots were two of the few readily available tools to enforce discipline. He also had a tendency to eccentricity that sometimes manifested itself in insubordination.

In the summer of 1824, Stuart sent Tod to McLeod's Lake, where he spent nine years as the clerk in charge. During his time there, Tod found time to read the many books the previous trader had left. Often

John Tod as a young man. He was able, but could be eccentric and insubordinate, sometimes violent. He later rose to a position of importance in the newly established colony of Vancouver Island.

lonely, he took up the fiddle—he already played the flute—to while away his hours. He also enjoyed the companionship of a "'singing girl' without whom life in such a wretched place … would be altogether insupportable."[242] She sang while he played the flute. She also gave him a child. Many years later, Tod would play a part in the colonial government of Vancouver Island.

Brown's Journey to Hotset

In December 2023, Chol led sop, the Wet'suwet'en chief at Hotset, arrived at Kilmaurs and asked Brown to go to his village to trade furs. He declared that if Brown did not go he would trade all his furs to a party of Atnahs who were expected at his village at the time of a coming feast.

Brown was now in a quandary. On the one hand, he did not want to miss the opportunity to acquire furs, but he knew he could only take a small party there, putting them all at serious risk should anything go wrong. He also wanted to meet directly with the Atnahs in the hopes of trading with them and encourage them to trade more with the HBC and less with the traders from the coast. It might also be useful, he told himself, to become acquainted with the Atnah Chiefs and, perhaps more importantly, for them to get to know him. This could be useful if he were to journey to the coast. On the other hand, he knew that Stuart would not approve. The cautious Stuart had already turned down his suggestions for journeying eastwards towards the coast and did not like officers to leave their posts. In spite of that, Brown decided to take the risk.

Brown, accompanied by a small party, arrived at Hotset on December 2. With a population of approximately 750, Hotset, about eighty miles southwest of Kilmaurs, was, he wrote, the most populous of all the Dakelh villages. It had about twenty Chiefs of various seniorities. Since the Atnah party had not yet appeared, the Chiefs there persuaded him to stay for four nights. He agreed on the condition he could trade with the villagers while waiting for their arrival.

Four days passed. Just as he was about to leave, news came that the Atnahs were at hand and would arrive in the morning. Brown decided to cross the river and camp in the woods about a mile from the village. The following morning, with three others, he went and traded in the village and then went a mile beyond, to where the Atnahs were engaged in ceremonies preparatory to coming into Hotset. The Atnah party consisted of seven or eight Chiefs and approximately thirty to forty young men, well armed with muskets or fowling pieces. Several also had pistols. What would they have thought when they saw Brown and his few companions coming towards them? It was a moment of high danger for Brown. But all went well. "They are a set of good-looking people, "he wrote, "and are much fairer than either the Carriers or Indians on the East side of the Mountains. Two or three of them had Blankets of 3 ½ Points and numbers of them Cloth, but both are much inferior to ours."[243]

His conversation with them was limited because no one in his small party spoke the Atnah language, and the Atnahs did not speak English or the Dakelh language. Brown recorded that

> I therefore made them a present of a little Gartering and Beads and took my leave of them. On my return to the Village [Hotset] I found that part of the residents and Atnahs of the Forks had Quarreled in consequence of some Gambling business on which account part of the latter had fled across the River, and the remainder were in the Village with their Guns in their hands and seemingly ready to fire. But none of them offered the least Violence or insolence to me.[244]

As far as Brown could judge, between 1,500 and 2,000 Indigenous people had gathered at Hotset for the feast. "The whole of whom behaved with the greatest decorum so that I had not a word with them," he wrote, "neither did I lose the most trifling article. But my situation was extremely dangerous, and I had to act with the greatest degree of caution. For a very small mistake would, in all probability, prove fatal to the party."[245]

He left them, rejoined his companions across the river and started on the journey back to Fort Kilmaurs. When Brown reached Kilmaurs, he sent his report of December 15 to Stuart with misgivings. He expressed the hope that even if Stuart did not approve of his journey, he would not altogether condemn it. He waited anxiously for the reply. He was right. Stuart did not approve. "I then opened your letter," Stuart wrote to him,

> and however much I may disapprove the measures you adopted, and I certainly think them reprehensible, I am not disposed to think it arose from any wish of distressing the rest of the Department; but rather from a laudable desire on your part to perform more than the existing circumstances of the case could lead to expect. But had [you] considered the consequences that would result from a miscarriage and that success could not warrant the adoption of a measure in itself wrong, I am sure you would not risk your own life and the safety of those men committed to your care, for the vanity of adding a few Skins (not one of which would be lost to the Company) to the returns of Kilmaurs.[246]

Stuart went on to say he was disappointed with the returns from the Babine district and that he now firmly believed that the sooner the Babine country and Fort Kilmaurs were abandoned the better. They had given it a fair trial and perhaps it was now time to close it. "That cursed place," he wrote to his old friend James McDougall, "has caused me more trouble and anxiety in the space of not fifteen months it has been established, than the rest of Western Caledonia during the seventeen years it has been established."[247] Nevertheless, he told Brown, since the governor and council had appointed him to Fort Kilmaurs, it wasn't up to him to close it.

Stuart had reason to be discouraged. The winter was one of the harshest they had ever known. The spirit of wine in the thermometer, he wrote, registered fifty-two degrees below freezing. The feet of a clerk and of another man froze because they were out travelling without snowshoes. One of them was likely to lose his toes. Stuart also complained his eyesight was failing and he could no longer write at night. Moreover, both the salmon and the whitefish failed. "We scarcely take a fish & live miserably," he wrote. "I have never known the Fraser's Lake Salmon to be so bad. And the few brought here from the Babine Country are to my taste worse. I cannot swallow a morsel of them."[248]

Discontent and More Alarms

In addition to obeying (or disobeying) Stuart's orders about liaisons with Indigenous women, HBC men in New Caledonia had other reasons to be discontented. Simpson had embarked on a program to cut costs. He reduced not only the number of employees but also the supplies of those that remained. He thought sails in the boats that were by now being used in New Caledonia were unnecessary because the men could paddle, which was better for them. He didn't use a tent on his own travels, so why should the men have tents on theirs? So, no tents. And he resented the expenditure on provisions for the families of men in the forts, and so, like Stuart, he made some attempts to stop men having country wives.

On March 10, 1824, another serious incident occurred at Fort Kilmaurs. A man from a group of Dakelh people from Fort St. James who were about the fort had gone into the fort's kitchen and stolen tobacco and a steel from Joseph Whitman's fire-bag. Caught, he was kicked out of the fort. Shortly after, several Dakelh men pushed their way into Brown's room. More flooded into the hall. Brown, who was trying to finish writing a letter, said he would come out shortly and see what the matter was. Suddenly he heard Whitman call out an alarm in the hall. Brown rushed out. He saw his men grabbing their muskets. Under the mistaken idea that one of the Dakelh men had stabbed someone, he ordered them to fire and ran back into his room for the double purpose of turning out the men still there and to get his firearm. While he was doing this, a gun went off, but the shot, luckily being high, did not harm anyone. Since the intruders were now flying from the hall in all directions, he told his men not to fire.

Brown then assembled the men to find out what had happened. Apparently, one of the Dakelh men had struck Whitman in the face, momentarily stunning him. This, it later turned out, was to be the sign for a general massacre. They had particularly wanted to murder Brown in his room. They faltered, though, when they found him alone and wanted to draw him into the hall to kill him there with axes. Their plan miscarried because Whitman had given the alarm quickly enough for his companions to seize their muskets. None of the intruders had guns, although a few had hatchets concealed beneath their robes.

When questioned, the Elders from the nearby village of Nah tell cuss told Brown they were appalled at what the young men from Fort St. James had been intending to do and said they had no prior knowledge of the attack. If this attack had been premeditated, Brown concluded, they would have come better armed and would have attacked when the men were dispersed not when they were gathered together so close to their muskets. Even though it appeared to have been an eruption of spontaneous anger, Brown mounted guard at night and told all his men to carry pistols and bayonets in their belts.

RECONCILIATION

Stuart and Brown now buried their differences and became friends again. Stuart commented in the post journal that he was pleased with Brown's conduct of late and had full confidence in him "now that he seems to be aware that practical experience is preferable to theoretic knowledge."[249] Brown wrote a letter to Stuart that pleased him so much it seemed to repair any bad feelings that may have existed. Since Brown's letters to him in the records at this time concerned mundane matters of business, it is possible that Brown had written him a separate, warmer letter that has not survived. "To say I perused it with pleasure," Stuart replied,

> would fall short of the sensations I felt on perceiving how different it was from our correspondence of the preceding year—always painful to my feelings. It revived in my mind a tender recollection of your letters from Fraser's Lake that used to delight me so much, and now that we once more appear to have no difference in opinion I flatter myself with the hopes that we shall continue to remain so.[250]

Brown, not to be outdone in civilities, replied that Stuart's letter "gave rise to sensations which my breast had been a stranger to for this last eighteen months. But as a perfect understanding is now established, I hope it will continue, for which purpose no exertion on my part will be omitted and I shall feel happy if I can only meet with your approbation."[251]

In July 1824, Simpson moved Stuart to Athabasca and appointed William Connolly to replace him as HBC superintendent in New Caledonia. Connolly was one of the Nor'Westers that Governor Williams and Brown had seized at the Grand Rapid in June 1819. Not having a warrant for his arrest, they had allowed him to proceed on his journey. It was Connolly who had doubled back and watched them from across the river, from where he sent the warning upstream to his colleagues. Connolly was altogether a harder man than Stuart. He may not have forgotten or forgiven Brown for his part in the ambush at Grand Rapid.

13

Disaster

1825-1826

"I am rejoiced to find that you are preparing to undertake a Voyage of Discovery towards the Coast."

George Simpson to William Brown, April 4, 1825

Brown had not by any means abandoned his idea that the traders from the coast posed a threat—ruin even—to the HBC's trade in the interior. He argued that the HBC should send an expedition to the Atnah villages on the Babine River, go down the river to the Forks and then on to the coast. We may speculate that mixed in with his intention to protect the interests of the HBC was a desire to make his name as an explorer. One of the books in his library was *Travels in Africa* by fellow Scotsman Mungo Park. This best-selling book, published in 1799, and one of the first travel exploration books, described Park's travels in West Africa. For Brown, it could have been inspirational.

Brown had made preparations for a journey to the sea in 1824, but for various reasons—including sickness—had postponed the trip until the following year. He now had the highest authorities in the HBC supporting his proposal. In March, the committee in London had written to Simpson saying that having HBC traders operating on the coast would strengthen the hand of the British government in the discussions it was having with the Russian government.[252] Following this, in April, Simpson wrote to Brown.

> I am rejoiced to find that you are preparing to undertake a Voyage of Discovery towards the Coast. It is an object of great moment that a friendly understanding should be established with the Natives as 'tis probable the Committee will direct that Posts be settled both in the Interior and on the Coast as far to the Northwards as far the British territorial rights extend, which we suppose to be about Latitude 60 and that a coasting trade will be entered into by Shipping connections with our Mainland business. We therefore look with much interest and anxiety to the result of your exertions and trust they will be crowned with success.[253]

Connolly told Brown in May that Simpson had written to him the previous September telling him it was important that

> every facility should be rendered Mr. Brown for the prosecution of his Discoveries down the Babine River. The Russian Settlements can be no great distance from where he went last year. The Committee and Government are anxious for every information that can be collected in respect to that Country and if Mr. Brown could even push his way to the sea, it would be highly gratifying.[254]

Simpson gave Brown permission to come out of New Caledonia to York Factory the following year. Nevertheless, for this summer of 1825, he instructed him to embark on his Voyage of Discovery to the Sea, as it was called. The heavy weight of expectation now lay on Brown's shoulders. He knew from his winter in Athabasca that the unsentimental Simpson was not likely to tolerate failure.

Preparations for the Voyage to the Sea—May and June, 1825

In the early spring of 1825, Brown went on an excursion up the Babine River as far as the Atnah village of Chil do cal. (He gave one hint that he might have gone as far as Weep Sim, but since he left no record of this journey, we cannot be sure.) While there, he had come to the conclusion that it would be an easy journey downriver to the Forks. And then perhaps to the ocean?

The spring of 1825 was a busy time at Fort Kilmaurs. While Brown was making preparations for the expedition to the coast—waiting for the extra men needed for the journey, assembling the provisions and the like—he continued with the fort's routines. At the beginning of May, he was at McLeod's Lake having discussions with Connolly. Charles Ross, in charge of Fort Kilmaurs during his absence, continued with the building work at the fort. The men were working on a new house. Baptiste Arionga and Duncan Livingston (murdered a few years later) hauled back logs from the woods, cut them, erected the walls and roofed the house. Then they had to collect stones for the chimney, mud it and hope it would stay up. In mid-May, Baptiste Arionga fell ill. He said it was a rupture, supposedly a recurrence of an old injury but Ross, writing the post journal, wrote that it was "really the P–x."[255] He felt better in a few days, though, and finished making the wheelbarrow he had been working on. He started on the door of the house, but soon fell sick again. Then Livingston had to be confined to the house because he had put a nail into his foot. Brown arrived back at

Kilmaurs on May 24, together with five men, four women and five children. Nail in his foot or not, Livingston soon entered into a country marriage with one of the women.

In June 1825, Pierre Chrysologue Pambrun arrived at Fort Kilmaurs to be the new clerk. Waccan, who was going to accompany Brown on his Voyage of Discovery, came with him. Pambrun brought mail with him, including from friends in Europe "which being of an agreeable nature," Brown wrote, "place this amongst the few happy days we enjoy in these dreary wilds."[256] While waiting, Waccan made himself useful by making furniture—a bed for Brown's room and a table and cassette for Pambrun. On August 2, they had just completed one more chimney when it collapsed top to bottom as a result of the rain pouring in from the top. This was a bad omen.

Personal Disaster

At Kilmaurs, Brown was still making preparations for his expedition when disaster struck. He fell seriously ill. The first sign that anything was wrong was noted on May 13, when the clerk John McDonell wrote to him saying he was sorry to hear he was unwell. On May 19, Brown excused his bad handwriting by saying he had rheumatism in his right arm that nearly prevented him from holding a pen. "My health is much better since I wrote you last," Brown wrote to McDonell in June, "but I am tormented with a most inveterate Rheumatism in my Legs and Arms, which gives me no peace, neither night nor day."[257] Ross wrote in the Fort Kilmaurs post journal on July 5 that, "Mr. Brown continues indisposed and is severely afflicted with the Rheumatism."[258] By that Friday, he was unable to get out of his bed. On July 16, he had to postpone the Voyage of Discovery, though he had firm hopes he would recover quickly and be able to carry on. He continued to collect supplies and asked Fort St. James for calico, flannel and cloth, with red being the colour the Indigenous traders most favoured. By July 21, though, he had lost the use of his legs and could get out of bed only with the help of crutches.

Consequently—probably to no one's surprise—Brown had to give up his plan of journeying to the coast.[259] His health went from bad to worse. On August 8, writing on his behalf, Ross reported that "Mr. Brown, in addition to his other complaints, is now troubled with a pain & dimness in both Eyes. So that it is really painful to behold the condition he is in at present, being not only completely deprived of the use of his Legs, but also threatened with the loss of eyesight.[260] Although it would have been obvious to everyone for a while that he was in no condition to lead the proposed expedition, it was only now that he formally cancelled it.

And it wasn't just his health that had imperiled the expedition. Brown had also been worried about the safety of travel in the Atnah country. The Dakelh and the Atnah peoples were in a state of conflict that summer, with murders, alarms and general hostility. The salmon were late coming up the Babine and Simpson's Rivers. Whenever this happened, the Dakelh men assumed the Atnah men were barricading the river at the Forks to prevent the salmon from coming upstream. On June 25, Brown learnt that a large Dakelh war party was heading down the Simpson's River towards Hotset. Travelling through these lands might be dangerous.

While Brown was ill that summer, the men he had collected at Fort Kilmaurs to go with him on the expedition were doing little. This was a serious problem for the cost-conscious company. To try and make good use of them, Brown sent a number of them to build a good horse track from Fraser's Lake to Fort St. James.

Chief Factor Connolly warned Brown that the council would be extremely disappointed that the Voyage of Discovery to the Sea had not happened.[261] Brown understood this. He replied that it might be wise to have a successful journey to report to the council when it met in the summer of 1826. He suggested that early in the following year he could make an attempt to reach the Forks, going by way of the Babine River: "For if it should so happen that I have not the means to go as far as the Forks in the Winter after not being able to go as directed in the Summer, it will most undoubtedly give rise to remarks, which tho' unjust may be both disagreeable & prejudicial to me."[262] Here then is the genesis of his next journey. Brown needed a success.

Connolly knew that Brown's failure would be held against him as well as against Brown. He was after all the chief factor for New Caledonia. He now appears to be trying to put as much space between himself and Brown as he could. His criticisms grew stronger, both of Fort Kilmaurs and of Brown personally. He wrote that Fort Kilmaurs had not proved itself: "It has been a continual source of expense and vexation to the District from the number of hands that have always been kept about it to the great inconvenience and frequently prejudice of the other posts."[263]

Having criticized Fort Kilmaurs, and by implication Stuart, whose idea it had been to establish the fort, he carries on to criticize Brown. On October 30, he wrote that Brown had been unable to proceed on his voyage as a result of illness.

> Although it is much improved from what it was during the summer, it having confined him to his bed for the space of three months & totally incapacitated him from attempting the Voyage of Discovery upon which he was

ordered, and for which every preparation was made in the spring at an expense of £376 in wages to extra servants who were left inland for the purpose of accompanying him.

That Mr. Brown was unable to perform this service I have not the least doubt. But I am much of opinion that it might have been entrusted to the management of Messrs. Yale, Pambrun & Ross, assisted by Waccan, the Interpreter, & the men originally intended for that voyage. To suppose these Gentlemen incapable of conducting an operation of this kind ... is to suppose them good for nothing at all and unfit to serve the Company. Thus it should appear from the Circumstance of them having been kept idle the whole summer is Mr. Brown's opinion of them.

The men, eleven in number, were also kept idle or doing trifling jobs about the Babine Fort until the 12th August, when five of them were sent to clear the roads between Fraser's Lake & McLeod's Lake. The other seven remained at the Babine [Fort Kilmaurs].... From the period that Mr. Brown was confined to his bed & determined as he was that no one should head the intended voyage but himself, he might safely have given over all idea of it. Without being gifted with the power of divination, he could possibly have foreseen that his health would not be sufficiently established this season to enable him to perform a voyage in which sound health at least was required.[264]

Connolly criticized Brown's management and his demands for men and supplies. He commented that Brown's ideas about the district and how it should be managed must have been extraordinary if he thought he was entitled to one-third of all the men in it. He also criticized Brown for staying too long at Fort St. James: "From Mr. Brown's long intended stay at this place, one would infer that he is not very anxious for his own post.... I am clearly of opinion that every one should attach to the duties of their Post and that Mr. Brown would be much better occupied in conducting the affairs of his own than remaining here in idle speculation of what is going on."[265]

Connolly had now accused Brown of mismanagement, bad judgement and neglect of his duties. He may have thought he had insulated himself from criticism.

The year 1825 ended with Brown in an unsettled state. He would have understood there was a dark cloud hanging over him. The members of council and George Simpson were not forgiving people, and he needed to show he had complied with their directions. Brown thought he could perhaps redeem his reputation by being able to report he had actually stood on the point at the Forks where the two rivers merged. That at least would be something to show for his efforts when he went back east the following summer. But would it be enough?

Journey to the Land of the Atnahs—March 1826

Brown's plan was to go up the lake to the Babine River and then follow it down to the Forks. Then, if all went well, he could even go down river as far as the coast. After numerous setbacks and the need to recover fully from his illness, he was ready to start by March 1. That day the weather was clear and pleasant.

The next day, it snowed for most of the day. With ice still on the lake, the weather was not good for travelling, but that had never stopped Brown or any other HBC man from making a journey. He took Waccan with him. He reached the village of Nass Chick at 2:00 p.m. that afternoon, and, after negotiating with a guide and interpreter who needed persuading to stick to a previously established agreement to come with them, carried on at sunset. He camped at nine but found the men he had sent ahead had taken all the axes, and he had none to cut firewood. No fire: no warm food. He and his men would have had a cold and cheerless night.

After setting off at sunrise, he rejoined his men near the Small Lake [Nilkitwa]. The river here was open and turbulent so they had to use an extremely bad portage trail. That evening, they reached Ack koo shaw's river [Nichyeska], where they camped for the night. One of the men had traded goods for a dog, which they killed and cooked for a good supper.

They were now at the boundary between Dakelh and Atnah territory. Farther downriver were the principal Atnah villages of Need Chip, Chil do cal and Weep Sim.[266] In addition, as Brown noted, a few Atnah hamlets and salmon fishing camps lined the river.

Brown and his party made their way along the edge of the river. This was a rough path, sometimes along the riverbanks and sometimes up and over the cliffs along the river. They had to cut down trees to enable them to get through. Although the currents in the river were strong, Brown considered it would be possible to navigate the many rapids without particular difficulty. On March 7, the party reached the Atnah village of Need Chip, where they found fresh tracks but no people. Brown stayed to make breakfast there. Approximately forty villagers then appeared and told him—as

Gitksan smokehouses near a canyon in Kisgegas, British Columbia, 1920. Brown came close to here in his unsuccessful attempt to reach the Forks of the Skeena River. At the time it may have been called Weep Sim.

far as he could make out—that they had traded all their furs with traders from the coast. The Chief persuaded Brown to stay the night, giving him a dog, a piece of berry cake and salmon as presents.

Starting an hour after sunrise the following day and after walking for three hours, Brown and his men reached the large village of Chil do cal. Here Brown stayed "in my old residence of last spring," which shows he had reached Chil do cal at that time. The next day they left Chil do cal in clear and pleasant weather an hour after sunrise. A couple of hours later they reached the village of Weep Sim, approximately five miles farther on. Brown noted that this village had about three hundred men in their prime. Weep Sim could possibly have been the village later called Kisgegas, or close to it, which was not far from where the Babine River enters what is now called the Skeena River. The weather had turned and was now cloudy, with falling snow.

Quo em, the Chief at Weep Sim, greeted them and welcomed them with a ceremonial dance and protestations of his poverty, which Brown saw as a negotiating strategy. One of the Atnah men gave Brown sixteen prime marten pelts, three common martens and a dog. In return, Brown gave him a small moose skin, one scalping knife, half a dozen brass rings, half a dozen brass thimbles, six strings of beads, one flint, one gun, one awl, a half foot of tobacco, a half pound of powder, one pound of shot and eight balls.

Brown believed that the Babine River, with perhaps a few portages at difficult times of the year, was navigable. He thought a moderately loaded canoe could travel from Fort Kilmaurs to the upper Atnah villages (Weep Sim and Chil do cal) in three days and from there to the Forks in another three. Based on reports from Indigenous Chiefs, he estimated it would then take five days to reach the coast. Even allowing five days to come up for every one day going down, he believed a party could make the round-trip journey to the coast and back in no more than two months. Nevertheless, he also concluded that it was not a practicable route to take furs to the coast on a regular basis. For one thing, they would need a relay of horses to take goods over the Babine Portage. For another, the Babine River would never be reliable for regular canoe traffic, requiring a mixture of running rapids, portaging, poling and canoe pulling.

Brown then made the surprising decision to return to Fort Kilmaurs. The following day, Friday, March 10, he started back. "According to my resolution of last night," he wrote, "I this morning a little after daybreak directed our canoe homeward in place of proceeding on to the Forks as I had at first intended."[267] The reason he gave for turning back and not continuing down to the Forks was that the Atnah people on the Babine River had few or no furs and he did not want to waste the men's time going any farther. The traders from the coast had, he said, been there before him and gathered all the furs.

This explanation is unconvincing. After all, this was primarily a journey of exploration, not one of trading. The lack of furs should not, therefore, have been a reason to turn back. Possibly Brown was not fully over his illness and was feeling the fatigues of the journey. Furthermore, his men may not have been fully supportive. Strictly against his (and the council's) orders and regulations, they were trading on their personal accounts with the Indigenous people. Brown caught one man trading and angrily threw the man's goods into the river. He said that he would split with his sword the head of any man he saw trading. This effectively ended this practice but would not have made the men more well-disposed to him. Could they have become insubordinate? Might they have refused to continue downriver into unknown and possibly dangerous territory?

Whatever the reason, they were on their way back to Fort Kilmaurs. Working against the flow of a river in the first days of spring, full of breaking ice and early snow melt, the journey would have been wet and laborious. On the way back, they found that wolverines had raided one of their carefully built caches of salmon and stolen half. The party arrived back at Fort Kilmaurs on March 14 in over a foot of new snow that was, Brown wrote, very fatiguing to walk through.

BACK AT KILMAURS

At the fort, they found all in good order. That night, though, a two-and-a-half-year-old Indigenous boy struck his younger brother over his nose with a big stick. Tragically, the child died. Worse was to come.

Brown now turned his mind to his trip back across the country to York Factory. He started making up the packs and packing his cassette with his personal possessions and papers. He sent a party of nine men to go ahead to Fort St. James before the spring thaw made the journey more difficult. They took with them packs and his personal cassette.

Later that month, Brown happened to look into the "Necessary [privy] spring" at the fort to see if the water was rising in it. He noticed something that looked ominously like the body of a small baby. He called Ross to come over and tell him what he thought it was. He thought the same as Brown, as did another man. They dug the object out, cleaned it and found to their horror and distress that it was indeed the body of a new-born female child. "The left arm was stretched out," he wrote, "and the hand firmly clenched. Part of the neck was discoloured, and the upper part of the head forced in."[268] Brown had the poor mite wrapped in a piece of "embossed serge" and buried a little distance from the fort.

They interrogated all the women at the fort about whose baby it might have been. At first, the women said it might have been that of a woman who had passed by the fort in January. Then they spoke to Margaret or the Boiteuse (the lame), who said that Mr. Pambrun's woman had every appearance of being big with child till within a short time of her departure, at which time all her bigness was gone. Though "bigness" could, she agreed, have come from another cause, many had been suspicious at the time. Brown wrote that "she was then asked if it seemed to her to be still born, to which she answered no, but supposed from the state of its head that it had received a blow in the delivery, as if it had fallen on the ground for want of a person to receive it."[269] Moreover, her being with child had apparently been the subject of gossip at the fort—even among the men. (The fact that Brown had not been told of the rumour speaks to his relationship with his men.) "Whether this woman may be guilty or innocent," Brown wrote, "the present impressions are so strong against her that nothing will be able to do them away except that of her being delivered of a child since her arrival at St. James, which I sincerely hope for the sake of her reputation has been the case."[270] And there, with suspicions but no proof, the matter rested. The post journal shows no evidence that Pambrun was interrogated about any part he might have had in the matter.

In making this journey down the Babine River, Brown had attained two of his objectives—to find out if the Babine River was navigable and how long it would take to reach the coast, but he did not achieve his other goals, which were to explore the land of the Atnahs as far as the Forks and if possible to reach the coast. In truth, he had not gone much farther than he had before. If Brown's intention had been to reach the Forks to be able to report a success to Simpson and the council, he had failed.

Connolly for one was certainly not impressed. "Mr. Brown informs me," he wrote,

> that he has made an excursion from the Babine River to some of the Atnah villages. The only satisfaction he draws therefrom is ascertaining that the Babine River is navigable as far as he went. A circumstance which, considering the very short distance that River is from the Babine Fort [Kilmaurs], it is rather surprising should it not have been sooner known.[271]

Brown's years at Fort Kilmaurs were coming to an end. Soon it would be time to start the long journey by canoe across the country to York Factory. As he prepared for his departure, he continued to supervise the regular business of the fort—all the familiar routines of trading, finding food and cutting wood. The men cleared rubbish from the yard. Duncan Livingston was run over by his traineau and was coughing up blood. The snow started melting. Rooks started to make their reappearance after winter. The rivers and streams became ice-free. Time to leave.

14

Homeward Bound

1826

"I bade my old friend Mr. Tod and my little Girl adieu."

William Brown, May 11, 1826

By April 17, Brown was ready to depart. He lists as going to Fort St. James "my little Boy and Fanny."[272] And here the mystery about Brown's women deepens. Who was Fanny? We may speculate she might have been either Josette called by another name or another woman altogether. That Fanny was Brown's country wife is evidenced by a reference in the Fort St. James post journal in 1843. This recorded that Fanny Brown, widow of chief trader Brown, had died.[273] The questions remain unanswered.

The day before he left Fort Kilmaurs, Brown sat down and wrote in the fort's post journal. Noting that Kilmaurs had been his home for over four years, he said:

> A place which I found covered with strong woods, but now leave a plane [plain] with a good Fort upon it. Here I have spent some as anxious moments as ever I have done in my life. And for the greatest part of the last two summers I was confined to bed with sickness. Still, I leave the place with regrets as I never have had the means to carry the business to that degree of perfection which I often wished I could have done.

Referring to his plan of reaching the Forks, he continued, with a touch of asperity,

> while it is more than probable that some other will be amply furnished with the means, and accomplish that end, by which he will reap the fruits of my labour. But let him Voyage amongst strange Indians with very small parties. After which sit down and boast.[274]

He was not to know that, in a twist of poetic injustice, the person to do this would be Simon McGillivray, his Nor'Wester adversary from Fort Wedderburn.

The following day, Wednesday, April 19, he wrote his last entry in the Kilmaurs post journal:

> In the course of an hour, I leave this place, which I do with reluctance, for though I have been here for four years, I have not during that time had the Means of Carrying the trade as far, or procuring such returns, as I might have done.... These evils I hope will ere long be removed, and another will have an opportunity of doing what I never had. When this is accomplished let him not be too rash in attributing all the merit to himself until he compares the means he employed with those I have had.[275]

He then put his pen down and went out into the fort to bid farewell to the men remaining there and to the Indigenous people from the vicinity who had "assembled to see me go and seemed to be sorry that I was leaving them, which I was also myself from being so long amongst them."[276] After a short ceremony, he set off down the lake. He must have known he would never return.

Journey to York Factory

Brown reached Fort St. James a short time before sunrise four days later. Here he busied himself with preparations for his long journey. The fort would have been buzzing with men gumming canoes and pressing the furs into packs. Clerks would be finishing the official journals for Brown to take back to York. Many would also be finishing personal letters home, either to Scotland or Montreal. At Fort St. James, Brown would have crossed paths with young James Douglas, another former Nor'Wester with a reputation for not holding back from scraps. Douglas, who was to marry Connolly's daughter Amelia, rose through the ranks of the HBC to become Sir James Douglas and the founding father of British Columbia.

Brown left Fort St. James for McLeod's Lake on April 27. William McBean, going with them, wanted to hire a porter to carry his property. So Brown sent him, with Josette as his interpreter, to a large village to see if they could find someone to help, which they couldn't. This indicates that Josette was accompanying Brown at this stage of his journey, along with their son, Daniel. (There was no mention of anyone called Fanny.)

When Brown went to York Factory, he took with him the furs from the New Caledonia posts and some from the Columbia District farther to the south. The original plan had been for all the Columbia furs to be taken down to the coast, but because so many horses had died at Alexandria that winter James McDougall was bringing up part of the district's furs for Brown to take. Connolly wrote in the post journal on May 5:

> Every arrangement being completed both for the voyage to York Factory.... At 8:00 o'clock this Morning, Mr. James McDougall with 8 men took their departure from Stuart's Lake for ... Mcleod's Lake, where they will join Messrs Brown & McBean with the people already there, with whom they will proceed, under the command of Mr. Brown, for York Factory.[277]

Brown arrived at McLeod's Lake on May 3. Here he found his old shipmate John Tod in charge. Everyone there was well, although Tod and his men were short of food. While waiting for McDougall to arrive, the men gummed the canoes and made more paddles.

On May 11, the brigade, with Brown in charge, left McLeod's Lake by canoe for the long journey to York Factory. It was cloudy, with showers of hail and rain. "Some time before sun rise," Brown wrote, "I bade my old friend Mr. Tod & my little Girl adieu."[278] Could "my little Girl" have been his country wife, Josette? If this was her, the farewells between Josette on the one hand and Brown and Daniel on the other may well have been emotional. They would have known the chances of ever meeting again were low.

THROUGH THE ROCKY MOUNTAINS

After he left McLeod's Lake, Brown planned to go down the Parsnip River, join the Peace River and cross the Rocky Mountain Portage. This was the way he had come into New Caledonia and he knew what to expect. They would then journey down the Peace River to Fort Chipewyan. From there they would take the same route to York Factory that Brown had taken with George Simpson in 1821. The route would have been familiar, though the rigours of it nonetheless demanding.

The journey was arduous and fast. For much of the time, they travelled by night as well as by day and so were able to make good progress. By May 13, they reached the Rocky Mountain Portage. Twelve miles long, steep and bestrewn with fallen trees, this was the most difficult part of the whole journey. After trading with the Indigenous people at the portage, they carried on across it. Brown set four men to carry the canoes and the other thirteen men, using tumplines, to carry the packs of furs, each of approximately ninety pounds. He also shared the provisions he had acquired in the trade "so that they have plenty to make them live well for two days, which I am glad of, as the poor devils were much in want of it, on account of the badness of the salmon."[279] On May 16, Brown left two dozen skins, a

Peace River close to Fort Dunvegan. It was close to here, on the way back to York Factory and then Scotland in 1826, that Brown lost his little white dog.

leather capot, eight deer snares, some babiche and his copy of Mungo Park's *Travels in Africa* in a cache at Tete de Boeff. By the evening, with the help of two local Indigenous men and their wives, the canoe carriers and men had taken their loads over the second ridge.

ON TO YORK FACTORY

By May 20, they were over the portage and heading downstream to Fort Chipewyan. Seeing a bear close to the riverbank, Brown wrote he "put ashore to breakfast when I sent Portalance to attack him, which he did and killed him. Embarked the meat and proceeded on our Journey until sunset when we went ashore. Had supper & allowed the men to cook a Kettle of the Bear, after which we renewed our Voyage."[280]

They came to the deserted fort at Dunvegan and stopped to have supper before intending to drift downstream during the night. At one of these stops, Brown lost his little white dog. It went ashore with them but refused to be caught when the time came to leave. Brown eventually lost his patience and left it behind. They paddled and progressed downstream, sometimes slowly pushing against a wind, other times bumping over rocks in low water, all the while passing familiar places. At Fort Vermilion on May 24, Brown received mail being held there for him, including letters from his friends in Europe. His letters to them, he noted ruefully, seemed to have been lost somewhere en route.

At Fort Chipewyan they had been wondering where Brown was. "I cannot account for the non-arrival of C. Factor Brown," wrote James Keith, "& the other Gentlemen and Engagés (supposed to be about 14) whom by C. Factor Connolly's letter of last autumn we were desired to make provision for."[281] Brown and his party arrived not long before midnight on May 29 and found everyone in bed. Visiting this fort must have been a strange experience for him. For a couple of years, it had been enemy territory and the Nor'Westers there had had a warrant for his arrest. Now it was the major HBC fort in Athabasca. He could look out over the lake to Potato Island and see Fort Wedderburn, now abandoned and rotting away. His old adversaries of the North West Company—Simon McGillivray, Samuel Black, John George McTavish—had meanwhile become respected officers of the HBC.

Since he was joining other canoes that were on the point of leaving, he did not have much time to look around and reminisce. Hugh Faries, a former Nor'Wester, was travelling in the same brigade. "It has been settled to make two Light Canoes and two Loaded Canoes," Brown wrote. "Some of the former men, Mr. Keith, Smith & I take one passage and in the other Mr. Faries & McDougall with their families and baggage with my Desk and Cassette, as I can take nothing with me save my papers and a change. In the other 2 Canoes are to be embarked 48 pieces and Mr. McBean with my Little Boy."[282] Faries, therefore, had the carriage of Brown's personal journals.

The brigade left Fort Chipewyan on May 31, and continued on the journey. Landmarks slipped by: the entrance to Athabasca River on June 3 and Methye Portage on the 5th. They reached Île à la Crosse at 2:30 p.m. on June 7 and stayed for a day. Here they needed to gum the canoes and rearrange the cargo again. By now, the men were exhausted. "They are very much fatigued with the want of rest," Brown wrote, "not having had more than three hours sleep in the twenty-four and such hard marching [paddling] so that I am very doubtful they will not be able to hold out to Norway House."[283]

George Back, *Îsle à la Crosse, February 28, 1820*. This was one of the main HBC river forts in Athabasca.

Brown was not going to let them rest for long. At 2:00 a.m. on June 8, they set out again. They nearly came to disaster at Rapid Croche. In the thick fog that lay on the river, the foreman could not see the right channel to take and took the wrong one. They ran over the rapids and were within what he called an ace of being upset. "In doing which we had a most narrow escape," he wrote. "For if the Canoes had been two feet farther into the Cascade, we would all have gone to eternity."[284] Some rapids they ran: some they didn't. Sometimes their packs became wet, and they had to unpack and dry them out.

They reached Cumberland House on June 14. Here they met other brigades from posts on their way to York Factory. Brown mentions one brigade that carried twenty-two women and children who were leaving the country with their men folk. From these he would have learned all the news and gossip of the day. He learned, for example, that over a dozen settlers in the Red River Settlement had recently perished from starvation. Many of the others there had been obliged to kill their livestock for meat and eat the grain they had saved for seeding the next year's harvest.

By Friday, June 16, they were at the Grand Rapid and encamped at the entrance of the Saskatchewan River where it flowed into Lake Winnipeg. Brown doubtless would have recalled the two notable occasions he had been there before—Governor Williams's ambush and later when he and Simpson had heard about the merger. From there it was a straightforward journey to Norway House, and then on to York Factory, where the brigade arrived on June 24.

YORK FACTORY AND THE NORTHERN COUNCIL

York Factory was still the throbbing heart and thinking head of the HBC in North America. Here canoes arrived from forts in every corner of the HBC territory, with pelts and castoreum for loading onto a ship to be taken to the markets in Europe. And here also members of the Northern Council were assembling for their annual meeting.

The council met on June 26. George Simpson was there, of course, and unlikely to be sentimental about having spent almost a year with Brown five years before. Among the eight members attending were old Nor'Westers Brown would have been familiar with—Edward Smith from Fort Resolution and George and James Keith, as well as John G. McTavish, who would not have forgotten his encounter with Brown at the Grand Rapid in 1819. His old boss John Stuart was also present. The council invited Brown to attend the meeting as a guest. At the meeting he may have had a surprise, or he may have been expecting it. Either way, it may have been an uncomfortable experience.

Though this is necessarily speculative, the questions might have been blunt. And why, Mr. Brown, did you not obey our instructions and proceed to the Forks? And if you were so ill, why did you keep valuable HBC employees idle about Fort Kilmaurs all summer? Could no one else have led the expedition, which after all was an important one? Connolly was not there in person but clearly he had written to the council giving his side of the story. The council deliberated and announced its decision.

The minute read:

> The reasons assigned by C.F. Connolly and C.T. Brown for not employing the party of 2 clerks and 8 men left inland in New Caledonia District last summer for the purpose of exploring part of the Babine Country (agreeably to the Resolve of Council 1824) not appearing satisfactory to this Council, as it must have been evident to both that the state of C.T. Brown's health would not permit his undertaking that voyage, Resolved that both these Gentlemen receive the censure of Council for such management which has been productive of much loss, inconvenience and disappointment.[285]

Brown may have felt the rebuke to be undeserved, but he may have derived some consolation from the fact that Connolly was included in the council's censure. Connolly's attempt to shift all the blame onto Brown clearly had not been enough to absolve him.

In a letter rippling with dissatisfaction and lack of compassion, Simpson communicated the decision to Connolly at Fort St. James. "I am very much upset," he wrote in July,

> and am by no means satisfied that the Voyage of Discovery intended to have been performed between the Babine country and the Coast, and for which ample means were provided, was not undertaken as, altho' Mr. Brown's health did not permit of his conducting it, some of the other Gentlemen who attached to the expedition were surely capable of that duty.... You should either have abandoned the enterprise and employed the people on some other service or have arranged that the party should be provided with a leader equal to the undertaking.... The loss and disappointment occasioned by such ill-timed delicacy on your part and injudicious non-compliance & overcaution on the part of Mr. Brown being very serious.[286]

Simpson was not known for generosity of spirit. "Worn out Indian Traders," he wrote in a letter in 1826, "are the most useless helpless class of men I ever knew and the sooner the Company can get rid of them after their days of activity and labour are over the better."[287] Perhaps he was thinking of William Brown.

Whatever Brown may have felt about the rebuke from the council, his feelings may have been mollified by another decision the council made a few days later. His old adversary from Fort Wedderburn, Simon McGillivray, was present at this meeting. When leaving Fort Chipewyan, Brown had left his cassette in the custody of Hugh Faries, who was to bring it with him in his canoe to York Factory. He hadn't. Brown complained to Simpson that Faries had left it at Fort Chipewyan, bringing instead more of his own possessions as well as his family. Included in that cassette would have been the personal journals Brown had been keeping for years. Never was he to see them again. This, Brown complained, had caused him pecuniary loss and considerable aggravation. The council disapproved of Faries's improper conduct and fined him £10, which it awarded to Brown as compensation. Brown had not forgotten his comrades from Nelson Encampment and other families who had gone to establish the settlement on the Red River and who were now starving. He donated the money to alleviate their distress.

Brown and Simon McGillivray would, if they had been so inclined, have had much to talk about. McGillivray, having been Brown's prisoner at Fort Chipewyan in 1820, could, for example, have told him how he had really escaped. A few years later, McGillivray was himself the chief trader at

Fort St. James. And it was he who made the journey overland to Hotset and then on to the Forks. On June 20, 1833, McGillivray walked out on to the stony point where the Simpson's [Bulkley] River joined the Babine [Skeena] River and fulfilled Brown's ambition. McGillivray was the first non-Indigenous person recorded as having visited the Forks.[288]

While waiting for the ship to take him back to Scotland, Brown spent his time at York Factory sorting and drying the New Caledonia furs, a number of which had become wet on their passage from Norway House. The *Prince of Wales* arrived on September 4 and the busy work of unloading the cargo and loading the furs for Europe began. When the ship was ready for the passengers, Brown and his son, Daniel, went on board. At 11:00 a.m. on September 29, the *Prince of Wales,* under the command of John Davison, the supercargo whom Brown would have recalled from the *Edward and Ann* in 1811, got under way and stood out to open sea with a fine breeze from the northwest.

The *Prince of Wales* crossed the North Atlantic, passed the Scilly Lighthouse on October 16 and continued up the English Channel. Brown and his son, Daniel, together with James Sutherland and George Keith, two HBC chief factors, took the pilot boat into Portsmouth and made their way by land to London. From there they journeyed back home to Scotland. As far as we know, this was the first time Brown had been to London, which may have been as bewildering for him as it likely was for Daniel.

SCOTLAND

We know little of what Brown did when he arrived back in Scotland. We may presume he took Daniel to see his grandparents in Kilmaurs. We do not know where Brown's legal wife, Elizabeth, was, but if she was in Kilmaurs there may perhaps have been an awkward moment or two when Brown introduced Daniel to her.

Brown was ailing. In the will he made on February 5, 1827, he stated that he was living on Princes Street in Edinburgh. Sutherland and Keith were witnesses. Keith, a former Nor'Wester, had been an adversary in Athabasca in those long-ago days before the merger. Declaring himself sound of mind but weak in body, Brown provided for his children and Josette, but not Fanny. The fact that he made no mention in his will of his legal wife, Elizabeth, either as a beneficiary or as an executor, raises the question of whether she was still alive.

The end of Brown's life was approaching. In early March 1827, the HBC secretary wrote to George Simpson and informed him that Brown, on furlough, was in a dangerous state with dropsy and other disorders, and that his death was expected daily.[289] William Brown died in Edinburgh on

Alexander Nasmyth, *Princes Street with the Commencement of the Building of the Royal Institute, Edinburgh*, 1825. William Brown was living on this street when, in March 1827, he died.

March 19. At the time of his death, he was thirty-six or -seven years old, depending on the month of his birth. His son, Daniel, who went to live in Kilmaurs with his relatives, died in November 1829 and is buried in Kilmaurs churchyard. His daughter Elizabeth died in 1887 and his daughter Jenny (Janet) in 1890. We do not know what happened to Josette or her daughter Margaret.

William Brown's life was not spectacular. He was not a grandee of the Hudson's Bay Company, with a seat on the Northern Council. He was not a great explorer, famous artist, or military hero of the wars with the French or Americans. He had his failings. His life may even be said to have ended in failure, with ill-health and censure for not reaching the Pacific Ocean. He was merely someone trying to do his best. His life in these years, though, is the stuff of which a country is built. The fifteen years he spent with the HBC were among the most contentious and pivotal ones in Canada's mostly peaceful history. They were the years that the territories west of what is now Ontario started to come together and establish an identity other than American. Short though it was, Brown's life was one of service, endeavour and survival. His determination and loyalty all helped to build the land that became Canada.

APPENDIX 1

Key Dates in William Brown's Life

1790   William Brown was born in Ayrshire, Scotland. This is the best estimate of his birth year.

1810   November 10: Elizabeth Armour gave birth to their daughter Elizabeth.

1811   July 26: The *Edward and Ann, Prince of Wales* and *Eddystone* left Stornoway with the first group of Lord Selkirk's recruits for the Red River Settlement.

1811   September 11: Brown arrived in Hudson Bay and transferred to the *Eddystone.*

1811   September 27: Brown landed at York Factory.

1811–1812   Brown spent the winter at Nelson Encampment.

1812–1815   Brown spent three years at Reindeer Lake.

1815   Autumn: Brown returned to Scotland on the *Prince of Wales.*

1816   August 17: Brown married Elizabeth Armour in Kilmaurs.

1816   October 25: Elizabeth Armour gave birth to their daughter Janet (Jenny).

1817   March 6: Brown applied to rejoin the HBC.

1818   Summer: Brown sailed from Scotland to York Factory on the *Prince of Wales.*

1818–1819   Brown was District Master in the Manitoba District.

1819   June 18–24: Brown participated in the ambush at Grand Rapid.

1819–1820   Brown was stationed at Fort Resolution, on Great Slave Lake.

1820–1821   Brown was in charge at Fort Wedderburn, on Lake Athabasca.

1820   October 23   Brown participated in the arrest of Simon McGillivray at Fort Wedderburn.

1821   After the merger of the HBC and the North West Company, Brown was made a chief trader in New Caledonia.

1821–1826   Brown was in New Caledonia, based at Fort Kilmaurs.

1822   October 10: Brown went to Babine Lake to set up a new fort, which he named Fort Kilmaurs.

1822   November 26: Brown proposed a journey to the Forks of the Skeena and the Pacific Ocean.

1825   Spring: Brown made a trip to the Atnah villages on the Babine River.

1825   May 11: First mention of his illness.

1825   July–August: Brown was bedridden at Fort Kilmaurs.

1826   March 1: Brown left Fort Kilmaurs for his second attempt to reach the Forks.

1826   April 19: He left Fort Kilmaurs to journey to York Factory.

1826   April 28: Brown arrived at Fort St. James and left a few days later.

1826   June 26: Brown attended the meeting of the Council of the Governors of the Northern District.

1826   September 20: *Prince of Wales* sailed from York Factory, with William Brown and his son Daniel on board.

1826 or early 1827   Brown returned to Edinburgh and took up residence on Princes Street in Edinburgh.

1827   March 19: William Brown died in Edinburgh from "dropsy and other disorders."

Glossary of the Fur Trade

babiche: raw-hide lacing used for making snowshoes and for tying bundles

buffalo: more properly, American bison

Canada: during the years covered by this book, Canada did not include Rupert's Land, Athabasca or New Caledonia; the term applied only to Upper and Lower Canada, roughly equivalent to today's southern Ontario and Quebec

capot: a coat.

cariole: a light vehicle on wheels or toboggan pulled by dogs or a horse

cassette: a box that officers used for their personal possessions

castoreum: the orange-brown substance that came from the pear-shaped scent glands located in the beaver's anal region used by them to mark territory and by humans for an array of purposes, medicines being one of the main ones; these "beaver-stones" were highly valuable and one of the primary articles of the fur trade

committee: the six-man committee that ran the Hudson's Bay Company from Fenchurch Street in London, England

council: the Council of the Northern Department of Rupert's Land that was established after the merger in 1821

derouin, en derouine: the term used when the North West Company and HBC men went out to the Indigenous communities to trade there

factor: a steward or agent in charge of an estate

factory: a term used for some HBC posts, most notably York Factory; called thus because it was under the charge of a factor

fathom: a unit of measurement of approximately six feet, usually to measure depth but in the HBC was also used to measure tobacco, which came in ropes or strings

fort: term used for HBC posts

gum: a resin used to repair canoes

livre: French coin in circulation, based on the currency in New France

made beaver: the term used as a measurement of money in the HBC; wooden and brass tokens denominated in made beaver were used

marching: commonly used to describe travelling by canoe

marriage à la façon du pays: "in the fashion of the country," a term that referred to the country marriage in which a non-Indigenous man took an Indigenous or Métis wife but was not married by a clergyman in church

outfit: the trade goods for any one particular year

peltry: undressed or raw pelts

pemmican: pemmican is a dried meat, traditionally made from buffalo, pounded with coarse powder and usually flavoured with berries; high in protein and edible for a long time, it was the staple and essential food that fed the North West Company and later the HBC; it was mainly produced in the district that was granted to Lord Selkirk for the Red River Settlement

pièce: one pressed pack of furs, generally weighing 90 lbs (41 kg)

porkeaters: these were the Nor'Westers engaged from May 1 to October 1 to take goods between Montreal and Fort William; this nickname came from the fact that salt pork was an important part of their diet

portage: the connecting link between rivers or lakes over which canoes and loads had to be carried

regale: rejoicing, merry-making

reindeer: caribou were often called reindeer; hence Reindeer Lake

siffler or siffleur: the mountain marmot

shaganappy: a rawhide strap

stroud: a blanket manufactured for barter or sale in trading with Indigenous people, probably being made in the textile industry in Stroud, Gloucestershire

traineaux: sledges, usually pulled by dogs

tumpline: a tumpline is a strap that crosses the head (sometimes the chest) and is used for carrying a pack; loads were carried over portages using these

Endnotes

Preface
1. Stephen R. Bown, "Canada Needs a Revival of Popular History," *Financial Post*, December 19, 2023.

Chapter 1: A Second Chance at Reindeer Lake
2. Topping to Sutherland, July 22, 1812, Fort Churchill Correspondence Book, 1811–1812, B/42/b/58, p. 7, Hudson's Bay Company Archives (hereafter HBCA).
3. Reindeer Lake Post Journal, September 18, 1812, B/179/a/8, p. 8, HBCA.
4. Fishing lodges on Reindeer Lake today hold out the prospect of catching large fish and many of them. In 1812, though, the post journals of Reindeer Lake recorded how difficult it was to catch fish, with starvation the consequence of failure.
5. James Parker, *Emporium of the North: Fort Chipewyan and the Fur Trade to 1835* (Regina: Alberta Culture and Multi-Culturalism/Canadian Plains Research Centre, 1987), 48.
6. Madge Wolfenden, ed., "John Tod: 'Career of a Scotch Boy,'" *British Columbia Historical Quarterly* 18 (July–October 1954):141 (hereafter "Tod: Career of a Scotch Boy").
7. Peter C. Newman, *The Company of Adventurers* (Markham, ON: Penguin Books Canada, 1987), 247.
8. Reindeer Lake Post Journal, July 5, 1813, B/179/a/9, p. 4, HBCA.
9. Reindeer Lake Post Journal, January 7, 1813, B/179/a/8, p. 15, HBCA.

Chapter 2: Chaos in Stornoway Harbour
10. Macdonell to Lord Selkirk, July 4, 1811, in Macdonell, Miles, *Selkirk Settlement: Letterbook of Captain Miles MacDonell to the Rt. Hon'able, the Earl of Selkirk,* (hereafter *Macdonell's Letterbook*).
11. Macdonell to Selkirk, July 25, 1811, *Macdonell's Letterbook*.
12. Macdonell, July 17, 1811, Selkirk Collection, C-16, image 94.
13. Macdonell to Selkirk, July 25, 1811, *Macdonell's Letterbook*.
14. Father Bourke, July 13, 1811, Selkirk Collection, C-17, image 233.
15. Macdonell to Selkirk, July 25, 1811, *Macdonell's Letterbook*.
16. Miles Macdonell, *Journal of a Voyage from London to Stornoway & From There to York Factory*, July 24, 1811, image 100, Selkirk Collection, microfilm C-16 (hereafter *Journal of a Voyage*).
17. Macdonell to Selkirk, July 25, 1811, *Macdonell's Letterbook*.
18. Father Bourke, July 28, 1811, Selkirk Collection, C-17, image 235.
19. Macdonell, *Journal of a Voyage*, July 25, 1811, image 102.
20. "Tod: Career of a Scotch Boy," 138.
21. "Tod: Career of a Scotch Boy," 138.
22. Macdonell, *Journal of a Voyage*, July 25, 1811, image 103.
23. Macdonell, *Journal of a Voyage*, July 26, 1811, image 104.

Chapter 3: Survival, Scurvy and Strife on Nelson River

24. "Tod: Career of a Scotch Boy," 138.
25. Macdonell to Lord Selkirk, October 1, 1811, *Macdonell's Letterbook.*
26. Macdonell to Lord Selkirk, October 1, 1811, *Macdonell's Letterbook.*
27. Macdonell to Selkirk, October 1, 1811, Selkirk Collection, C-1, image 49.
28. Macdonell to Selkirk, October 1, 1811, Selkirk Collection, C-1, image 51.
29. "Tod: Career of a Scotch Boy," 139. In the original, Tod called Cook Cookson and recalled, incorrectly, that the head man's name was Jameson.
30. Macdonell to Auld, December 25, 1811, B/42/b/57, p. 117, HBCA.
31. Macdonell, October 5, 1811, *Journal of a Voyage,* image 117.
32. Macdonell, October 7, 1811, *Journal of a Voyage,* image 117.
33. Father Bourke, October 8, 1811, Selkirk Collection, C-17, image 248.
34. Newman, *Company of Adventurers,* 233.
35. Auld, a note on a letter by Macdonell to Auld, December 25, 1811, B/42/b/57, p. 21, HBCA.
36. Auld to Cook, November 3, 1811, B/42/b/57, p. 10, HBCA.
37. Auld to Cook, November 19, 1811, B/42/b/57, p. 13, HBCA.
38. Macdonell to Auld, December 25, 1811, B/42/b/57, p. 17, HBCA.
39. Macdonell, October 15–20, 1811, *Journal of a Voyage,* images 121–122.
40. Auld to Macdonell, October 16, 1811, B/42/b57, p. 7, HBCA.
41. Macdonell, October 31, 1811, Selkirk Collection, C-16, image 125.
42. Cook to Auld, February 29, 1812, B/42/b/57, p. 24, HBCA.
43. Auld to Cook, March 18, 1812, B/42/b/57, p. 25, HBCA.
44. Dr. John Buchan, *Buchan's Domestic Medicine,* Newcastle, 1812, 447.
45. Cook to Auld, December 17, 1811, B/42/b/57, p. 16, HBCA.
46. Cook to Auld, December 23, 1811, B/42/b/57, p. 16, HBCA.
47. Macdonell to Auld, December 25, 1811, B/42/b/57, p. 19, HBCA.
48. Macdonell, November 30, 1811, *Journal of a Voyage,* image 132.
49. Macdonell, December 2, 1811, *Journal of a Voyage,* image 133.
50. Macdonell, December 11, 1811, *Journal of a Voyage,* image 134.
51. Father Bourke, January 14, 1812, Selkirk Collection, C-17, image 259.
52. Father Bourke, November 30, 1811, Selkirk Collection, C-17, image 255.

Chapter 4: Mayhem and Mutiny

53. Macdonell to Auld, February 27, 1812, B/4/b/57, p. 22, HBCA.
54. Father Bourke, January 1, 1812, Selkirk Collection, C-17, image 258.
55. Magnus Spence per David Halcrow, Testimony, Selkirk Collection, C-1, image 270.
56. James Taylor, Testimony, Selkirk Collection, C-1, image 269.
57. John Randall, Testimony, Selkirk Collection, C-1, image 270.
58. Note by Auld on Macdonell's letter to Auld, February 27, 1812, B/42/b/57, p. 23, HBCA.
59. Macdonell, *Journal of a Voyage,* January 13, 1812, image 140.
60. Macdonell, *Journal of a Voyage,* February 8, 1812, image 149.
61. Macdonell to Auld, February 27, 1812, B/42/b/57, p. 22, HBCA.
62. Macdonell, February 10, 1812, *Journal of a Voyage,* image 150.
63. Macdonell, February 12, 1812, *Journal of a Voyage,* image 151.

64. Note by Auld on Macdonell's letter to Auld, February 27, 1812, B/42/b/57, p. 22, HBCA.
65. Auld to Macdonell, April 30, B/42/b/57, p. 37, HBCA.
66. Father Bourke, February 28, 1812, Selkirk Collection, C-17, image 267.
67. Auld to Macdonell, May 10, 1812, B/42/b/57, p. 44, HBCA.
68. Auld to Macdonell, May 13, 1812, B/42/b/57, p. 47, HBCA.
69. Hillier to Auld, May 15, 1812, B/42/b/57, p. 47, HBCA.
70. Insurgents to Auld, May 13, 1812, B/42/b/57, p. 49, HBCA.
71. Macdonell to Auld, May 15, 1812, B/42/b/57, p. 48, HBCA.
72. Macdonell to Auld, June 19, 1812, B/42/b/57, p. 60, HBCA.
73. Macdonell, June 26, 1812, *Journal of a Voyage*, image 176.
74. Auld's note on a letter to him from Macdonell dated April 18, 1812, B/42/b/57, p. 35, HBCA.
75. Auld to Macdonell, May 10, 1812, Fort Churchill Correspondence Book, 1811–1812, B/42/b/57, p. 44, HBCA.
76. Macdonell to Auld, April 18, 1812, B/42/b/57, p. 33, HBCA.
77. Note by Auld on Macdonell's letter of May 24, 1812, B/42/b/57, p. 57, HBCA.

Chapter 5: Brown Proves His Worth at Reindeer Lake

78. John Charles, *Nelson House & Deer Lake Districts Report*, B/141/e/1, p. 7, HBCA.
79. Reindeer Lake Post Journal, June 21, 1813, B/179/a/9, p. 4, HBCA.
80. Reindeer Lake Post Journal, November 2, 1813, B/179/a/9, p. 9, HBCA.
81. Reindeer Lake Post Journal, April 5, 1815, B/179/a/10, p. 14, HBCA.
82. Reindeer Lake Post Journal, April 17, 1815, B/179/a/10, p. 15, HBCA.
83. Reindeer Lake Post Journal, May 29, 1813, B179/a/9, p. 3, HBCA.
84. Reindeer Lake Post Journal, September 16, 1813, B/179/a/9, p. 7, HBCA.
85. Reindeer Lake Post Journal, September 20, 1813, B/179/a/9, p. 7, HBCA.
86. Reindeer Lake Post Journal, June 13, 1815, B/179/a/10, p. 3, HBCA.
87. Reindeer Lake Post Journal, June 26, 1814, B/179/a/10, p. 4, HBCA.
88. Reindeer Lake Post Journal, January 28, 1815, B /179/a/10, p. 12, HBCA.
89. Reindeer Lake Post Journal, June 15, 1815, B/179/a/10, p. 17, HBCA.
90. Fort Churchill Post Journal, 1814–1815, July 15, 1815, B/42/a/141, HBCA.
91. Fort Churchill, Officers & Servants, A/30/14, HBCA.

Chapter 6: District Master and the Pemmican War

92. *Report of the Manitoba District*, by William Brown for 1818–1819, November 11, 1818, B/122/e/1, p. 5, HBCA.
93. *Report of the Manitoba District*, by William Brown for 1818–1819, B/122/e/1, p. 9, HBCA.
94. *Report of the Manitoba District*, by William Brown for 1818–1819, B/122/e/1, p. 10, HBCA.
95. Peter C. Newman, *Caesars of the Wilderness* (Markham, ON: Penguin Books Canada, 1987), 232.
96. *Report of the Manitoba District*, by William Brown for 1818–1819, B/122/e/1, p. 5, HBCA.
97. *Report of the Manitoba District*, by William Brown for 1818–1819, B/122/e/1, p. 12, HBCA.

98. Manitoba District, Post Journal, February 18, 1819, B/122 /a/2, p. 12, HBCA.

99. *Report of the Manitoba District*, by William Brown for 1818–1819, November 11, B/122/e/1, p. 12, HBCA.

Chapter 7: Arrest and Ambush

100. Simpson, *Journal of Occurrences in the Athabasca Department by George Simpson, 1820 and 1821, and Report*, 19, B/39/a/18, HBCA.

101. Newman, *Caesars*, 170.

102. Newman, *Caesars*, 172.

103. *Robertson Correspondence*, 76–77. Other versions of his capture do not vary in essentials. Fort Chipewyan Post Journal, 1818–1819, B/39/a/14, HBCA.

104. Robertson to Keith, March 3, 1819, Fort Chipewyan Correspondence Book, B/39/b/1, p. 15, HBCA.

105. Newman, *Caesars*, 244.

106. Williams to Selkirk, January 2, Governor Williams—Correspondence Book Outwards, 1819, D/1/1, p. 6, HBCA.

107. Williams to the governor of the Southern Department, Governor Williams— Correspondence Book Outwards, July 25, 1819, D/1/1, p. 24, HBCA.

108. Connolly, Statement about the events at Grand Rapid, RG4-B46, vol. no. 620, Library and Archives Canada (hereafter LAC).

109. Connolly, Statement about the events at Grand Rapid, RG4-B46, vol. no. 620, LAC.

110. Voyageurs, Statements about the events at Grand Rapid, RG4-B46, vol. no. 620, LAC.

111. Voyageurs, Statements about the events at Grand Rapid, RG4-B46, vol. no. 620, LAC.

112. McTavish, Statement about the events at Grand Rapid, RG4-B46, vol. no. 620, LAC.

113. William Williams, *Robertson Correspondence*, 287.

114. Voyageurs, Statements about the events at Grand Rapid, RG4-B46, vol. no. 620, LAC.

115. McTavish, Statement about the events at Grand Rapid, RG4-B46, vol. no. 620, LAC.

116. Shaw, Statement about the events at Grand Rapid, RG4-B46, vol. no. 620, LAC, setting out the words of the participants.

117. McTavish, Statement about the events at Grand Rapid, RG4-B46, vol. no. 620, LAC.

118. Shaw, Statement about the events at Grand Rapid, RG4-B46, vol. no. 620, LAC.

119. William Williams, *Robertson Correspondence*, 288.

120. William Williams to the governor of the Southern Department, Governor Williams—Correspondence Book Outwards, July 25, 1819, D/1/1, p. 24, HBCA.

121. McTavish, Statement about the events at Grand Rapid, RG4-B46, vol. no. 620, LAC.

122. William Williams, September 20, 1819, *Robertson Correspondence*, 289.

123. Robertson to Moffat, ca. mid-July, 1819, *Robertson Correspondence*, 95–96.

Chapter 8: Privations at Fort Resolution

124. Robertson to Moffat, September 29, 1819, letter 32, *Robertson Correspondence*, 106. A hanger is a particular type of hunting sword or long knife that hung from the belt.

125. Robert McVicar to Governor William Williams, December 1, 1819, Fort Resolution Post Journal, B/181/a/2, p. 23, HBCA.

126. Fort Resolution Post Journal, October 1, 1819, B/181/a/2, p. 6, HBCA.

127. Fort Resolution Post Journal, October 4, 1819, B/181/a/2, p. 7, HBCA.

128. Fort Resolution Post Journal, October 6, 1819, B/181/a/2, p. 8, HBCA.

129. Fort Resolution Post Journal, October 14, 1819, B/181/a/2, p. 14, HBCA.

130. Fort Resolution Post Journal, October 11, 1819, B/181/a/2, p. 11, HBCA.

131. Fort Resolution Post Journal, October 14, 1819, B/181/a/2, p. 14, HBCA.

132. Fort Resolution Post Journal, October 27, 1819, B/181/a/2, p. 18, HBCA.

133. McVicar to Robertson, December 1, 1819, Fort Resolution Post Journal, B/181/a/2, p. 30, HBCA.

134. William Todd to McVicar, January 6, 1820, entered in the Fort Resolution Post Journal, on January 20, 1820, B/181/a/2, p. 40, HBCA.

135. McVicar to McDonald, February 5, 1820, Fort Resolution Post Journal, B/181/a/2, pp. 42–43, HBCA.

136. McVicar to Williams, December 1, 1819, Fort Resolution Post Journal, B/181/a/2, p. 15, HBCA.

137. McVicar to Williams, December 1, 1819, Fort Resolution Post Journal, B/181/a/2, p. 66, HBCA.

138. Fort Resolution Post Journal, April 20, 1820, B/181/a/2, p. 66, HBCA.

139. Fort Resolution Post Journal, December 16, 1819, B/181/a/2, p. 34, HBCA.

140. Fort Resolution Post Journal, January 1, 1820, B/181/a/2, p. 36, HBCA.

141. Fort Resolution Post Journal, January 9, 1820, B/181/a/2, p. 37, HBCA.

142. Fort Resolution Post Journal, February 8, 1820, B/181/a/2, p. 46, HBCA.

143. Fort Resolution Post Journal, April 15, 1820, B/181/a/2, p. 63, HBCA.

144. Fort St. Mary Post Journal, September 19, 1820, B/190/a/2, p. 22, HBCA.

145. Fort Resolution Post Journal, October 14, 1819, B/181/a/2, p. 13, HBCA.

146. Fort Resolution Post Journal, April 15, 1820, B/181/a/2, p. 64, HBCA.

147. Fort Resolution Post Journal, January 17, 1820, B/181/a/2, p. 39, HBCA.

148. Fort Resolution Post Journal, May 9, 1820, B/181/a/2, p. 74, HBCA.

149. Robertson to Brown, February 3, 1820, Fort St. Mary Post Journal, B/190/a/2, p. 70, HBCA.

150. Robertson to McVicar, February 5, 1820, Fort Resolution Post Journal, B/181/a/2, p. 70, entered on April 25, 1820, HBCA.

151. McVicar to Robertson, May 22, 1820, Fort Resolution Post Journal, B/181/a/2, p. 79, HBCA.

152. Robertson to Williams, February 4, 1820, Robertson Correspondence, p. 271.

153. Robertson to Moffat, May 28, 1820, Fort St. Mary Post Journal, B/190/a/2, p. 105, HBCA.

154. Robertson, May 24, 1820, Fort St. Mary Post Journal, B/190/a/2, p. 102, HBCA.

Chapter 9: Fort Wedderburn—George Simpson and Simon McGillivray

155. Fort Chipewyan Post Journal, 1820–1823, June 6, 1820, B/39/a/16, p. 6, HBCA.

156. Fort Chipewyan Post Journal, 1820–1823, September 7, 1820, B/39/a/16, p. 29, HBCA.

157. Fort Chipewyan Post Journal, 1820–1823, July 13, 1820, B/39/a/16, p. 14, HBCA.

158. Fort Chipewyan Post Journal, 1820–1823, September 6, 1820, B/39/a/16, p. 29, HBCA. Simpson was not yet governor of the HBC.

159. Simpson, *Journal of Occurrences*, 40.

160. Fort Chipewyan Post Journal, 1820–1823, December 9 and 10, 1820, B/39/a/16, p. 52, HBCA.

161. Fort Chipewyan Post Journal, 1820–1823, September 8, 1820, B/39/a/16, HBCA.

162. Brown to Simpson, September 22, 1820, Fort Chipewyan Post Journal, 1820–1823, B/39/a/16, p. 223, HBCA.

163. Simpson to Brown, October 17, 1820, Simpson, *Journal of Occurrences*, 84.

164. Simpson, *Journal of Occurrences*, 86.

165. Simpson, *Journal of Occurrences*, 87.

166. Fort Chipewyan Post Journal, 1820–1823, October 23, 1820, B/39/a/16, p. 41, HBCA.

167. Simpson, 128. Simpson recorded this conversation twice. The other record is on page 94. There is no substantial difference between them.

168. Simpson, who privately doubted the legality of the warrant, maintained that if the warrant had been intended for the senior Simon McGillivray, it would have described him as "of London" instead of "the parish of Montreal, Mercht." Simpson, *Journal of Occurrences*, 129.

169. Simon McGillivray's Diary, November 17, 1820, C-9165, LAC.

170. Simon McGillivray's Diary, November 18, 1820, C-9165, LAC.

171. Simon McGillivray's Diary, November 30, 1820, C-9165, LAC.

172. Simon McGillivray's Diary, November 19, 1820, C-9165, LAC.

173. Simon McGillivray's Diary, November 27, 1820, C-9165, LAC.

174. Simpson, *Journal of Occurrences*, 114.

175. Simon McGillivray's Diary, December 2, 1820, C-9165, LAC.

Chapter 10: Fort Wedderburn—Conflict Rising

176. Simpson, *Journal of Occurrences*, 180.

177. Simpson, *Journal of Occurrences*, 180.

178. Simpson, *Journal of Occurrences*, 181.

179. Fort Chipewyan Post Journal, January 1, 1821, B/39/a/16, p. 56, HBCA.

180. Simpson, *Journal of Occurrences*, 204.

181. Fort Chipewyan Post Journal, 1820–1821, January 1, 1821, B/39/a/16, p. 56, HBCA.

182. Fort Chipewyan Post Journal, 1820–1821, March 18, 1821, B/39/a/17, HBCA.

183. Simpson, *Journal of Occurrences*, 275. This is not a typographical error. The original text refers to Mr. Back (Lieutenant George Back), who was second-in-command of the Franklin expedition and was at the time visiting Fort Chipewyan.

184. Fort Chipewyan Post Journal, 1820–1821, April 20, B/39/a/17, p. 23, HBCA.

185. Fort Chipewyan Post Journal, 1820–1821, January 22, 1821, B/39/a/16, p. 59, HBCA.

186. Simpson, *Journal of Occurrences*, 43.

187. Simpson, *Journal of Occurrences*, 74.
188. Simpson, *Journal of Occurrences*, 82.
189. Simpson, *Journal of Occurrences*, 88.
190. *Report on the District*, B/39/e/3, p. 17, HBCA.
191. Stuart's Lake (Fort St. James) Post Journal, 1820–1821, June 10, 1820, B/188/a/1, p. 9, HBCA.
192. Simpson, *Journal of Occurrences*, 133.
193. Brown to Greill, February 9, 1821, Fort Chipewyan Post Journal,1820–1821, B/39/a/16, p. 63, HBCA.
194. Stuart to McDougall, February 25, 1821, Stuart's Lake (Fort St. James) Post Journal, B/188/a/1, p. 43, HBCA.
195. Simpson, *Journal of Occurrences*, 339.
196. Simpson, *Journal of Occurrences*, 349.

Chapter 11: Fort St. James and Fort Kilmaurs

197. Simpson, *Journal of Occurrences*, 349.
198. *Canadian Courant*, May 12, 1821, reprinted in the *Statesman* in London on July 2, 1821.
199. Fort Chipewyan Post Journal, 1821–1822, August 1, 1821, B/39/a/20, p. 12, HBCA.
200. Stuart to Keith, July 25, 1822, Fort St. James Correspondence, 1821–1822, letter 6, B/188/b/1, p. 12, HBCA.
201. Stuart to Brown, February 7, 1822, Fort St. James Correspondence, 1821–1822, letter 8, B/188/b/2, p. 12, HBCA.
202. Stuart to Keith, July 25, 1822, Fort St. James Correspondence, 1821–1822, letter no. 6, B/188/b/1, p. 13, HBCA.
203. Stuart to Brown, December 11, 1821, Fort St. James Correspondence, 1821–1822, letter 17, B/188/b/1/, HBCA.
204. Stuart to Nicholas Garry, April 20, 1822, Fort St. James Correspondence, 1821–1822, letter 3, B/188/b/1, p. 9, HBCA.
205. Brown to Stuart, December 7, 1821, Fort St. James Correspondence, 1821–1822, letter 16, B/188/b/1, p. 24, HBCA.
206. Brown to Stuart, December 7, 1821, Fort St. James Correspondence, 1821–1822, letter 18, B/188/b/1, p. 26, HBCA.
207. Brown to Stuart, February 3, 1822, Fort St. James Correspondence, 1821–1822, letter 23. B/188/b/1, p. 31, HBCA.
208. Stuart to Garry, April 20, 1822, Fort St. James Correspondence, 1821–1822, letter No. 3, B/188/b/1, p. 9, HBCA.
209. Babine Post Journal, 1822–1823, October 26, 1822, B/11/a/1, p. 11, HBCA.
210. Babine Post Journal, 1822–1823, October 29, 1822, B/11/a/1, p. 13, HBCA.
211. Babine Post Journal, 1822–1823, October 31, 1822, B/11/a/1, p. 13, HBCA.
212. Babine Post Journal, 1822–1823, November 5, 2022, B /11/a/1, p. 14, HBCA.
213. Brown to Stuart, November 12, 1822, Babine Post Journal, 1822–1823, B/11/a/1, p. 18, HBCA.
214. Babine Post Journal, 1822–1823, December 21, 1822, B/11/a/1, p. 31, HBCA.
215. Babine Post Journal, 1822–1823, December 25, 1822, B/11/a/1, p. 32, HBCA.
216. Babine Post Journal, 1822–1823, December 28, 1822, B/11/a/1, p. 33, HBCA.

217. Babine Post Journal, 1822–1823, January 13, 1823, B/11/a/1, p. 40, HBCA.

218. Brown to Stuart, January 17, 1823, Babine Post Journal, 1822–1823, B/11/a/1, p. 42, HBCA.

219. Brown, Report on Babine District, B/11/e/2, p. 14, HBCA.

220. Stuart to Brown, November 29, 1822, letter 10, B/188/b/2, p. 15, HBCA

221. Brown to Stuart, November 30, 1822, letter 11, B/188/b/2, p. 16, HBCA.

222. Stuart to Brown, December 2, 1822, letter 12, B/188/b/2, p. 17, HBCA.

223. Stuart to Brown, December 2, 1822, letter 12, B/188/b/2, p. 18, HBCA.

224. Simpson to Brown, July 27, 1822, Governor George Simpson, Correspondence Book Outwards, D/4/1, HBCA.

225. Brown to Simpson, December 3, 1822, Governor George Simpson, Correspondence Inwards, 1822–1823, letter 10, D/4/117, HBCA.

Chapter 12: Alarms and Excursions

226. Stuart to Brown, January 27, 1823, Fort St. James Correspondence Book, 1822–1823, letter 14, B/188/b/2, p. 19, HBCA.

227. Brown to Stuart, February 10, 1823, Fort St. James Correspondence Book, 1822–1823, letter 16, B/188/b/2, p. 22, HBCA.

228. Brown to Stuart, February 10, 1823, Fort St. James Correspondence Book, 1822–1823, letter 16, B/188/b/2, p. 23, HBCA.

229. Stuart to Brown, March 7, 1823, Fort St. James Correspondence Book, 1822–1823, letter 19, B/188/b/2, p. 30, HBCA.

230. Brown to Stuart, March 6, 1823, Fort St. James Correspondence Book, 1822–1823, letter 20, B/188/a/2, p. 30, HBCA.

231. Stuart to Brown, January 27, 1823, Fort St. James Correspondence Book, 1822–1823, letter 14, B/188/b/2, p. 21, HBCA.

232. Babine Post Journal, 1822–1823, February 1, 1823, B/11/a/1, p. 45, HBCA.

233. Babine Post Journal, 1822–1823, February 2, 1823, B/11/a/1, p. 46, BCA.

234. Brown to Stuart, May 16, 1823, Fort St. James Correspondence Book, 1823, B/188/b/3, letter 39, B/188/b/3, p. 28, HBCA.

235. Stuart to Brown, May 16, 1823, Fort St. James Correspondence Book, 1823, B/188/b/3, letter No. 38, B/188/b/3, p. 27, HBCA.

236. McLeod's Lake Post Journal, 1823–1824, October 24, 1823, B/119/a/1, p. 13, HBCA.

237. McLeod's Lake Post Journal, 1823–1824, B/119/a/1, October 26, 1823, p. 16, HBCA.

238. Stuart to McDougall, December 9, 1823, McLeod's Lake Correspondence Book 1822–1824, letter 13, B/119/b/1, p. 14, HBCA.

239. McLeod's Lake Post Journal, 1823–1824, October 26, 1823, B/119/a/1, p. 15, HBCA.

240. McLeod's Lake Post Journal, 1823–1824, February 6, 1824, B/119/a/1, p. 33, HBCA.

241. Stuart, John, Western Caledonia Report, B/119/E/1, p. 8, HBCA.

242. "Tod: Career of a Scotch Boy," 232.

243. Brown to Stuart, December 15, 1823, McLeod's Lake Correspondence Book—1823–1824, letter 95, B/119/b/1, p. 74, HBCA.

244. Brown to Stuart, December 15, 1823, McLeod's Lake Correspondence Book—

1823–1824, letter 95, B/119/b/1, p. 74, HBCA.

245. Brown to Stuart, December 15, 1823, McLeod's Lake Correspondence Book—1823–1824, b/1, letter 95, B/119/b/1, p. 75, HBCA.

246. Stuart to Brown, January 10, 1824, McLeod's Lake Correspondence Book—1823–1824, letter 96, B/119/b/1, p. 75, HBCA.

247. Stuart to McDougall, December 30, 1823, McLeod's Lake Correspondence Book—1823–1824, letter 20, B/119/b/1, p. 20, HBCA.

248. Stuart to Brown, January 17, 1824, McLeod's Lake Correspondence Book—1823–1824, letter 97, B/119/b/1, p. 79, HBCA.

249. McLeod's Lake Post Journal, 1823–1824, March 29, 1824, B/119/a/2, p. 7, HBCA.

250. Stuart to Brown, February 23, 1824, McLeod's Lake Correspondence Book—1823–1824, letter 99, B/119/b/1, p. 81, HBCA.

251. Brown to Stuart, March 15, 1824, McLeod's Lake Correspondence Book—1823–1824, letter 102, B/119/b/1, p. 83, HBCA.

Chapter 13: Disaster

252. John Henry Pelley, Nicholas Garry et al. to George Simpson, March 12, 1824, Governor George Simpson, Correspondence Inwards, 1821–1826, D/5/1, HBCA.

253. Simpson to Brown, April 4, 1825, Babine Correspondence Book, 1825–1826, letter 2, B/11/b/1, p. 9, HBCA.

254. Connolly to Brown, May 11, 1825, Babine Correspondence Book 1825–1826, letter 12, B/11/b/1, p. 18, HBCA.

255. Babine Post Journal, 1825, May 13, 1825, B/11/a/3, p. 7, HBCA.

256. Babine Post Journal, 1825, B/11/a/3, June 12, 1825, p. 12, HBCA.

257. Brown to McDonell, June 24, 1825, Babine Correspondence Book 1825–1826, letter 14, p. 21, B/11/b/1, HBCA.

258. Babine Post Journal, 1825, July 5, 1825, B/11/a/3, p. 18, HBCA.

259. Charles Ross to James McDougall, July 9, 1825, Babine Correspondence Book 1825–1826, letter no. 18, B/11/b/1, p. 25, HBCA.

260. Babine Post Journal, August 8, 1825, B/11/a/3, p. 23, HBCA.

261. Connolly to Brown, November 2, 1825, Babine Correspondence Book 1825–1826, letter 36, B/11/b/1, HBCA.

262. Brown to Connolly, January 1, 1826, Babine Correspondence Book 1825–1826, letter 40, B/11/b/1, HBCA.

263. Connolly, Report on New Caledonia, 1826, B/188/a/5, p. 76, HBCA.

264. Fort St. James Post Journal, 1825–1826, October 30, 1825, B/188/a/6, p. 12, HBCA.

265. Fort St. James Post Journal, 1825–1826, February 6, 1826, B/188/a/6, p. 44, HBCA.

266. In the *Delgamuukw* trial about Indigenous title, a British Columbia court spent much time trying to locate exactly where these villages were. Even with the assistance of Arthur J. Ray (professor emeritus, University of British Columbia), the court had difficulty reaching definitive conclusions. (*Delgamuukw Trial Transcripts of the Supreme Court of British Columbia, 1989*. University of British Columbia Library Historical Books.) After much discussion, the court concluded that Brown had reached the area around Kisgegas but he had not

reached the confluence of what is now the Babine and Skeena Rivers, only a few miles away. This suggests that Weep Sim could have been at or near the place where the village of Kisgegas was.

267. Brown's Journal, March 10, 1826.
268. Brown's Journal, March 30, 1826.
269. Brown's Journal, April 1, 1826.
270. Brown's Journal, April 1, 1826.
271. Fort St. James Post Journal, 1825–1826, March 26, 1826, B/188/a/9, p. 54, HBCA.

Chapter 14: Homeward Bound
272. Brown's Journal, April 17, 1826.
273. Fort St. James Post Journal, 1843, December 27/28, 1843, B/188/a/19, p. 103, HBCA. A barely legible entry in this journal states that Fanny Brown, the widow of chief trader William Brown, "at present the wife of Qua's son" "took her departure to render an account of her good and bad deeds" in this world. It also recorded that she had a large family and that her daughter, not less than sixteen—was this Margaret?—did not seem much affected by her death.
274. Brown's Journal, April 18, 1826.
275. Brown's Journal, April 19, 1826.
276. Brown's Journal, April 19, 1826.
277. Fort St. James Post Journals, 1825–1827, May 5, 1826, B/188/a/8, p. 5, HBCA.
278. Brown's Journal, May 11, 1826.
279. Brown's Journal. May 13, 1826.
280. Brown's Journal, May 20, 1826.
281. Fort Chipewyan Post Journal, May 26, 1826, B/39/a/24, p. 33, HBCA.
282. Brown's Journal, May 30, 1826.
283. Brown's Journal, June 7, 1826.
284. Brown's Journal, June 9, 1825.
285. Minutes of Council, June 26, 1826, B/239/k/1, p. 95, HBCA.
286. Fort St. James Correspondence Book, 1826–1827, Simpson to Connolly, July 5, 1826, letter 29, B/188/b/5, p. 20, HBCA.
287. Simpson to Colvile, quoted in Newman, *Caesars*, 314.
288. Other non-Indigenous traders may have come up from the coast and visited the Forks before 1833, but if so, they did not record their visit in writing. When Simon McGillivray stayed overnight in a hut in the Wet'suwet'en village of Hagwilget, close to the Forks in 1833, he saw on the wall an accurately drawn picture of a European ship, with masts, sails and guns.
289. HBC Secretary to Simpson, March 12, 1827, paragraph 34, A6, Official London Correspondence Book, A.6/21, HBCA. Dropsy was an old name for what is now called edema, a build-up of fluid in the body's tissues. It has also been suggested that Brown may have suffered from multiple sclerosis. T. Jock Murray, *Multiple Sclerosis: The History of a Disease*, ch. 3, "The Palsy without a Name: Suffering with Paraplegia, 1395–1868" (New York: Demos Medical Publishing, 2005), 31.

Select Bibliography

Anderson, Nancy Marguerite. *The York Factory Express, Fort Vancouver to Hudson Bay, 1826–1849*. Vancouver: Ronsdale Press, 2021.

"The Affair at Stornoway, 1811." *The Beaver*, Spring 1982, 53.

Bell, Charles Napier. *The Selkirk Settlement and the Settlers: A Concise History of the Red River Country from its Discovery, Including Information Extracted from Original Documents Lately Discovered and Notes Obtained from Selkirk Settlement Colonists*. Winnipeg, 1887.

Belyk, Robert C. *John Tod, Rebel in the Ranks*. Victoria, BC: Horsdal & Schubart, 1995.

Bown, Stephen R. *The Company: The Rise and Fall of the Hudson's Bay Empire*. Toronto: Anchor Canada, 2021.

Brown, William. *Journal*. R 7759-0-0-E, MG 49-DB, Volume 1–2, Library and Archives Canada.

Bryce, George. *The Life of Lord Selkirk, Coloniser of Western Canada*. Toronto: Musson Book Company, 1912.

Bumstead, J.M. *Fur Trade Wars: The Founding of Western Canada*. Winnipeg: Great Plains Publications, 1999.

Burley, Edith. *Servants of the Honourable Company: Work, Discipline and Conflict in the Hudson's Bay Company, 1770–1789*. Don Mills, ON: Oxford University Press, 1997.

Elliott, Marie. *Fort St. James and New Caledonia, Where British Columbia Began*. Madeira Park, BC: Harbour Publishing, 2009.

Gibson, James R. *The Lifeline of the Oregon Country*. Vancouver: UBC Press, 1997.

Harmon, Daniel William. *A Journal of Voyages and Travels in the Interior of North America*. Andover, MA: 1820. Reprinted as *Sixteen Years in the Indian Country: The Journal of Daniel William Harmon, 1800–1816*, ed. William Kaye Lamb (Toronto, 1957). Reissued as *Harmon's Journal, 1800–1819*, foreword by Jennifer S.H. Brown. Surrey, BC: TouchWood Editions, 2006.

Hudson's Bay Company Archives, Archives of Manitoba Microfilms, held at the HBC Archives in Winnipeg, many of which are available online, listed by microfilm number.

Lower, Robert. *Unsettled: Lord Selkirk's Scottish Colonists and the Battle for Canada's West, 1813–1816*. Toronto: ECW Press, 2023.

MacDonell, Miles. *Selkirk Settlement: Letterbook of Captain Miles MacDonell to the Rt. Hon'able, the Earl of Selkirk*, Selkirk Correspondence (cited as Macdonell's Letterbook).

MacDonell, Miles. *Journal of a Voyage from London to Stornoway & From There to York Factory*, July 15, 1811–1812, Selkirk Collection, microfilm C-16, commencing at image 87 (cited as Journal of a Voyage).

MacDonell, Miles. MacDonell to Lord Selkirk, October 1, 1811. *Manitoba Pageant* 13, no. 1 (Autumn 1967).

Morton, Jamie. *Fort St. James, 1806–1914: A Century of Fur Trade on Stuart Lake.* Environment Canada Parks Service, 1988.

Newman, Peter C. *The Company of Adventurers.* Markham, ON: Penguin Books Canada, 1987.

Newman, Peter C. *Caesars of the Wilderness.* Markham, ON: Penguin Books Canada, 1987.

Parker, James. *Emporium of the North: Fort Chipewyan and the Fur Trade to 1835.* Regina: Alberta Culture and Multiculturism/Canadian Plains Research Centre, 1987.

Payne, Michael. *The Most Respected Place in the Territory: Everyday Life in Hudson's Bay Company Service, York Factory, 1788–1870.* Ottawa: National Historic Parks and Sites, Canadian Park Service, Environment Canada, 1989.

Ray, Arthur J. *Indians in the Fur Trade: Their Role as Trappers, Hunters and Middlemen in the Lands Southwest of Hudson's Bay, 1660–1870.* Toronto: University of Toronto Press, 1974.

Ray, Arthur J. *The Early Economic History of the Gitxsan–Wet'suwet'en Territory*, University of BC Special Collections. A report prepared by Professor Ray for the Gitxsan–Wet'suwet'en Tribal Council, January 16, 1985, Exhibit 960 to the Delgamuukw Trial Transcripts, Proceedings of the Supreme Court of British Columbia, 1989, for April 20, 1990.

Red River Settlement Papers in the Canadian Archives relating to the Pioneers, selected by Chester Martin, Archives Branch, 1910, R 7504-45-5-E, MG 29-C73, no.1, Library and Archives Canada.

Robertson, Colin. *Colin Robertson's Correspondence Book, September 1817–September 1822*, ed. E.E. Rich. Toronto: The Champlain Society, 1939 (cited as Robertson's Correspondence).

Selkirk Collection, Canadiana Heritage, Canadian Research & Knowledge Network, microfilms C-1–C-20, https://heritage.canadiana.ca/ (Selkirk Collection).

Simpson, George. *Journal of Occurrences in the Athabasca Department by George Simpson, 1820 and 1821, and Report*, ed. E.E. Rich. London: The Champlain Society for the Hudson's Bay Record Society, 1938. This is a transcript of Simpson's report in B/39/a/18, HBCA (cited as *Journal of Occurrences*).

Simpson, George. *Character Book of Governor George Simpson*, reprinted in *Hudson's Bay Miscellany, 1670–1871*, ed. with introductions, Winnipeg, The Hudson's Bay Record Society, vol. 30, 1975 (cited as Simpson's *Character Book*). In 1832, George Simpson wrote character sketches of the principal HBC employees. Brown was dead by then, and he did not write one about him. His comments were intended to be confidential and so he did not hold back on his assessments. John Stuart, for example, had criticized Simpson's putting aside his country wife, who was the sister of his own wife, after he married Frances in 1830. Simpson's report on him was very unfavourable.

Tod, John. "John Tod: Career of a Scotch Boy." This appeared originally in the *Victoria Daily Times*, September–December, 1905. The account was based on conversations between Tod, G.H. Wilson-Brown and Gilbert Malcolm Sproat before Tod's death in 1882 and was credited to Sproat, despite being written in the first person as if by Tod. On occasion, Tod's dates and names are not correct. Edited by Madge Wolfenden and with an appendix, it was reprinted in the *British Columbia Historical Quarterly* 18 (July–October 1954): 133–238.

Twigg, Alan. *Thompson's Highway, British Columbia's Fur Trade, 1800–1850, The Literary Origins of British Columbia*. Vancouver: Ronsdale Press, 2006.

Van Kirk, Sylvia. *Many Tender Ties: Women in Fur-Trade Society*. Winnipeg: Watson & Dwyer Publishing, 1980.

Younging, Gregory. *Elements of Indigenous Style, A Guide for Writing by and about Indigenous Peoples*. Edmonton: Brush Education, 2018.

Illustration Credits

Maps: All the maps were made for this book by Morgan Hite of Hesperus Arts, Victoria. The map of the Manitoba District is based on a map made by Peter Fidler in 1820 (Hudson's Bay Company's Archives, B/55/e/1).

Chapter 2: Stornoway Harbour
Kilmaurs and the Jougs, 1900, unknown author, William Harvey, Picturesque Ayrshire, 1900. Public domain via Wikimedia Commons.

William Daniell, RA, *Stornaway [sic] on the Isle of Lewis*, 1819, RA (1769–1837). Public domain via Alamy.

Chapter 3: Survival, Scurvy and Strife
Robert Hood (ca. 1797–1821), *The Hudson's Bay Company Ships* Prince of Wales *and* Eddystone, 1819. Courtesy of Library and Archives Canada, box A099-01, item 2836426, acc. no. 1970–188–1221, W.H. Coverdale Collection.

Peter Rindisbacher, *Departure of the Second Settler Transport from York Factory to Rock Fort* (Rock Depot), September 6, 1821. Courtesy of Library and Archives Canada, box A163-02.

Chapter 4: Mayhem and Mutiny
Miles Macdonell, from the original in Toronto City Hall. Courtesy of the Archives of Manitoba, photo collection, Personalities – MacDonnell, Miles, N16074.

Winter Couriers of the North-West Fur Company, 1877. Public domain via Wikimedia Commons.

Chapter 5: Brown Proves His Worth at Reindeer Lake
Peter Rindisbacher, *A Gentleman Travelling in a Dog Cariole in Hudson's Bay with an Indian Guide*, 1826. Courtesy of Library and Archives Canada, box A164-02, item 2837928.

Chapter 6: District Master and the Pemmican War
Peter Rindisbacher, *Cold Night Camp on the Inhospitable Shores of Lake Winnipeg, in October 1821*. Courtesy of Library and Archives Canada, box A163-01, item 2835791.

Chapter 7: Arrest and Ambush

Colin Robertson. Courtesy of Library and Archives Canada, box Op-0110, item 22080.

Soldiers of the De Meuron Regiment. Public domain via Wikimedia Commons.

Grand Rapid, Saskatchewan River, Head of Old York Boat Portage, 1890. Courtesy of Library and Archives Canada, box T-2421, item 3304412, Geological Survey of Canada, PA-050898.

Chapter 8: Privations at Fort Resolution

Peter Rindisbacher, *Extremely Wearisome Journeys at the Portage*, 1821. Courtesy of Library and Archives Canada, box A163-02, item 2895379.

Nathaniel Parker Wills, Rapids, *Canadian Scenery Illustrated*, vol. 2, 122. Illustrator, William Hughes.

George Back, RN, *Mountain Fall Rapid on the Slave River*, on July 17, 1825. Courtesy of Library and Archives Canada, item 2895648.

George Back (1796–1878), *Southeast View of Great Slave Lake from Fort Providence, the Nor'Wester Fort*, November 30, 1820. Courtesy of Library and Archives Canada, box BK-004, item 2963399.

George Back, *Winter Travelling on Great Slave Lake. Narrative of a Journey to the Polar Sea in the years 1819, 1820 and 1821*, by Sir John Franklin, published in 1823, 276.

Chapter 9: Fort Wedderburn—George Simpson and Simon McGillivray

Sir George Simpson, about 1850, photographer unknown, copied by William Notman Studio, 1872. Public domain via the McCord Stewart Museum Montreal.

Peter Rindisbacher, *Two of the Companies Officers Travelling in a Canoe made of Birchwood Manned by Canadians*, ca. 1824. Public domain via Wikimedia Commons.

George Back, *Fort Chipewyan, May 27, 1820*. Public domain via Wikimedia Commons.

Chapter 10: Fort Wedderburn—Conflict Rising

George Back, *Lake Athabasca with Fort Chipewyan on the Bluff on the Right*, 1832. Courtesy of Library and Archives Canada, box A009-02, item 2896936.

George Simpson, HBC Governor, on a Tour of Inspection. Courtesy of Archives of Manitoba, Walter Gordon Photograph Album, digital image No. HB-18-004211, Location Code H 4-195-1-4.

Chapter 11: Fort St. James and Fort Kilmaurs

Peace River in the Rocky Mountain Pass. From within the entrance of the Rocky Mountain Canyon—Looking Down. Courtesy of Archives of Manitoba, James McDougall Album 2, 1891–1892, Digital Image Number HB17–000248.

John Stuart. Illustration by Geoff Mynett, based on image A-01876 via the Royal BC Museum and Archives.

View on Lake Babine, BC, looking west, 10/8/91. Courtesy of the Archives of Manitoba, from the James McDougall album 2, 1891–1892, image HB17-000230.

Chapter 12: Alarms and Excursions

Outlet of Stuart Lake, Salmon Trap & Bush Fire in distance, 22/8/91. Courtesy of the Archives of Manitoba, from the James McDougall album 2, 1891–1892, image HB17-000231.

John Tod as a Young Man. Illustration by Geoff Mynett, based on item PDP 00117 via the Royal BC Museum and Archives.

Chapter 13: Disaster

Gitksan smokehouses near a canyon in Kisgegas, British Columbia, 1920, Canadian Museum of History, Marius Barbeau Fonds, item 49490.

Chapter 14: Homeward Bound

Peace River close to Fort Dunvegan. Reclus, Élisée, T*he Universal Geography,* vol. XV, London: J.S. Virtue & Co., 1876–1894, fig. 80, Peace River.

George Back, *Îsle à la Crosse, February 28, 1820.* Courtesy Library and Archives Canada, box BK-004, item 2837997.

Alexander Nasmyth (1758–1840), *Princes Street with the Commencement of the Building of the Royal Institute, Edinburgh,* 1825. Public domain via Wikimedia Commons, held in the Scottish National Gallery, part of National Galleries Scotland in Edinburgh.

Index

journey to land of the Atnahs, 152–53, 157–58, 160, 162–64, 166
marriage with Elizabeth, 67, 72, 123, 175. *See also* Brown, Elizabeth, née Armour
parents, 26
return to Scotland, 11, 15–16, 65–67, 175–76
relations with John Stuart, 15, 128, 131–33, 141–45, 147–56
Simpson's opinion of him, 5, 108–10, 121–22, 124, 126, 144

C

Connolly, William, 15, 80–83, 156, 158, 160–61, 166, 168–69, 171, 173–74
Cook, William, 35, 37, 41–42, 44, 46
country wives, 122–123, 150–51, 154, 159. *See also* Bolieu, Josette; Fanny *under* Brown, William
Cumberland House, 80–81, 85, 88, 126, 128, 172

D

De Meuron Regiment, 81–**82**–84, 114, 120
Douglas, James, 168
Douglas, Thomas. *See* Selkirk, Earl of

E

Eddystone, 28, 31, 35–**36**–37
Edward and Ann, 28, 33–34, 36, 47, 81, 147, 175

F

Forks of the Skeena, 12, 123, 129–30, 139–41, 143, 153, 157–58, 160, 162–64, 166–67, 175
Fort Chipewyan, 13, 22, 73, 76–**77**, 79, 89, 104–6, **110**, 119, 121–**122**–123, 127–28, 132, 169–71, 174
Fort Dauphin, a.k.a. Dauphin House, 69–71
Fort Douglas, 63, 72. *See also* Red River colony
Fort George, 129, 147–51
Fort Kilmaurs, 12, 133–39, 143–44, 148, 153–55, 158–61, 164–68, 173
Fort Resolution, 93–99, 102–3, 110–11, 173
Fort St. James, 12–13, 129, 133–38, 143–45, 154–55, 159–61, 165–68, 174–75
Fort Wedderburn, 73, 76–80, 86, 89–90, 94–95, 102–26, 128, 142, 144, 167, 171
Fraser, Simon, 131–32
Fraser's Lake, 129, 131, 141, 154–55, 160–61
Frobisher, Benjamin, 80, 82–83, 85

N

Nelson Encampment, 24, 38-**40**-50, 53–54, 60, 174
Norway House, 63, 81, 104, 124, 126–28, 148, 171–72, 175

O

Orkney, 28
Orkney men, 31, 40, 48–50, 52–53, 57–58, 67, 109

P

Pambrun, Pierre Chrysologue, 159, 161, 165–66
pemmican, 13, 21–22, 62, 65, 75
Pemmican Proclamation, 62
Pemmican War, 72–76, 105, 117–21, 127
Prince of Wales, 15, 28, 31, **36**, 65, 67, 81, 175

R

Red River colony, 22, 27–28, 30, 37–38, 40–44, 48, 57–59, 62–63, 67, 72–73, 172, 174
Reindeer (Deer) Lake, 17–19, 22–24, 59–65, 68, 72–73
Robertson, Colin, 15, 22, 63, 72, 72, 76, 78-**79**-80, 83, 85–89, 92, 94–95, 99–106, 111, 116
Rocky Mountain Portage, 77, 106, 128, 148, 169

S

scurvy, 13, 36, 44–46, 50, 54, 99
Selkirk, Earl of, 22, 27–28, 30–32, 34–36, 39, 45, 58, 62, 80, 106, 114
Semple, Robert, 63, 65, 67, 72, 82
Seven Oaks, Battle of, 72–73, 80, 82
Shaw, Angus, 80, 83–84
Simpson, Sir George, 12, 15, 78, 106-**107**-**125**-128, 133, 141–45, 147–48, 154, 156–58, 162, 172–75
Simpson's (Bulkley) River, 12, 129–30, 140–41, 148–49, 160, 175
Smith, Edward, 98, 100–1, 106, 171, 173
Stornoway, 22, 25-**29**-31, 34–35
Stuart, John, 13, 15, 73, 83, 88, 99, 124, 128-**132**-134, 137–38, 141–45, 147–56, 160, 173
Stuart's Lake, 12, 123–24, 129, 133–36, 139, **145**, 169
Sutherland, Richard, 17–19, 22–24, 60–63

T

Tod, John, 20, 27, 29, 33, 35, 37–39, 45, 147–48, **151**–152, 169

W

Waccan. *See* Boucher, Jean Baptiste
Williams, William, 67–68, 76, 80–88, 94–95, 102, 106, 124–25, 127–28, 156, 172
Witset. *See* Hotset

Y

Yale, James Murray, 73, 147–51, 161
York Factory, 12, 14, 17–18, 20, 22, 28, 36–**38**–46, 53–57, 67–68, 75, 81, 83, 85–87, 131, 147, 151, 165–66, 168–75

Acknowledgements

I am grateful for the unrivaled support and skill of my wife, Alice, who carefully read drafts of this book with a fine pencil and made many valuable suggestions, and Steve Mynett, Annika Reinhardt and Peter Mynett for their unstinting support and encouragement. I also want to thank Vici Johnstone, Sarah Corsie and Malaika Aleba at Caitlin Press for their continued support and for publishing my books. I thank Catherine Edwards for her sharp and incisive editing and Morgan Hite of Hesperus Arts for the maps that illustrate the text. And I also thank Maggie Wray in Scotland, a descendant of William Brown, for sending me useful information about her ancestor and Lisa Bobbie of North Roots Research for locating documents for me in the Hudson's Bay Company Archives in Winnipeg. This book is largely based on the original journals, documents and papers of the countless members of the Hudson's Bay Company and I acknowledge my debt to them for their tireless work and preservation of their histories.

About the Author

PHOTO STEPHEN MYNETT

Geoff Mynett was born in Shropshire, England, and qualified in England as a barrister. After coming to British Columbia in 1973, he requalified and practised law in Vancouver until his retirement. A believer in the importance of a rigorous search for and reliance on the facts, he is also an amateur artist. He and his wife, Alice, live in Vancouver.

In 2019, Ronsdale Press published his biography of a pioneer doctor in Hazelton in Northern British Columbia in the period 1900–1936: *Service on the Skeena: Horace Wrinch, Frontier Physician*. In 2021, it won the Jeanne Clark Award for Local History and the George Ryga Award for Social Awareness in Literature. Caitlin Press published his books: *Pinkerton's and the Hunt for Simon Gunanoot: Double Murder, Secret Agents and an Elusive Outlaw,* in 2021; *Murders on the Skeena: True Crime in the Old Canadian West, 1884–1914,* in 2021; *River of Mists: People of the Upper Skeena, 1821–1930,* in 2022; and *The Eventful Life of Philip Hankin: World-Wide Traveller & Witness to British Columbia's Early History,* in 2023.

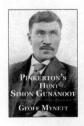